THE KENTUCKY

THE

KENTUCKY

by

THOMAS D. CLARK

Lexington, Kentucky

1969

TO MY DAUGHTER

ELIZABETH

Contents

The Kentucky first appeared in 1942 as the 16th book of the highly successful Rivers of America series. The series was planned and started by Constance Lindsay Skinner and edited by Stephen Vincent Benet and Carl Carmer. This edition has been revised by Dr. Clark for Henry Clay Press.

Special thanks is due J. Winston Coleman, Jr. for assistance in the illustration of this expanded edition. Most of the photographs are from Dr. Coleman's extensive Kentuckiana collection.

The Editors

THE KENTUCKY

I

The River

WHEN white men first appeared in the Kentucky country, they crossed and recrossed the Kentucky River or wandered through its maze of headwaters. Perhaps it would be nearer the truth to say that these first scouts of eastern land speculators blundered through the river's valley. Dr. Thomas Walker, the first Virginian to come land hunting, waded through the rugged Kentucky country and returned home to report a partial failure of his expedition. Christopher Gist, a romantic woodsman, was the next to record a visit through the same region, and before the century came to an end scores of other exploiters came looking for fertile farm land and easy opportunity in the Kentucky River's valley.

Later a continuous procession of Englishmen was to pass through pioneer Kentucky. Among these Anglocritics of the raw frontier country was John Ferdinand Dalziel Smythe, a hardy traveler who took to the western woods afoot. He set out from North Carolina through the woods toward the setting sun, and he entered Kentucky through the headwaters of the river. The valley's hypnotic spell befell him, and in a burst of enthusiasm most unlike an Englishman he wrote an appreciative description of it. His outpouring is no

13

halfway matter. He said that he traveled "the whole length of the Kentucky, including its meanders, from the source of the Warrior's Branch in the Allegheny Mountains, to the confluence of the Kentucky with the Ohio, it is certainly between four and five hundred miles, containing a body of land on each side, that cannot be surpassed, and scarcely equalled by any in the universe, for fertility of soil, abundance of game, excellence of climate, and every other beauty and advantage imaginable, except difficulty of access to it." This was a gallant introduction of the river to prospective pioneers from a man who otherwise found a great deal of fault with the Kentucky settlements. Settlers came quickly upon the heels of the good John Ferdinand. Here on the banks of the Kentucky was a thrilling place to start the long and eventful march toward the great West and to a new America.

The Kentucky is not alone a river or a drainage system, it is a way of life. In fact, before it injects its merry flood deep into the side of the Ohio at Carrollton, it becomes several ways of life. It would be an extremely imaginative person indeed who could stand down at its mouth and conjure up the story of the river and its numberless tributaries. How much humanity this story contains is difficult to explain. The pattern is both varied and complex.

Other rivers, much more pretentious in length and certainly so in girth, go drifting nonchalantly past large industrial cities. Or they dally along through wide and pleasant bottom lands. They can boast loudly of romantic days when men raced proud steamboats upon their currents to the sea, or of the grand parts played as rich pawns in both national and international politics.

No unusually proud paddle wheels have churned

the waters of the Kentucky, nor have any proud steamers been humiliated in the ceremony of having their horns stripped from them, because they were defeated. No momentous international decisions have interrupted the course of its history. Yet, the Kentucky is not a humble stream; rather, it is bold in its course. Like its buckskinned pioneers of another era, it wears no silver buckles at shoe tongue or knee, but it is American along every inch of it, and it personifies the American dream of rugged independence and self-determination. Steep palisades and deep rock-lined gorges are vigorous testimonials of a rugged, determined current. In its race to the Ohio it has cut a deep swath before it. The proud Bluegrass is pierced deeply through its heart, and as the river enters its last lap it rushes like a seasoned thoroughbred with a final burst of magnificent force past the finish line.

Good Kentuckians never go halfway, they are all Kentucky or none. So is the river all Kentucky. At the very base of the rigid wall of Pine Mountain two of its forks turn their haughty backs upon the near-by Virginia hills. A third fork, the north one, extends a slender tantalizing finger toward the Big Sandy, and, actually, where the farthermost branch greedily snatches the last drop of water from the dividing ridge, it lies deep in Big Sandy territory.

Wright Fork, named for that mountain combination of man and legend, "Devil John" Wright, tumbles down a rocky hillside above McRoberts to begin a river. It scampers, like a boy who has raided a neighbor's orchard, behind huge boulders and under cover of a thickly overgrown woodland until it is well out of its rival's clutches. Not far from where the first mountain rill breaks into the open, other branches tumble down

steep hillsides with crystal-clear water from bubbling mountain springs to speed on the race.

Before the youthful Kentucky has gone far in its swift journey through the narrow Kentucky mountain valleys, its bed becomes contaminated with the foul discharge of coal mine pumps which disturb the placid woodlands with their periodic coughing. Down past tipple after tipple flows the North Fork. Like a frontier Kentucky child who was forced to stand by and endure the horrors of seeing its mother scalped and disemboweled by Indians, the slender river puts off into the forest at Mayking with a gruesome impression upon it of bare, gutted and slate-covered hillsides. But before it meets its sister forks at St. Helens, it witnesses more horrors of squalid settlements and of naked hillsides, which mourn beneath deadening burdens of infertile slate and rock.

Coal is man's dream along the first hundred miles of the North Fork. Thousands of tons of soft black coal are dragged from the dark tunnels which run far back into the neighboring mountainsides. This grimy trade has ensnared nature and humanity alike. Miners are native sons who once strode the Kentucky's banks with long-barrelled rifles resting lightly in the crooks of their arms looking for squirrels or neighbors, or tended highland cornfields. At quitting time they stroll down the public highways clad in coarse denim overalls and jackets, with hard plastic fiber caps and lantern brackets atop their heads. Where once rifles rested in the crooks of their arms, they now lug huge dinner pails. They cast furtive glances at passing strangers, and the whites of their eyes give them the weird appearance of being actors in a vast outdoor blackface minstrel show. These dust-covered men dig for Kentucky's black gold —nearly $100,000,000 worth of it each year.

From the Hazard coal fields the North Fork begins its long swing northwestward to Jackson. It runs a merry race with the Troublesome as it flits in and out of deep coves. At last it reaches Jackson, but here it is spun around to an abrupt about-face. The onrushing current sets stubbornly against a rocky ledge and is rudely turned back to seek a way around seven tedious miles of jagged limestone bluff to return within fifty feet of its departure from a regular course.

In the midst of this pan bowl is a small family cemetery, now overgrown with honeysuckle vines and cedar trees. One large granite stone bears the simple legend telling that beneath it is buried "James Hargis, October 13, 1862, to February 6, 1908." This stone marks the end of a long and tragic story. Judge Jim Hargis was a powerful influence among the Breathitt hills and along the river. As storekeeper, logman, and officeholder, he had, also, money, power of granting credit, and was politically influential. He was a determined man, and would suffer no interference with his plans. It was he who did much to create the strife which gave Jackson and Breathitt County the unfortunate title of "bloody." Periodic bloodshed has placed the community in an unfavorable light before the nation. Dr. D. B. Cox, Jim Cockrill, J. B. Marcum, Jim and Tige Hargis, and Ed Callahan fell at the hands of murderous feudsmen. During the first decade of the present century, waters of the North Fork ran red with blood. On several occasions governors of Kentucky sent the state militia upstream to quell civil war, and to guarantee honorable and just trials in the courts.

South of the bloody North Fork, the middle one scampers along through the Big Laurel to Greasy Creek and then to an arbitrary point where temperamental mapmakers finally decide to imprint the name "Kentucky." Perhaps nowhere else in America does a stream drain a more genuinely rural or isolated area. In some respects the valley of this fork comprises America's human museum. Here the great westward movement eddied and then stood still. If it be true, as some sociologists have assured us, here are to be found America's "contemporary ancestors." Human life has changed little from what it was when the first settlers forced their way through the great pass at Pound Gap or wandered upstream from the "three forks."

So unchanged has much of the human life in this region remained that proud mountain gardeners share seed beans with visitors, and declare that some of them "were brought in by our folks when they came through Pound Gap from Old Virginia." Those which have tiny brown eyelets are called "bird's-eye," and the snow-white ones are "goose craw." Mountain housewives blush, as though they were afraid of shocking the polite visitor, when they tell you the legend that a frontier hunter killed a wild goose on the Poor Fork of Cumberland and found the original seed of these beans in its craw.

At St. Helens the North and Middle forks come together to form the main stream, and five miles below here the South Fork joins forces with its sisters.

Red Bird and Goose Creek are the headstreams of the South Fork. They dip deeply into eastern Kentucky and compete with the tentacles of the Cumberland and Rockcastle for floodwaters. In some respects the South Fork is the wayward sister. It rushes headlong toward the mother stream with little self-control, and in a self-destructive passion. At the "narrows" it fights valiantly against the crowding of stubborn hillsides. Here its waters churn furiously against the rocky ledge in protest against the restrictive hand of the mountains.

Really the lower fork should have been called "Troublesome." An astounding amount of human tragedy has marred its history. Stalking feudists have ambushed their victims along its banks. Bakers have killed Howards, and Howards have retaliated by laying Bakers low. Wagers, Bakers, and Whites have carried on an incessant warfare in which human blood has often been spilled for petty reasons, or for no reason at all.

Of one fact, however, the South Fork can be proud: Goose Creek in its early history yielded an abundance of fine salt to give savor to delicious Kentucky foods. Once clumsy salt barges drifted to the "outside," where their owners disposed of their cargoes. So prominent were the saltworks at Garrard that traders came from afar to purchase salt. Legend has it that the roistering cavalry leader, General John Hunt Morgan, in aiding the Confederacy swapped Yankee prisoners for sacks of Goose Creek salt.

Only a fragment of the story of the Kentucky's headwaters can be discovered by following the main streams. The real heart of the upriver country is to be found up the creeks. There is Hell-fer-Sartain, for instance, whose rock-strewn bed thoroughly justifies its realistic title. John Fox, Jr. first attracted the attention of American literary men by publishing a touching little story with this creek's name for a title. During the World War, quiet but courageous Willie Sandlin brought honor to Devil-Jump Branch, Hell-fer-Sartain Creek, and the United States Army by bayoneting, in 1918, twenty-four Germans at Bois-des-Forges. Too, there was Uncle Johnny Shell, who in his one hundred and twenty-first year exhibited a six-year-old son at the Bluegrass Fair in 1919. Uncle Johnny's formula for a long life and enduring virility is not without its virtues. In answer to a great Kentucky temperance leader's question of how he had lived so long, the old mountaineer replied that "many's the time I've laid out all night under a tree which had three or four coon in it. Didn't want the dogs to tear 'em up. I got drunk once. It was when I was about twelve years old. I was a right smart chunk of a boy in them days. They wuz having a logrollin' and everybody went down to the branch to get 'em some liquor, and I went too. They had to take me home. But I haven't drunk much since."

Troublesome Creek extends far into the upper river country, and as any eastern Kentucky politician can tell you, it is the "longest" little creek in the United States. This is a virile creek which reaches deep into the lives of many people. The origin of its name is somewhat obscured in legend. Some local historians have said that it rests upon a case of infidelity on the part of the first woman settler along its banks. This woman, so the story goes, was unfaithful to her husband and he traded her off to her lover, and she in turn became the paramour of her first husband. At Hindman the traveler has to decide which fork of Troublesome he will follow. There are the right and left forks. In 1902 three charitably inclined women, May Stone, Lucy Furman, and Katherine Pettit, followed the right fork to establish the first settlement school in the mountains. They went up the Troublesome to carry "larnin'" to the grand- and great-grandchildren of Uncle Solomon Everidge and his neighbors. Before these three gallant Bluegrass women came to the Troublesome, its people were without educational advantages. Uncle Solomon was an unusually wise old mountain patriarch, and it disturbed him mightily to see his people growing up in ignorance. He walked forty miles to the railroad town of Hazard to beg the "fotched-on" women to remain in the mountains and bring his people "larnin'."

There are a hundred or more other creeks. Their names are characteristic of the simple imagination of the people who live along them. Mountaineers, however, have used no more comical names for their creeks than have real estate men in naming streets in new subdivisions. For the mountaineer the creek serves the same purpose as the street for the city dweller. As examples of the imaginative naming capacity of the eastern Kentuckian there are Cutshin, Thousand Sticks, Defeated, Tom Biggs, Stillhouse, Upper and Lower Devil, Quicksand, Lost, Frozen, Squabble, Buffalo, and Betty Bowman creeks. Also the names are within themselves chapters in simple living and in the importance of commonplace in rural life.

Creeks to the mountaineers mean long and narrow ledges of bottom lands where houses and barns can be built, and where meager crops of corn can be grown. Likewise, every creek forms a cove and settlers have followed them in locating suitable spots for building cabins. Large families have been reared, and the increase has married and always pushed higher up the creek. Soon a community of people bearing the same name and all akin have come to exist. Natives along the Kentucky River and its tributaries speak of branches and creeks within the same range of meaning that city dwellers refer to streets and street corners. A traveler is always given directions by creek valleys and junctions with main streams. A native will announce that he lives at the "head of Ball" or the "mouth of Buffalo." In fact, the creeks have become highways. Nature was thoughtful in keeping most of the streams shallow and in lining them with firm rock ledges. A creek-bed road may not be so smooth or wide as a four-lane highway, but at least the traveler can follow it.

Back to the main stream at Beattyville, it spreads out into a dignified river which sets forth to its destination in a businesslike way. However, like a true Kentuckian, it never gives any sign of being in a hurry. Like a mountaineer making his way over a steep ridge, the Kentucky picks its way lazily but with determination around points of mountain ridges, and wears away rocky obstacles only when it has to. Yet because of its placidity, many natives living near its water line forget that it is neither indolent nor senile until they wake up and find it in bed with them.

Far below Beattyville the Red River, last of the large mountain streams, pours in a murky contribution, and at last the Kentucky starts its gallant swing through the Bluegrass. At Boonesboro, where Daniel Boone and Richard Henderson once dreamed of a western empire, the river begins to bite deep into the blue limestone ledge which sits across the rest of its route. In cutting its way, the river has embedded itself beneath deep limestone palisades which are picturesque every moment of the year. In spring, redbud, dogwood and crab-apple burst into bloom to form a perfect floral background for the flush emerald river. Summer months bring full-leafed bushes and trees which give the steep riverbanks the appearance of being luscious green velvet rolls in which a delicate slender necklace nestles. In the fall, flaming-red leaves of the sugar maples blend with the rich canary yellow of the water maples and the deep rich purple of the blue ash. Walnut and scaly-bark hickories add a softer shade to the rich colors of their gaudy fellows. Duck berries, or bittersweet, add another attractive detail to the extravagant panorama of fall. Tiny streams which pour their miniature rivulets headlong over the precipitous cliffs to the big stream below are finally caught in winter's tight grip. When this happens the deep palisades stand out in the morning sun as a vast wall of a natural crystal palace.

Many a traveler has halted in an ecstasy of enchantment when he has come within sight of the Kentucky River gorge for the first time. From a vantage point atop the high bridge where the Cincinnati-Southern Railroad crosses the river, the confluence of the Kentucky and Dick's rivers spreads out into a rare and beautiful landscape. Rolling back from the rocky crest of the steep embankments are thousands of acres of fertile Bluegrass land where fields of broadleaf burley tobacco are intermingled with rank fields of corn and luscious bluegrass pastures. Off to the southwest is Harrodsburg, where James Harrod and George Rogers Clark helped to entrench Mother Virginia on the Kentucky frontier. To the west is Pleasant Hill, where the Shakers prospered and then failed for want of leadership and converts.

At the headwaters of the Kentucky men make money from coal, oil, and gas, but from Fort Nelson to below Frankfort many secure an ample livelihood by making whisky. Many important distilleries, which capitalize upon the fact that they make and sell a famous "made in Kentucky" brand, owe thanks to the river for its supply of fresh water. Whenever men drink whisky the brand "E. H. Taylor, Jr." has real meaning. "Belle of Anderson" always meant fine quality whisky to native Kentuckians, and so have "James E. Pepper," "Old Crow," "Old Joe," "Old Prentice," "T. B. Ripy," "Cedar Brook," "Old Hoffman," and "Bond and Lillard." Historically, the Kentucky River has always been associated with the whisky business. Upstream it has been the moonshiner, in the Bluegrass it has been the licensed distiller, and before the advent of distilled water the Kentucky was a significant division point in whisky quality.

It was said that the sensitive gauger, Pat Lanpheer, who was called the man with a "golden nose," could tell not only by a whisky's aroma whether it was made on the Kentucky, but likewise whether upon the right or the left bank.

Like a frolicsome mountain lassie who glides through one last figure in a rollicking square dance, the Kentucky makes one grand final wing around the bluff on which east Frankfort sits. The river cuts so closely under the precipitous banks that one scarcely realizes it lies far beneath his feet. Yet, nature planned it this way perhaps for a purpose. Here she was to give peace to one of her great noblemen. Atop these rugged palisades stands a modest stone marker which tells the visitor that underneath its base lie the physical remains of Daniel and Rebecca Boone. Thousands of feet have worn the ground bare around the iron fence that guards the sacred spot.

Scores of people come daily to stand with bared heads before the resting place of these two people who dreamed and sacrificed for a home and an America west of the Appalachian Mountains. Daniel in his long wanderings in the Kentucky country visualized the day when his people would come to enjoy the fruits of its fertile soil. His faithful mate, Rebecca, symbolized in her struggle to make her family a home the courage of pioneer American womanhood.

If, in 1845, Daniel Boone had served on the committee to select his final resting place, he would have been pleased with the spot at the top of the big Frankfort hill. The old pioneer would have loved the beautiful landscape which spreads out before the cemetery toward the governor's mansion and the new state capitol into the setting sun.

In the state cemetery there are the graves of dozens of other Kentucky men and women whose lives are inseparable parts of the valley's rich history. Not far from the Boone monument are the graves of John Brown and his wife, Margaretta Mason. John Brown's influence is still a live factor in the state's political history. It was he who represented the struggling Kentucky District in the Congress of the Confederation when it was trying to disengage itself from Virginia. Close by on the same ledge overlooking the river is the grave of John Jordan Crittenden, who wished to preserve the Union by compromise in the dark days of '60. He lies here amid kinsfolk and governors overlooking the political happenings of the new state capitol.

Down near the entry to the cemetery is the grave of the political martyr, William Goebel. It is marked by an upright figure proclaiming to visitors in bronze, as Goebel did in life, the evils of railroads and textbook companies. Crowning the ridge is the shaft memorial to Kentucky's braves who were killed in many wars, and within its shadow is Theodore O'Hara's modest tomb. At last he has bivouacked with the heroes of whom he sang in his famous poem.

Down around the lower bend, the Kentucky River whips around a corner of Frankfort which has withdrawn itself from the workaday world of the state capital. Here linger many memories in lavender of another and doubtless grander day. Liberty Hall, built in 1796, on Virginia tidewater lines, by the proud Senator John Brown, is an eloquent testimonial to the good taste of an early Kentucky aristocracy. Its gardens run back to the river, and in the spring its flowers blend with the green stream in perfect harmony.

Near by is Wilkinson Street, reminiscent of the town's founding father, and not too far away on top the gently rolling tongue of land reaching back from the river to where the bluff takes a "nigh cut" stands Gideon Shryock's beautiful Greek revival masterpiece. The old state capitol stands as stately as a Kentucky colonel who has retired from active affairs, but who dawdles away his days pleasantly digging into his family's history. Frankfort is the river's chief city, and since 1793 Kentucky's capital.

No one who saw the Kentucky lash out at Frankfort in 1937 will ever forget how furious the stream can be. Its murky waters covered the lower parts of the town and washed mercilessly at the doors of the old penitentiary where 2,900 convicts were confined. West Frankfort was left a shambles. A thick coat of upriver silt was deposited over everything. In the doorways of humble homes lay pieces of cheaply veneered furniture. Furniture manufacturers stood exposed by their sins of both omission and commission in the doorways of drenched houses in the slums of Frankfort. It was a heartbreaking sight to see poor victims returning to their homes to pick at the soggy remains of household furnishings which had required a lifetime to accumulate. The Kentucky, like a pet dog suddenly gone mad, had left calamity and ruination in its rampant path.

Again in 1939, a tributary of the Kentucky struck a deadly blow at the folk in its valley. The quiet little Frozen Creek in Breathitt County came up so rapidly during the night of July 4th that fifty-one victims were swept downstream to death. A whole village was washed away in this "flash" flood, and steel highway bridges were twisted into worthless masses of scrap.

State roads were washed in two, and corn crops were completely ruined within an hour.

This is the Kentucky, a thing of beauty and strength, but like Samson's Delilah, treacherous. Its story is varied, but never dull. Much of America's history is intimately tied up with the land that lies within its rugged valley.

2

John Swift's Silver

Young Jim Rose was sent out to sprout his
father's hillside cornfield up in Wolfe County. Jim cut
the stubborn sassafras and scrub oak sprouts, and mashed
the horseweeds from stumps and stubs which had been
bruised by several generations of reluctant Rose grub-
bers. Clint, the father before him, had "brushed" that
hillside as a lad, and doubtless he had, in the solitude
of his work, dreamed of Swift's rich silver lode which
was said to be cached somewhere in near-by Tight Hollow. If a man could only discover the big haul of silver
which Old Sailor John had hidden away under a Kentucky ledge he could forget, forever, hillside cornfields
and determined sprouts which had aggravated the
Roses every spring. Perhaps Young Jimmy's mind, like
that of his father, dwelt pleasantly on the subject of the
great silver legend which the old-timers delighted in
telling over and over.

Rising and falling with a degree of lackadaisical
regularity, Jim's grubbing hoe struck rocks and bushes
alike. When it came in contact with the flinty stones
of the Wolfe County hillside sparks flew, but that
was customary with stones and grubbing hoes in their
seasonal conflict with each other. On this June morning in 1937, however, young Rose's hoe struck a stone

30

that didn't give off flinty sparks, and the sound was different. The freshly made scar on the "rock" revealed a yellow streak. He had struck gold! At least, he had struck one nugget of gold.

Lying before Clint Rose's boy was a huge lump of gold said to have assayed 85 per cent gold and 15 per cent silver. In the language of the region here was "pyore" gold and silver worth, so it was said, $950,000 a ton.

Barefooted Jimmy Rose brought to life an old Red River legend, which, in reality, had never been relegated to the archival scrap heap of local history. People of the valley had only to recall that such names as Campton, Swift's Creek, Upper and Lower Devil's Creek, Trace Fork, Tight Hollow, and Pine Ridge were associated with silver and gold to once again become excited.

Just as Clint Rose's boy caused the excitement in 1937, another young adventurer had created an interest in the region nearly two hundred years earlier. George Munday, the first boy, seems to be of legendary origin. Some say he was Spanish, some know for certain that he was a Frenchman, and others take for granted that he was an Englishman. Anyway, it is said that his first association with Wolfe County silver was at the mouth of a bear's den. His party had shot a bear and it had rushed into its den. When the miners dragged their prize from the hole, they discovered that it had dug into a rich vein of silver.

Before Munday's party could exploit their newly found prize, everyone except George was killed by Indians. The savages took the boy with them, and through their frequent visits to the region of the crags in the Red River valley he helped his Shawnee companions mine huge stores of pure silver.

Later Munday fell into the hands of the Cherokees, and they, too, knew the secret of the silver lode. When the Shawnees were absent, the Cherokees sneaked in and engaged themselves in mining.

In time, Spanish miners from Mexico appeared on the scene to gather precious cargoes of the beautiful white metal. Munday worked and chatted with these ravenous fortune seekers. Their stories went back to De Soto. When this explorer tramped through the southern Tennessee wilderness Indians told him, so it is claimed, of vast silver deposits to the north. It was from this source that the Mexican conquistadores of the eighteenth century learned of the Kentucky Quivira.

Even doughty French coureurs de bois knew of the fortune to be had without much labor in the Kentucky River country. On many occasions George Munday saw the subjects of King Louis digging for the coveted nuggets. These Latin soldiers of fortune were talkative and historically minded. From them young George secured a full account of the vast silver deposits.

The French were friends of the Indians, but they hated with vengeance the high and mighty British officials who were trying to drive them out of the western country. Likewise they detested the land-clearing, home-building, cattle-grazing American backwoodsmen. They were determined to fight this unscrupulous combination until their last lance was broken. In turn, the British and their American backwoods subjects were ready to sweep the jabbering Frenchmen out of their path westward.

In 1754, the Virginia governor sent the adventurous Washington west, with old Christopher Gist as guide, to spy on the French posts.

French woodsmen were obstinate. They wished to

hold onto their furs and silver, and to their glorious
western woods. This drew fire from the imperial-
minded British. In 1755, General Braddock went on his
blundering march toward the headwaters of the Ohio.
Fighting on the side of the victorious French, on that
day when the redcoats were hurled back, was George
Munday. Unlike his French comrades-at-arms, it was
not a day of victory for him, for he was led away a
captive.

When Washington's men moved back toward Virginia they took their "white Indian" captive with them.
Munday drifted with them until he landed in Alexandria. At civilized Alexandria this boy of the Kentucky woods roamed the streets in search of food. It
was while suffering the pangs of hunger that he met
the robust English sailor, John Swift. Swift was ready
to sail for Cuba, but before he left he provided a room
and food for his new friend. When Swift's ship had
sailed to Havana and back he found his young charge
thriving.

Munday was so grateful to his rugged benefactor
that he told him of the rich silver lode in Kentucky.
He told Swift that the Indians had left the mines for
the open country, and the war had driven the French
from the Kentucky valley. George offered to go as
Swift's guide and interpreter if he wished to work the
mines. This was in 1757, but John Swift wanted to
delay the journey westward until he could fetch seasoned Spanish miners from Havana to assist him.

At Havana, Sailor John engaged the services of
two Peruvian prospectors, named Gries and Jeffrey. On
June 21, 1761, Swift, Munday, Gries, and Jeffrey left
Alexandria for Kentucky. They fought their way
through the trackless western Virginia woods, across

the deep streams, and over the mountainous crags to the rugged canyon of the Red River tributaries.

For eight years John Swift and his three companions dug for silver ore. It is said that in those years they mined and smelted $273,000 worth of silver bullion. There was a magic charm over this silver, however, for the party was unable to leave Kentucky with $200,000 worth of it, and today it lies buried somewhere in a Kentucky cove. Along the trail back to Virginia $70,000 more was hidden.

Fortunately for future and wealth-seeking generations, John Swift's years at sea had disciplined him. He knew the importance of records, and he kept a journal of his venture. Too, he drew a map of the middle Kentucky River country, designating the location of the mine. Today copies of this old journal are to be found in many hands. Perhaps it is because they have been copied from the same original that they all partially agree. The maps are scarcer, and are indefinite as to matters of exact location.

Back in Alexandria, Swift and his merry companions swore strict secrecy, and they promised that three years hence they would meet in that place and journey back to Kentucky. Again the sea called to Sailor John, and he departed for London.

Before Swift left America he sensed that there was dissatisfaction with the English rule in the colonies. Here and there bold persons were speaking critically of the crown's colonial policies. On the streets of London he was so indiscreet as to give voice to his personal views upon colonial government. He spoke critically of the king and his colonial exploiters. For his ardent outbursts of American partisanship he was led away to a darkened cell where he was forced to remain until the end of the Revolutionary War.

Fifteen years after his departure from Alexandria, poor blind John Swift returned to work his Kentucky silver mines. While he was serving time in an English cell his companions of the first journey had organized an expedition and returned to Kentucky, but they were ambushed and killed by the Indians. With Munday, Gries, and Jeffrey dead, Swift selected as his right-hand man Colonel Tye. It was to him that his records were entrusted, and he became the active leader of the expedition. After an arduous journey back to Kentucky the party went searching for the silver mines, but they never found them.

Blind John, once more in Kentucky, was unable to go into the woods by himself. He went exploring on the arm of his constant companion, Anderson. It was pitiful to see the old man hobble over the rocky ground, up the cliffs, and across the mountain streams, searching frantically for the site of his former mining adventure. For fourteen years he searched for the Kentucky El Dorado, but never with success. In 1800 the old man died broken in spirit and body. As he lay dying he admonished his companions: "It is near a 'peculiar rock.' Boys, don't never quit hunting fer it. It is the richest thing I ever saw. It will make Kentucky rich."

In a land where words uttered on the deathbed are highly prophetic, Swift's dying words have rung in the ears of prospectors as a certain promise of riches. The "boys" have never given up the search. First there was Old Man Cud Hanks at Campton who tramped the hills about the town looking for Swift's silver lode. Uncle Cud claimed that he knew Sailor John, and that he had firsthand information of the mine. But death overtook him, too, before he could find the precious cache.

When Cud Hanks was in his grave, Old Mrs. Anderson, whose husband had been intimate with Swift, took up the search. She had the records and the maps, and she went looking for the "remarkable rock." Death prevented her from succeeding. Her intimate friend, Aunt Becky Timmons, took up the search where she left off. Aunt Becky came into possession of the journals and maps which Swift had kept. These were first given to Colonel Tye, and then to Colonel Torwood, and in 1863 to Mrs. Timmons.

Aunt Becky had the advantage over her fellow searchers after the rich ore because she was a mystic. She could place her hands under the ledge of a table and by a series of taps the spirit would impart direction by which she could search for the treasure. Her table, however, was a fickle thing and she was never able to find the "turtleback" rock where the three white oak trees grew from a common stump.

Becky Timmons's successor was "Long George" Spencer, of Glen Cairn. His search was that of a musically inclined philosopher. He had learned to play the fiddle better than anybody else in the Red River valley. When the Mountain Central Railroad was built up the gorge he took to storekeeping. Uncle George had the best setup of any of the silver hunters. He divided his time among his interests of reading the Bible, storekeeping, fiddling, and prospecting. In his long hours of reading the Bible he began to wonder about some of the stern passages found there.

Searching for the "remarkable rock" always held a fascination for Long George, and he spent many days among the lonely crags of the Pottsville gorge. He knew where the "remarkable rock" with the turkey-foot impressions was. Likewise he had seen the grave of Swift's partner, J. C. Blackburn, and above it the stone bearing the date 1825. All these things the fiddling Bible scholar knew, but he knew even more. The Lord did not want anyone disturbing the rich silver deposit—of this Uncle George was certain, for did not the vigorous old Hebrew prophet Haggai remind his readers that the Lord said "I will shake all nations, and the desire of all nations shall come." Then with a note of positive triumph the prophet warned that "The silver *is* mine, and the gold *is* mine, saith the Lord of hosts."

When a learned Ohio State University professor appeared on the scene in 1937 to study the possibility of there being a rich deposit of precious minerals in the Kentucky valley, Long George was unimpressed by the wise man's statements. He *knew* that there was silver in the hollow, but that to search for it was a sin in the sight of the Lord.

Every time the Glen Cairn philosopher went searching for John Swift's silver something queer happened to him. There was the time when he dug a pit, taking precautions to prevent a cave-in or other accident, and a rock from a foreign formation fell in upon him. On another occasion the old man had dug down deep into the earth when a weird female stranger appeared at the mouth of the pit above him and shouted "get out and quit looking for silver." This was enough. Uncle George recalled the harsh command of Haggai and he grew afraid to work against the Lord's will. "Things," he said, "happened when I couldn't see anything wrong."

Obviously the silent actors, the Indians, played a part in this Kentucky River legend. There are almost as many versions of the appearance of Indians in the regions as there are repetitions of the story. One account repeated often along the river is that of the two Cherokee braves and a squaw who came back to Kentucky in 1871 from the West. These Indians appeared at

Irvine, and from this place they went to the farm of Jacob Crabtree. The young chieftain was a polite man who spoke, so it is said, English with an Oxford polish. He talked intelligently of minerals, and hinted that their visit was prompted by the presence of Swift's silver. The whole thing was mysterious to the good people of the upper Kentucky. At Crabtree's farm the braves left their feminine companion and made their way up the Little Sinking Creek to the Big Sinking, and thence several miles upstream. Far up this latter creek they hitched their horses and went on foot to "the mines."

After the Indian braves had been absent from the Crabtree farm for several days they returned with two buckskin sacks filled with a "heavy substance." One of them stood anxiously watching over the precious bags with cocked revolvers. They had found the fountain-head of their tribal ancestors' fortune. Again the river country was alive with rumors of the silver mine. At Ashly and Bone Cave on Lower Devil Creek a prospector, in the year the Indians came, found twenty-seven pots each about eighteen inches in diameter.

Another story gives an account of two Spaniards who came to a sugar furnace on Upper Devil Creek. They went into "the canyon" and in a few days they returned with two sheepskin sacks filled with "something heavy."

Lower downstream, in Clark County, there is an eerie tale of John Swift. This version makes the blind sailor a murderer. Here, it is said, Swift and his men had hidden their rich burden and gone back to Virginia. Before the party was disbanded the members had agreed that they should return to the mine as a party. At least John Swift and three companions should be present in the returning group.

In 1790 the survivors of the company were brought together and prepared for a journey into the Kentucky wilderness. There were in this party George Munday, a Scotchman named McClintock, two Frenchmen, and two Shawnee Indians. When this band had arrived in Kentucky it found the mines and their hidden treasure. Here was a fortune, and an everlasting source of supply of ore to replenish it. The sight of so much silver went to John Swift's head; he became selfish and crafty. He wanted the fortune for himself. He rapidly forgot George Munday's kindness in taking him into his confidence by telling him of the mine. McClintock and the Frenchmen were to share in the spoils. The old sailor lost control of his will and, like so many men of the sea, chose to take the path of blood to a realization of his ambitions. While his weary companions slept he thrust his flashing blade into their hearts one by one until he stood alone in the midst of the gore, but in full possession of his precious silver.

From the scene of his bloody deed John Swift crept through the woods back to Virginia. At last he was a rich man, but a curse of unhappiness accompanied his riches. His eyes failed him, and he groped afraid and friendless through eternal darkness with his guilty conscience weighing heavily upon him.

John Swift's wicked soul was damned. He had left most of his riches behind in Kentucky. Until this date no one, except James Rose, has found any part of the murderous John's rich prize.

When Sunday editors in the Ohio valley run short on feature stories they can always count on the Swift legend as a popular filler. Time and again this old legend has been dressed up and spread before the Sunday supplement-reading public. Several times the Louisville *Courier-Journal* has published accounts of this famous legend. In 1894 it carried a story by the parson-editor Dickey of the Jackson *Hustler*. This story brought an interesting response which attempted to deflate the Swift legend with reasoning even more fantastic than the original story. The author explained that John Swift was a counterfeiter who came to Kentucky to debase the coinage of the crown. He put sufficient alloy into the coin silver which he brought with him to make three coins out of one. So profitable was the business that soon he had "understrikers" throughout the mountains of Kentucky and Virginia. Each year these sharpers stirred anew the silver legend, and palmed off their devaluated coins upon innocent receivers. In 1841 and 1842 they stirred up much excitement around Campton and on the Red River by claiming that they had discovered the mine.

This defaming story went unheeded. Why should Swift come all the way to Kentucky to counterfeit coin in 1760 to 1770 when there were numerous isolated mountain valleys nearer the center of eastern civilization?

It seems now that the curse of John Swift has settled down upon the Kentucky valley. Hundreds of Kentuckians have searched frantically for the mines. Hundreds of "dry holes" bear silent testimony of frustrated hope. In 1937 the Swift Mining Company was formed, and the crowds which gathered at Roscoe Tyler's Cash and Carry Store were eager to buy stock in the new venture. Young Jim Rose's discovery of gold had brought promise of great riches to Tight Hollow.

For more than a hundred and twenty-five years Colonels Tye and Torwood, Old Lady De Jarnette, Granny Anderson, Aunt Becky Timmons, Long George Spencer, and J. J. Hughes have tramped over the rugged face of the valley looking for the "turtle back rock with the turkey tracks," but they, along with the Swift Mining Company, have ceased to look. A new generation has come on to be tantalized by the extravagant story of buried fortunes. With the stern command of Haggai that "The silver *is* mine, and the gold *is* mine, saith the Lord of hosts," and the dying words of Sailor John that "It is near a 'peculiar rock.' Boys, don't never quit hunting fer it. It is the richest thing I ever saw. It will make Kentucky rich," ringing in their ears they still hope to make a fortune the "easy way."

3

Boonesborough, Frontier Outpost

GATHERED on the narrow Sycamore Shoals Island in the Watauga River in East Tennessee, the proprietors of the newly formed Transylvania Land Company passed out the last of their gaudy trinkets to their Indian friends. For several weeks the Transylvania proprietors, led by the ingenious Judge Richard Henderson, had dazzled the eyes of the Cherokees with $10,000 worth of fancy baubles. In return for these articles, the whites asked that the Indians trade them the vast stretch of wilderness territory which lay between the Alleghenies and the Ohio, and south of the Kentucky River and north of the Cumberland. One friendly conversation followed another, and the gracious Henderson used all his excellent persuasive powers to get the chiefs to give up this part of their hunting ground. All but one of the Indian leaders consented with enthusiasm to the exchange. One young chieftain, Dragging Canoe, was in a surly mood. He realized that his people had been too hasty in selling their lands. Stamping his feet and pointing toward Kentucky, Dragging Canoe muttered prophetically through his teeth to Henderson: "You have bought a fair land, but you will find its settlement dark and bloody!"

In the first flush of success, Henderson and his col-

leagues were not too much disturbed by the ominous
warning of the surly young chief. One matter more
was to be settled before the council disbanded. The
Transylvania Company purchased from the Indians
a path to their land through Cumberland Gap. On
March 17th, the land of southern Kentucky had passed
into a new ownership, and the Kentucky River was to
become the company's frontier line of action.

A week before the proprietors of Transylvania
concluded their treaty with the Cherokees, Daniel
Boone and a party of twenty-nine companions started
for the Kentucky River to begin a settlement. These
men hurried northwest along the Wilderness Trail,
which had been worn by the tramping of animals, Indians, and long hunters. They were instructed by their
employers to cut back the limbs, to blaze trees indi-
cating the best route, and to locate the most favorable
fording places in the rivers and creeks. At the head
of the party was the natural-born woodsman, Daniel
Boone. He had the happy inborn faculty of being able
to locate the most favorable route without spending
too much time in comparing locations. Even today the
wisdom of his choice of route is to be seen.

It was a happy experience indeed to set off into
the woods to blaze a trail to the new settlement which
was to spring up deep in the Kentucky country. Traveling with Boone was a literate young pioneer, Felix
Walker. As the party moved deeper into the woods,
Walker paid more and more attention to the journal
which he kept. Once over the Allegheny ridges, he became intoxicated with the beautiful natural scenery
spread out before him. If it had not been for the fact
that the footsore Walker carried only a limited supply
of paper, his lyrical outbursts would have labeled him
as the first of the notable western prevaricators. He

found the woods so full of turkeys that he declared they belonged to one universal flock which covered the whole Transylvania grant. "We felt ourselves," he wrote, "passengers through a wilderness just arrived at the fields of Elysium, or at the garden where there was no forbidden fruit."

There was to be, however, both evil and forbidden fruit in this Elysium field of Felix Walker's. Before the party could reach its destination on the Kentucky River, Captain William Twetty and a Negro slave had fallen victims to the Indians' arrows. Even the journalist Walker, himself, was to be brought down seriously wounded.

The Indian raids caused Boone to hasten on to the bank of the Kentucky, and to make preparations to protect his party from further exposure to the savages. Felix Walker, wounded and suffering the pangs of death three hundred miles from medical aid, recorded in his journal a note of fading dreams. For twelve days he lingered between life and death in the cold March snow.

If Walker's dream was fading, that of Boone was not. Boone wrote his employer, Henderson, with cool assurance on April 1, 1775, that, "If we give way to them [Indians] now it will ever be the case." Boone's determination to establish a settlement in the western country was strong. With the vigor of a courageous man he wrote: "This day we start from the battle ground, for the mouth of Otter Creek, where we shall immediately erect a fort—" This was the assuring note of a man who, unhappily, had once been turned back when he had tried to locate a settlement in the West. He gave evidence in this communication that he knew his expedition was to be of the utmost importance to

the expansion of white settlement west of the mountains.

Boone and his companions traveled up the Kentucky River from the scene of their disaster. Near the
mouth of Otter Creek the Kentucky straightens out
into a long and placid stream. The steep river hills
which hover all the way down from the mountains
fall back on the south side in a protecting elbow below the mouth of the Otter. Here was a safe place to
erect a fort. There was fresh water in abundance, and
near by was a salt lick. Roaming over the prairies were
buffalo. This truly was a land which possessed all the
advantages a frontier settler could desire. So attractive
was the spot that Felix Walker, who had been transported there on a litter carried between two horses, rose
from his bed of pain long enough to see the buffalo
rush playfully away from the salt lick.

Struggling along behind the Boone party were
Judge Richard Henderson and his companions. News
of the Indian raids on the men at the Kentucky reached
them. Timid settlers were turning back, and every day
the party met people hastening back east of the mountains in order to save their lives. It was with fear and
uncertainty that Henderson and his men trudged
through the Kentucky wilderness toward Boone's camp
on the river. In the party was the hardy Virginian,
William Calk. Like Felix Walker, Calk realized that
their journey was to be important, and in his clumsy,
half-illiterate way he attempted to keep a record of
it. On a piece of foolscap paper, with one corner torn
away, he made a day-to-day entry of the journey. This
journal, an heirloom of the Calk family today, is a
humble testament of the growing pains of western
America. Conserving every spot of paper, Calk de-

tailed the trials and woes of frontier travel. Beginning without ceremony, he announced:

1775, March 13 monday I set out from prince Wm to travel to Caintuck on tuesday Night our Company all got together at W. prises on Rapedan which was Abraham banks Philip Drake Eanoch Smith Robert Whitledge & my self there abrams Dogs leg got Broke by Drakes Dog. . . .

thurs 23 we start early and travel till a good while in the Night and git to Major Cornwels on holston River:

friday ye 24th we start early and turn out of the wagon Road to go across the mountains to go to Danil Smiths we loose Driver come to a turrible mountain that tried us all almost to death to git over it & we lodge this night on the Laurel fork of holston under a grait mountain & Roast afine fat turkey for our supper & Eat it without any Bread.

thursday 30th we set out again and went down to Elk gardin and there supplied our Selves with Seed Corn and irish taters then we went alittel way I turned my hoss to drive afore me & he got scared Ran away and threw Down the Saddell Bags & Broke three of our pouder gourds Abrams flask burst open a wallet amongst the reast of the horses Drakes mair Ran against asapling & noct it down we cacht them all again on & lodged at John Duncans.

William Calk's sentence structure, capitalization, and punctuation perhaps left much to be desired, but his power of description within a limited space was vivid enough. He wrote as a man who had suffered the loss of three precious "pouder gourds," and as one who had kept an anxious eye on his pack of "Seed Corn & irish taters." While Calk worked laboriously about the night campfires scribbling line after line of his clumsy vernacular into his journal, Judge Henderson wrote a more elaborate and graphic account of the journey. He wrote always in a spirit of optimism, even in the face of the most trying adversities and delays. His interest was that of the speculator who had staked a small fortune on the venture, and he, of necessity, looked forward to the future. While Calk wrote of so small a commonplace as a dog's broken leg, Henderson wrote of plans for a stanch fortification on the Kentucky.

On ahead of Judge Henderson's party at the end of the newly blazed trail near the mouth of Otter Creek, Boone and his companions had begun to build cabins. For the moment the Indian raids had passed, and Boone's men paid more attention to the location of good land than to the building of a fort. It was difficult to get ambitious men to look ahead to the days when they would need the protecting shelter. Land was the thing that had brought the men west, and to them it was an all-consuming passion. They were the first on the ground, and it was they who would have the choicest plots. Also, Boone was a wilderness scout, not a military engineer. He paid too little attention to the strategic location of his camp. Fresh water was important, and he located his cabins near the Kentucky. This was enough attention to location, he thought, but he was not to foresee the grave trials to come.

Quickly, upon his arrival, Richard Henderson located a new fortsite. He was a man with conservative tendencies and soon he was having built a strong fortification. He, perhaps like Boone, lacked complete appreciation of the importance of terrain in the location of a fortification. His plans, however, of Boonesborough Fort are those of a thoughtful man. Henderson took great care with important protective architectural details. Spaces between the cabins were filled in with a strong puncheon wall. There were projecting walls out from the second stories of the blockhouses, and the roofs of the intervening cabins were slanted inward. Once the fortress was begun at Boonesborough, it became a symbol of permanence of white settlement in the Kentucky country. Here the white man was to fight many of his hardest battles for the possession of the land.

The Transylvania Company was composed of ambitious men. They looked forward to the time when their huge territory would become a fourteenth colony. Already Judge Henderson was being denounced as a "pyrate" by Governor Martin of North Carolina, and he was being watched by Governor Dunmore. Both these royal officials anticipated the day when the Kentucky settlers, like those at Watauga, would try to escape the control of the crown. For English colonial government in America, those simple log cabins forming the crude outline of Boonesborough Fort were an evil sign of dissolution. Henderson did not wait to quibble with jealous colonial officials over the legalistic aspects of his colonial title. He called a meeting of delegates to attend the Boonesborough assembly on May 22, 1775. Already the Virginia backwoodsmen were penetrating the western woods. They were building settlements at Harrodstown, Boiling Springs and St. Asaph at the head of the Dick's River.

Judge Henderson called the assembly together at Boonesborough for the expressed purpose of establishing representative government, and of imparting to the delegates some knowledge of the rights of the proprietors. After the legislature had gathered in the open and it had passed its nine famous laws, Judge Henderson performed the ceremony "livery of seisin." While he stood as the pompous and authoritative head of the Transylvania Colony, yeoman John Farrar cut a slice of green Kentucky River sod from the soil and handed it to him. This was an ancient feudal token of possession, and it was exhibited to impress the American backwoodsmen with the fact of Transylvania Company's ownership of the soil.

One act more was performed before the abortive legislature gathered under the spreading branches of the giant sycamores and the Boonesborough assembly passed out of existence forever. Transylvania Colony had gone through all the extra-legal formalities of becoming the fourteenth American colony by 1776. It did not, however, receive colonial recognition from the crown, and after July of that year it failed to be accepted as a colony by the continental group of states. On Sunday morning John Lythe of the Church of England read the Episcopal service. He raised his voice in loud supplication for the health of the British king. This was the first and last time such a prayer was uttered on Kentucky soil. Before other Boonesborough assemblies could be held, George Rogers Clark and his Harrodsburg neighbors had stirred up opposition against the North Carolinians at Boonesborough. This was the beginning of the downfall of Transylvania Colony.

From the very beginning of the western movement there had been bitter rivalry between Virginia and North Carolina. Virginians poured through Cumberland Gap into the Kentucky River valley to encroach upon the lands of the Transylvania claim. East of the mountains royal governors, Dunmore of Virginia and Martin of North Carolina, were apprehensive about Henderson's activities in Kentucky. Governor Martin was issuing one tirade after another against the "outlaw" company. He was denouncing Henderson as a "land pyrate." Governor Dunmore, interested in land speculation, was jealous of the encroachment upon territory which he contended had always been Virginia's. James Harrod and his men had already established a priority claim, and this fact was embarrassing to the

Transylvania officials. The long days and nights at Boonesborough were anxious ones for Richard Henderson. He was coming to realize that the West was to be a source of free land for the man who either had the blessing of Virginia or who was willing to defend his claim with his own rifle or ax.

News of the Declaration of Independence from the British crown by the colonial radicals at Philadelphia was received at Boonesborough with mixed feelings of joy and apprehension. Henderson was extremely doubtful of his influence before a colonial assembly in which Virginia was such an important part. Before the year had ended George Rogers Clark and John Gabriel Jones, spokesmen for the Harrodsburg settlers before the Virginia legislature, had brought the Transylvania dream to a close. There was to be no manorial colony in the West controlled by the stockholders of a joint-stock company. Henderson was given 200,000 acres of land on the Ohio River, and in December, 1776, Transylvania was quietly transformed into a Virginia settlement.

While the Virginia and North Carolina governors quarreled with Henderson and his associates, Daniel Boone turned his attention to his own personal ambition. Since 1773 he had dreamed of settling in Kentucky. Before 1775 had ended, he had brought his wife and children across the mountains to the settlement on the Kentucky River. Daniel was a strange mixture of carefree adventurer and sentimental homebody. His West of the future was one with women and children in it. When he prodded his fellows at Boonesborough to busy themselves with the completion of the fortification he was reminding himself of that happy morning, on September 8th, when he had led Rebecca and Jemima out to the Kentucky to be the first white

women to see that stream. In later years Boone told
the first Kentucky historian, John Filson, of this incident. It was, Boone intimated, one of his outstanding
achievements. A week after the Boone women arrived
on the Kentucky, Colonel Richard Callaway and
William Poage came with their womenfolks. Boonesborough was beginning to show definite signs of becoming an island of civilized permanence in the western woods.

A dark cloud was to hang over the West in the
immediate years following the establishment of Boonesborough. As a part of "rebel" Virginia, Boonesborough
and Harrodsburg were to become in fact the revolutionary back doors of the eastern seaboard. Three hundred miles west of the upper Piedmont, the crude
puncheon walls of Fort Boonesborough were to withstand the savage assaults of the British and their red-
skinned allies. Even before the end of 1775 Indians were
raiding the country around Boonesborough. Two settlers were killed, and warlike signs were becoming more
evident every day. At Harrodsburg, George Rogers
Clark was beginning to make a plan to stop the Indian
menace to Kentucky by procuring Virginia aid.

Before Clark and his stalwart companion could
get back to Virginia to lay their claims for protection
before the legislative assembly, the Indians were to
come again to Boonesborough. On the quiet Sunday
afternoon of July 14, 1776, the Kentucky River fort
was stirred from its Sabbath lethargy by the kidnaping
of Jemima Boone and the Callaway girls. One of Jemima's feet had been injured by a cut from a cane, and
she and Elizabeth and Frances Callaway had gone for
a canoe ride on the Kentucky. The three young girls
had paddled downstream and then had drifted toward
the opposite bank, which was shaded by a heavy growth

of underbrush coming down to the water's edge. When the prow of the canoe eased in near the bank, a Shawnee warrior rushed out, caught the buffalo-thong tug and started ashore with it. Behind him were four other warriors. When fiery little Frances Callaway saw the predicament they were in, she belabored with the paddle the slick head of one warrior tugging at the boat. The girls were dragged from the boat and made captives of the five braves who had lain in wait for them.

When it was discovered back in Boonesborough that the girls were gone, there was great excitement. John Guess swam across the river under the immediate danger of being fired upon by Indians in ambush and rescued the canoe. Daniel Boone took to the woods barefooted. When the cry went up that Jemima Boone and the Callaway girls had been captured, the gallant Samuel Henderson was shaving. He had shaved one side of his face and was about to begin on the other, but he had no time to finish. The other men of the fort were dressed in their "Sunday" homespun clothes, and they did not take time to change.

Across the Kentucky, Boone was able to pick up the trail of the savages and the girls. Quickly he mapped out a plan of strategy. One party was sent directly to the fording place at the Blue Licks on the Licking, and a second followed closely upon the heels of the kidnapers. Night came before the searching party got far on the trail. Again the courageous John Guess volunteered his services, and went back to the fort to secure buckskin woods clothes for the party, and a pair of moccasins for the barefooted leader.

Relying upon the keen woods instinct of Boone, their leader, the searching party moved quickly behind the Indians. Tracks ahead of them began to appear fresher. Then there was the still-warm carcass of a

freshly killed buffalo. A little farther on was the wrig-
gling body of a snake which had just been killed. The
trail disappeared abruptly. Boone, long experienced in
the habits of the savage in the western woods, read ac-
curately the meaning of this sign. The Indians were
hungry, and they had waded up the middle of a near-by
clear-water stream to a place where they could cook
their buffalo meat.

Moving cautiously along the creek, the searching
party found Boone's judgment to be correct. There
were the five Indians about the campfire, and the girls
were seated near by. The two younger girls were resting their heads in Betsey Callaway's lap. Prematurely
one of the whites fired his gun at the Indians. Shots
from the guns of Boone and John Floyd knocked down
the sentry and the Indian cooking the buffalo meat.
The others fled into the brush, but before they ran for
cover one of them threw his tomahawk at Betsey Callaway's head. The men from Boonesborough were
highly excited over the capture, and before they could
be calmed one of them had almost knocked Betsey
Callaway's brains out with the butt of his rifle. He had
mistaken her, with her dark complexion and head tied
up in a bandanna, for an Indian.

The rescue of the kidnaped girls was a tender affair
here in the wild Kentucky woods. Samuel Henderson,
with two more days' growth of beard on one side of
his face than on the other, was there to rescue his
fiancée, Betsey. Within a month after they returned to
the fort they were married. Too, Flanders Callaway and
John Holder, gangling boys, romantically rescued from
the clutches of savage warriors their fourteen-year-old
sweethearts, Jemima Boone and Frances Callaway. It
was with a high spirit of triumph that the bedraggled

rescue party delivered the three girls back at Boonesborough.

This was the famous year of the "three sevens," and it was to be a trying one for the people at Boonesborough. The man power had dwindled to an insignificant number. Food was scarce, and the continuous danger of Indian raids kept the settlers from properly tending their fields and gardens. News came in throughout the year that the Indians were menacing the settlers all up and down the Kentucky valley. Breadstuff became exceedingly scarce, the supply of gunpowder was exhausted, and in the dead of winter salt gave out. It seemed that the ragged, half-starved band of settlers hovering about the smoldering fires in the Boonesborough cabins would have to give up and go back to their friends across the mountains. Again it was the indomitable will of the old woodsman-dreamer that saved the day. Boone had not wavered in his purpose since the day he wrote Henderson, in April, 1775, of his intentions to settle in Kentucky.

In January, Boone took thirty men and the fort's saltmaking equipment to the Lower Blue Licks on the Licking River to make salt. Once at the famous salt wells, he left his companions to their labors while he scouted and hunted game for the party. In the afternoon of January 7th, Boone killed a buffalo, and near sundown as he was making his way to the camp he was surrounded and captured by a band of Shawnee warriors. This was Boonesborough's hour of sorrow because Boone was the guiding spirit among the settlers. Now he was a captive of the Indians. As a matter of strategy to save the settlement Boone led his captors to the salt camp, where they captured all but four of the men. Within the hearing of his associates Boone persuaded the Indians to give up the idea of capturing the fort. He said it was strongly fortified and that the Indians would be defeated. They had, as Boone said, twenty-five prisoners and a good bit of loot. If they would wait until spring to attack the fort he would go with them and help bring about its capture. These were treacherous words for Boone's companions to hear, and years later, after he had helped so nobly to defend Boonesborough, he was called into court to answer to a charge of traitorous duplicity at the Lower Blue Licks.

Boone's logic was convincing to the Indians and they agreed to go away without attacking the fort. The crafty woods diplomacy of the hunter had saved the fort, and perhaps the white settlements in the West. His craft and clever understanding of the woods were to impress his captors. They thought it great fun that they had captured the white hunter. For some reason Boone appealed to the Shawnees' sense of humor, and at times they made it appear that they had played a huge joke on the Kentuckian by capturing him. Chief Black Fish became fond of the famous captive. When Boone was made to run the gantlet he did so with such cleverness that he came out at the end of the line without injury. He ran too close to one line for the braves to trounce him with their clubs, and he was too far away from the other line for the warriors to reach him.

Making their way through the woods from Kentucky to the Shawnee village at Chillicothe, and then to Detroit, Black Fish and his braves delivered their captives to the old "ha'r buyer," Governor Henry Hamilton. Boone already knew Hamilton, and to impress both the English official and his Indian allies he displayed his British captain's commission issued by Governor Dunmore. When Chief Black Fish and his braves left Detroit, however, they took Boone with them. The old chief had been offered a hundred pounds for Boone by the governor, and he refused to take it. Boone was going home to Chillicothe to become the chief's adopted son, and a favorite member of the tribe. Boone, no doubt, was happy enough about his prospect of living with the Indians. Doubtless he could have been completely happy had not the haunting fear of the annihilation of Fortress Boonesborough by his "brothers" bobbed up frequently to torment him. He knew quite well that his people on the south bank of the Kentucky River were without adequate protection.

Runners through the woods from the Lower Blue Licks carried the disheartening news that Daniel and his men had been captured. This was almost too much to bear, and if it had not been for the determination of a few stout souls, the Boonesborough settlers would have given up and gone home to Virginia and North Carolina. Rebecca Boone, poor soul, had suffered so many disappointments on the frontier. At Cumberland Gap she had buried a son, who was killed in 1773 by the Indians, and she had gone back with the party of settlers to remain in the Clinch River valley until 1775, when she came on to Kentucky. She could not bear to live on the frontier without Daniel, and she and the children went back to North Carolina.

While the settlers at Boonesborough were struggling to overcome the misfortune which had befallen them, their leader Daniel was having his body vigorously scrubbed by squaws so as to rid it of the last vestige of contaminating white blood. As a member of Black Fish's tribe, Boone became a good and dutiful red-skinned son. He listened intently to all that was said in his hearing. Always he was careful to ingratiate himself with his father. When he went hunting he brought back the choicest meat for Black Fish. Soon he was to discover that the Indians with British assistance and encouragement were to attack Boonesborough. The situation was desperate. Daniel had to make his escape and go home to warn the settlers. The chance came on July 16th when the braves were returning from a saltmaking expedition. Boone's captives became interested in a flock of turkeys and they went off and left "Big Turtle" with two old squaws. This was his opportunity. He cut the salt kettles loose, jumped astride his horse, and made off through the woods toward the Kentucky.

Few rides in American history equal the dash of Daniel Boone away from Black Fish's braves. Four days after he had slipped away from his Shawnee brothers near Little Chillicothe, he was knocking frantically for admission on the gate at Boonesborough. He had ridden through the woods, swum several rivers, including the Ohio, without any considerable supply of food. Fortunately he arrived at Boonesborough in time to help save it.

Immediately upon Boone's arrival the settlers began to strengthen the fortification. New sections of strong puncheon wall were placed into position. Cabins were reinforced and prepared for a siege. Guns were cleaned and their locks were picked. The meager supply of gunpowder was parceled out as judiciously as possible. A well inside the courtyard was begun, but when the attack did not come immediately the work was left off before the diggers reached water.

Inside Fortress Boonesborough every settler's nerves were on edge. Momentarily the Indian attack was expected, but luckily for the whites it was delayed. Boone's escape from the Indians had changed their plans. A scouting expedition was organized, and Boone led a party of whites back across the river to see what was happening. On this journey the Kentuckians fought a brief skirmish with the Indians. One of Chief Moluntha's sons was killed, and it was said that Boone had fired the fatal shot. The whites learned that the Shawnees and British were moving toward Boonesborough, and that soon the long-awaited siege would take place.

Early on the morning of September 7th, Chief Black Fish, Dagnieau de Quindre, his slave Pompey, and a dozen French Canadians were before Boonesborough. During the night they had quietly crossed the Kentucky a half mile below the fort.

Chief Black Fish and his associates had come to take Boone and his companions back to Detroit. They did not rush upon the fort with loud mad yells, nor did they begin sniping at the whites. Perhaps the chief and de Quindre believed that Boone would surrender the fort to them as he had the party of saltmakers in January at the Blue Licks. A brave carrying a white flag of truce was sent up to the gate to communicate with the whites. Apparently no one was astir inside the fortification. It appeared to be deserted except for the lazy streamers of smoke which curled upward from the cabin chimneys. Behind the walls, however, anxious eyes followed every move made by the approaching Indian. Boone used good psychological strategy. He allowed the brave to "hallo the fort" twice before he answered. The brave's communication was received as calmly as if he were an everyday caller. The attackers were asking for a conference with the whites in which they could talk over Boonesborough's fate. When the messenger returned to his superiors with a favorable message he was again sent to the fort gate with presents of roasted buffalo tongues as tokens of good faith.

When the three fortress representatives to the con-

ference came out to meet Black Fish, de Quindre and
Moluntha, Boone was a bit embarrassed. He had just
run away from his father Black Fish, and just a few
days before he had shot, so it was said, Moluntha's son
in the skirmish beyond the Ohio. Black Fish greeted Big
Turtle with "Well, Boone, howdy?" Boone answered
"Howdy, Black Fish?" "Well, Boone, what made you
run away from me?" "I wanted to see my wife and
children so bad that I could not stay any longer." "If
you had only let me know, I would have let you go at
any time, and rendered you every assistance."

This exchange of greetings indicated that the Indians were exceedingly patronizing. The whites were
warned that they were about to be subjected to a wily
bargain. Luckily the Boonesborough conferees were
equal to the occasion, one of their number appeared at
the conference dressed up as a pompous Virginia military dignitary. In the conversation, Black Fish and de
Quindre were too obsequious. Black Fish made known
the significant fact that they had brought forty horses
with which to take the white women and children back
to Detroit. He felt certain that the fort would be sur-
rendered at once. Boone asked for a two-day truce in
which to consider the matter.

These were two precious days. The whites now had
some tangible knowledge of what their opposition was
like. Black Fish had indicated, also, that he believed the
fortress garrison to be much larger than it really was
when he told the whites that he had brought along
forty horses for the women and children. While the
white leaders were studying the information they had
gained they were likewise preparing the fort for a
siege. Water was brought from the Lick Spring. As
much corn and other food as could be brought from
the outside without causing suspicion was stored in the

fort. The days immediately ahead were gloomy ones at best. The whites had only one advantage and that was the protecting wall of the fort, but it could be destroyed by fire and scaled with ladders. At the end of two days the whites and Indians once again conferred outside the fort wall. Men, women, and children inside the fort paraded as armed men when the Indians and their Canadian friends approached the council ground. This was fine military deception, and doubtless it impressed the enemy. Again the Boonesborough representatives filed outside to seek a delay of activities. Under the great sycamores they spent the day drinking, smoking the fraternal pipe, and eating the feast prepared by the women of the fort. At last Boone and his companions were forced to announce their adverse decision to Black Fish's proposition. The Indian chief then resorted to sham. He proposed that they sign a treaty of friendship anyway. This was agreeable to the whites, but when it was observed that the chiefs had exchanged their older braves for young and stronger ones Chief Black Fish replied in a defiant manner. Upon signing the treaty it was proposed that the whites and Indians shake hands, but since the Indian was an inferior it would require two Indians to one white man to make the agreement binding. This was a clever ruse, but the whites saw through it before they fell into the young braves' strong grasps. When it was seen that the Indians were resorting to duplicity, the whites waved their hats, a signal for their sharpshooters at the loopholes to open fire.

For eight days Black Fish, his brother chiefs, and de Quindre maneuvered their forces in an effort to seize the fort. On one occasion they attempted to give the impression that they had withdrawn the siege. De Quindre had his bugler go across the river and sound his bugle in such a way as to give the impression that the Indians were giving up and going home. It was by that shrewd seventh sense of an embattled people that the Boonesborough leaders were not caught off guard. The gates were kept barred, and vigorous preparations went on for the defense of the fort. There was genuine anxiety among the settlers, however. They were almost out of food, water, and gunpowder. The courage of many of them was at its lowest ebb. Boonesborough, they knew, must surely fall into the hands of the Indians. Several of the men were wounded, and one was dead, and the Indians continued to pound away at the fort.

Several days before, Daniel Boone had leveled his famous rifle on the Negro slave Pompey and had dropped him out of the forks of a tree near the fort. Pompey, from his point of vantage, was able to pour an effective fire in on the whites. When he was killed the whites were cheered. On another occasion Flanders Callaway had fired a wooden cannon at a knot of Indians with some success. But all these things failed to alleviate the emergency.

In the enemy's camp there was desperation. Every effort to take the fort had failed and Black Fish's braves were becoming discouraged.

De Quindre persuaded his red-skinned allies to make one last effort to capture the fort. The Indians began digging a trench from the edge of the Kentucky toward the center of the fort's commons. They threw the fresh dirt into the river, and the broad muddy streak which it made was soon discovered by the lookout mounted atop the crude tower which had been erected in the courtyard. This was bad news indeed. From this trench the savage attackers could blow up the fortress and overrun the whites. Boone and his companions started a countertrench to meet their enemies. In the meantime much badinage was shouted back and forth over the wall between the Indians and the whites.

As the Indians dug closer and closer to the surface beneath the courtyard, the whites waited in fear and trembling of the horrible fate which perhaps would befall them. The rain fell in torrents, and everywhere was a sea of mud. Livestock staggered about in the mire, and a man could hardly make his way from one cabin to another without being buried in it. If this kept up everyone in Boonesborough would drown. Over the wall the muddy streak widened. Darkness came on, and still there was the monotonous, nerve-racking thud of the savages' picks and shovels. Still the heavy rain splashed in the murky courtyard. Scarcely an individual, including Boone himself, believed that an hour later his scalp would still be on his head.

Outside, the situation was equally disturbing. Black Fish's braves were wet and impatient. Their tunnel trick had been discovered, and they believed that if they dug into the courtyard that the whites would make good their wild boast "to bury five hundred" of them. Some of their braves were dead. Pompey, the dusky interpreter, had fallen a victim to the white man's gun. It began to appear that the whites inside the fort led charmed lives. The moment had arrived when the restless braves no longer would listen to the pleas of de Quindre. They had experienced enough of the stubborn resistance of the Boonesborough settlers. On the night of the eighth day the Indians withdrew in defeat. Their methods of attack were not adaptable to long sieges. Inside Fortress Boonesborough, Big Turtle and his people were exhausted. They were hungry, wet, and sleepy. One more day of the siege and the people in Boonesborough would have had to surrender because of their physical inability to resist any longer.

Along the north side of the fort, the Kentucky again ran clear. Where a day before the telltale streak of muddy water had drifted away from the fort in a wide fan-shaped pattern there was now the cheerful green surface of the fresh, flush stream. Boonesborough had held out against heavy odds. When its gates creaked open the next morning its success was assured. The salvation of Boonesborough was the salvation of Kentucky and the American frontier. Boonesborough on the south bank of the Kentucky became a symbol of hope and security in America's great westward movement.

4

Off To 'Orleans

A SUAVE gentleman presented himself at the Spanish governor's mansion in New Orleans in June, 1787. He had come down the river aboard a Kentucky River flatboat especially to visit Don Esteban Miro, colonel of the royal armies, political and military governor, and intendant general of the province of Louisiana. It was quite an exciting occasion in the governor's household to receive so distinguished a personage as a former general officer of the American Patriots' Army. The two officers bowed and scraped to each other. Each of them, however, was slyly sizing up the other. James Wilkinson, Kentuckian, was a shrewd man, and he had come to ask a big favor of Don Esteban.

Kentuckians met with serious reverses when they attempted to run the vigilant blockade of the Spanish down the river and to deliver their farm products in New Orleans. Kentucky fields were producing an abundance of choice crops. At the time the urbane Wilkinson sat in Governor Miro's parlor at New Orleans sipping sparkling imported wine with his gracious Latin host, Kentucky cribs and smokehouses were crammed with the produce of three years. Tobacco, when it could be sold, brought only $2.50 per hundred pounds. Pork products were a drug on the market.

Flour, another important commodity, was almost worthless; in fact, it was hardly worth enough to pay the cost of grinding. Everybody had flour; no one wished to buy it.

In April of that year General James Wilkinson had left Frankfort aboard his flatboat, which was loaded with tobacco, hams, butter, and other produce. The boat ran the gantlet of snags, Indians, and wild currents to pull in to the water front at Natchez. Spanish officials were afraid the day would come when the American backwoodsmen would attempt effectively to run their blockade on the lower river. Time and again lone traders had attempted to do so, but most of the times their boats and goods were confiscated and the boatmen locked up for their trouble. But Wilkinson's boat was different. It was not the property of an ordinary Kentucky backwoodsman, but that of a general officer. The intendant of the Natchez District was in a quandary. Spanish gentlemen respected any man who had the rank of "general," even when he was a flatboatman. The Natchez official was certain that his superior officer at New Orleans would not want him to commit a breach of diplomatic etiquette. Wilkinson's boat was permitted to continue its journey. General Wilkinson, however, set forth overland on horseback to New Orleans.

His boat arrived before he did, and it was only by adroit manipulation that Daniel Clark, an American merchant, prevented confiscation of its cargo. When its owner reached the port city he began negotiations with Governor Esteban Miro to open the port of New Orleans to the rich Kentucky trade. At least Wilkinson hoped Miro would open the trade to his monopoly. Miro was poorly informed about economic and political conditions in the upriver country. He scarcely knew where Kentucky was nor how powerful was the American district. The governor had spent most of his time in a pleasing round of society in New Orleans instead of working diligently at the task of his governorship. Advantages of exact geographical knowledge were with the proud Kentuckian. Quickly Wilkinson sized up the situation, and then through the medium of suggestion, veiled threat, closeted whispering, and much gentlemanly shoulder shrugging he secured valuable trading concessions. To James Wilkinson, gentleman, of what consequence was a little cargo of hams, butter, and tobacco? It did not matter about his flatboatload of produce then at the waterfront, except, "that the property belonged to many citizens of Kentucky, who, availing themselves of his return to the Atlantic States by way of 'Orleans, wished to make a trial of the temper of his government, that he on his arrival might inform his owners what steps had been pursued under his eye, that adequate measures might be afterward taken to produce satisfaction." He went on to say that, of course, if Governor Miro was forced to obey the orders of the court then he would have to govern within the law. Yet, no one could guarantee what the Kentuckians would do. One thing Wilkinson knew quite well—Miro did not want an eruption of Kentuckians. The suave Kentuckian made assurances that he could do a lot toward preventing trouble. In fact, it has been said that he promised to shape the formation of the new state of Kentucky accordingly.

A short time after his conferences with Governor Miro, James Wilkinson sailed around the Atlantic Coast to Philadelphia. With him he carried a generous amount of cash from the sale of his products and a secret trade agreement from the Spanish officials. The agreement was so secret, in fact, that the parties communicated only by code. Key words were located in pocket dictionaries. Soon after Wilkinson's return to Kentucky, the intendant at New Orleans pored over his miniature dictionary by the hour. He was checking the arrival of flatboats loaded with rich cargoes from the Bluegrass.

Back in Kentucky the farmers were excited. Quickly they rushed their fine products to Curd's, Scott's and Shryock's ferries, and to Frankfort. Early in 1788, James Wilkinson's agents were off for New Orleans. They carried between forty and eighty hogsheads of tobacco along with large shipments of hams, butter, and flour, which were sold for good prices. A third cargo was taken down by the general in person in 1789. Much of this latter shipment was made up of tobacco which he sold to the Spanish crown monopoly. Young Philip Nolan and John Ballinger were sent back to Kentucky overland with 6,000 silver dollars saddled on two mules. Ballinger became ill in Natchez, but Nolan was able to deliver safely his precious freight to his employer in Frankfort.

James Wilkinson failed to make a large personal fortune out of his rich southern trade, but he did aid in opening the southern market to Kentucky farmers. Along the Kentucky River business boomed, warehouses were built at every significant point: at Hickman Creek, Curd's Ferry, Scott's Landing, Shryock's Ferry, Frankfort, Leestown, Forks of Elkhorn, Gratz, and Drennon's. It was a profitable business to sell a year's produce at the great New Orleans market. If a farmer could take his boat safely through the trials of a difficult voyage he could realize a handsome profit on his year's work.

In 1791, Wilkinson wound up his shipping business and prepared to return to the army. During the four years he was in the business of trading down the river he sent more than $100,000 worth of Bluegrass prod-

Kentucky hemp fields.

ucts to New Orleans in his boats. The last year he sent down the *Royal Oak, Dreadnaught* and *Union,* which carried cargoes of 120 hogsheads of tobacco weighing 122,000 pounds.

Within a few years the Kentucky was lined with boats on their way to New Orleans. Most of them were of a similar type to the one built for James Wilkinson by William Pope and Hugh Ross. Its specifications called for gunwales "fifty feet long and six inches square, the bottom planks two inches thick, twelve boards to be put across the boat, the side planks to be one and one-half inches thick. The stanchions or studs to be three by six, five feet high and five to a side. The boats to be finished in a workman-ship-like manner, to be pinned with seasoned white oak pins and bored, and the sides to be five feet high and the whole to be of oak timber." This was the structural description of the "Kentucky boat." A stout cabin, a pair of ornamental deer horns, a pair of side sweeps, and a long steering oar topped off the equipment.

In these sturdy, but clumsy craft thousands of rugged red-horse Kentucky backwoods farmers floated to New Orleans with their rich cargoes. At every bend of the river, during the fall, winter, and early spring months, were Kentucky boats. In October, 1795, the so-called Pinckney treaty between the United States and Spain was signed. Western American products were permitted to enter the port of New Orleans free from Spanish interference for a period of three years. This was exciting news in Kentucky, and activity on the river increased by leaps and bounds. In 1797, William Hart wrote his relative, Colonel Thomas Hart of Lexington, from Natchez that he had just reached that place with a sailing vessel loaded with Kentucky products. The next year M. Umstead informed Colonel Hart that he had heard "a piece of news of what must be a valuable acquisition to the western world, (viz.) a boat of considerable burthen making four miles and a half (an hour) against the strongest current in the Mississippi River worked by horses." All up and down the Kentucky, business was booming. Farmers and mill men like old John "2-9" Scott at the mouth of Hickman Creek were developing prosperous businesses. Bluegrass lands were planted to tobacco and hemp. Wheatfields yielded thousands of bushels of plump grain to be used in making flour for southern purchasers. Smokehouses were filled with curing meat for the slave and shipmasters' trade at New Orleans. Kentucky newspapers carried numerous bits of southern commercial information. Prices from the great Mississippi markets were frequently listed. An example of this commercial activity is the report of August 25, 1802, which appeared in the *Kentucky Gazette*. Kentucky products shipped during the first six months of that year were: 841 barrels of apples; 7,971 gallons of beer, cider, and ports; 80 barrels of beef; 3,300 bushels of corn; 1,237 bushels of corn meal; 85,570 barrels of flour; 85 gallons of flaxseed oil; 272,222 pounds of hams and bacon; 42,048 pounds of hemp products; 55,052 pounds of lead; 2,-482 barrels of pork; 342 bushels of potatoes; 2,399 pounds of soap; 2,640 pounds of manufactured tobacco; 503,618 pounds of loose tobacco; and 13,666 feet of lumber. This was a rich trade indeed. It was offering close competition to Spanish and French business interests in New Orleans. Kentucky goods and Kentucky boatmen alike had become infamous by 1803. The port was closed by the Spanish governmental officials in that year, and the Kentuckians were ready to go to war to open it again.

Long before the beginning of international wrangling over the Port of New Orleans at the time of the Louisiana Purchase, the Latin population of that city was casting scurrilous epithets at the Wild Kentuckians who drifted down the river aboard their slow-moving Kentucky broad-horns with their heavy cargoes. They came to the city to sell their goods, to get drunk and to gamble, and to shoot up the town. They were a rowdy lot. Later that year New Orleans and Louisiana became American territory. The river was opened free to all American trade. Kentucky products could go downstream to market without fear of interference, if the Spaniards could be removed from New Orleans. For a time it seemed that those Spanish subjects who felt that Napoleon had overreached their government were going to hold on to Louisiana at any price. Kentuckians armed themselves and made plans for a campaign against these rebels. Before the issue was settled many upriver volunteers were on their way to free the great market city.

When the last of Spanish rule was destroyed in Louisiana, a vast number of heavily laden flatboats drifted down the Kentucky to the Ohio, to the Mississippi, and to New Orleans. It was a wild lot of devil-may-care native sons who sawed back and forth on the long boom poles to avoid snags, eddies, sandbars and boat wreckers. The long days drifting were hot and unexciting. Boatmen piled up their energy to the "spilin' " point, and they were ready for any little fun that might appear. Along the way they "joshed" greenhorn bank squatters, bantered other boatmen, and stole chickens, pigs, and lambs from the banks. All along the way they were tempted to gamble and to drink at the dives which lined parts of the river. At Cave-in-Rock, boatmen were maneuvered into stopping. Down at Memphis, Paddy Meagher's Bell Tavern swarmed with upriver Kentucky bullies. Sally Meagher, belle of Pinch Gut,

was a flashy siren who could lift a rafter's roll of cash
almost with her eyes. She was a "fancy gal" indeed when
it came to dancing. Not far away was Sam Stodger's
Padraza Hotel on "Smoky Row," where boatmen
caroused for a night before going on down the river.

By the time the Kentuckians got to Natchez and
New Orleans they were "bilin' over" with meanness, or
so it seemed to the dignified citizens of those cities.
Kentucky's aristocratic son, James Brown, who was to
become one of the first United States senators from
Louisiana, was not at all proud of his "jeans-britchied"
fellow statesmen. As far as he was concerned, they were
a dirty, stinking, coarse, mad lot. In one of his many
letters to his father-in-law, Thomas Hart, in 1805 he
expressed himself freely on the subject of both Kentucky boatmen and Kentucky products. He was not the
usual obsequious son-in-law when he told Colonel Hart:

. . . prepare yourself therefore to be amused and amusing
for the visit to Kentucky will be principally on account of
yourself and a few chosen friends, and the length of my stay
will depend upon the mode of my reception.

In a country like yours overstocked with unprincipaled
speculators, lying jockies, peddling retailers and idle whiskey
drinkers, I am not surprised that you should offer us a shipment by the first spring flood. Most of the articles sent from
your country to our market are of the same fraudulent rot-
ten stamp; and the very name of Kentucky is an epithet of
reproach in every port of the Mississippi. Go on then and
send us decayed hemp, sour weevil-eaten flour, tainted meats
and tainted characters. They can do no harm here. Your
productions, and your people are alike unknown and dis-
trusted. The *former* will bring no cash, the *latter* will get
no credit. By these observations I would not be understood
as reflecting upon the inhabitants of your country generally.
No, I have left behind me a class of men who, if they were
known here would in part wipe away the stain which many

of your Mississippi boatmen and traders have stamped upon
the character of Kentucky.

Family records do not tell what Colonel Hart's
reactions were to this frank letter. At least he kept it
in his family papers. Doubtless the wild boatmen off
on a spree did leave much to be desired in the way of
decorum.

If the people along the streets of New Orleans
looked upon the Kentucky boatmen as wild customers,
it was because they failed to understand what these men
had to face on their journey to the city. At Louisville
they had to run the treacherous falls of the Ohio, and
south of that point they were forced to watch out for
trouble in every form. Boat wreckers were in hiding beyond every bend and snags bobbed up under the surface
of every ripple. At old Fort Massac and at Cave-in-
Rock there were gangs of cutthroats who murdered
boatmen and pillaged their rich cargoes at will. Among
these bloodthirsty river pirates was the heartless old
reprobate, Colonel Plug (M. Flueger). The colonel was
a nutmeg Yankee from Rockingham County, New
Hampshire.

A favorite trick of old Plug's was to pick the
oakum calking out of a seam of a boat below the water
line so that the boat would sink beneath its cargo. When
barrels of whisky, cider, pork, and hogsheads of tobacco floated free, they were captured by the river
thugs and shipped south in their boats. Native boatmen
were knocked in the head and their bodies dropped,
with weights about their necks, into the river. Colonel
Plug, his brown sloven wench Pluggy, his henchman
"Nine Eyes," and three or four other rogues became
known up and down the river for their thievery.

Kentucky boatmen may have lacked culture, but

lack of courage was not one of their social failings. There would be a day, they said, when they would play Colonel Plug's game with him, and they would throw in a few little personal touches for good measure. On a spring run a vigilante committee came looking for the Massac sharpers. They were mistaken, as they intended they should be, for greenhorn farmer-boatmen on their first drift down the river. Plug invited them to stop and to play a "social game" with him. When they were comfortably seated under the massive cottonwoods which shaded the old pirate's lookout, he gave a soft whistle, a signal for his gang to come out of hiding and attack the boatmen. The Kentuckians, however, were ready for the assault, and when Plug's cutthroats came out of the woods, more Kentuckians appeared on the scene. This was indeed unusual. It was a little hitch in his procedure which the methodical Colonel Flueger had not expected. His henchmen were embarrassed, four of them were captured and thrown into the river, one was killed, and Colonel Plug was taken prisoner.

The Kentucky boatmen had their own individualistic ideas of what was the most effective manner of chastising the old murderer. Mosquitoes were so thick in the Mississippi bottoms that they turned the air blue. Plug's clothes were stripped off, and his arms and legs were tied in an affectionate bear's hug about a likely sapling. His tough sunburned hide was softened up for the mosquitoes by a generous application of cowhide. There tied to his sapling, the pirate was left by the boatmen to atone for his numerous sins committed against the Kentucky boatmen over a period of many years. Mosquitoes by the thousands dug their sharp bills deep into the prisoner's bloody back. Scarcely a spot of skin remained untouched. He writhed and groaned in pain until it seemed that he would lapse into a state of coma.

Then the wench Pluggy came to his rescue. Perhaps a woman, even a slow-witted one like Pluggy, never asked her spouse a more exasperating question than did she. Pluggy came upon her husky New England lover tied to his tree of punishment and being sapped to death by the stinging mosquitoes. In her broken Cajun-English, she blurted out, *"Yasu Chree! O mio carissimo sposo* what for like a dem fool, you hug de tree, and let the marengoes suck all your sweet bred?"* Even in his direst moment of adversity the colonel could not refrain from cursing his simpering mixed-breed mistress.

He had paid a price at the stake, but Pluggy had saved her husband from his tormentors' full revenge. There were to be many other days of robbery and murder in his life. Other Kentucky half-horses and half-alligators were to drift past Massac with heavy cargoes of farm products only to be murdered and robbed. In one final grand act Flueger was to lose his life. He was engaged in the meticulous task of plucking the oakum calking from a flatboat when a storm blew up. So intent was he upon his thieving business that he was unaware of the approaching gale and was drifted out to midstream. Soon he was caught in the same fatal trap which he so often set for his hapless victims. The waves of the river were choppy, and the barge sank fast. There was one chance of being saved, and that was for the high-jacking Flueger to ride ashore aboard a barrel of bourbon whisky. This proved to be impossible. Flueger could not hold onto the tossing barrel. He sank to the bottom before Massac, where his bones were picked clean by the catfish and snapping turtles. His days were ended, and the Kentucky boatmen had one less snare to run past on their way down to 'Orleans.

A contemporary has left a fine description of the old days when boatmen struggled with the river in order to sell their rich products from the Kentucky valley.

Hard and fatiguing as was the life of a boatman, it was rare that any of the class ever exchanged vocation. There was a charm in the excesses, the fightings, and the frolics which boatmen anticipated at the end of their voyage, which cheered them on. Such an effeminate expression as "I am tired" never escaped the mouth of a boatman. After the labors of the day, he went to rest highly stimulated with whiskey, rose from his hard bed with the first dawn of day, and with a large draught of bitters reanimated his exhausted powers, and was ready to obey the order, "Stand to your poles and set off." As the boats were laid to for the night in an eddy, a part of the crew could give them headway on starting in the morning, while others struck up a tune on their fiddles, and commenced their day's work with music to scare away the devil and secure good luck. The boatmen, as a class, were masters of the fiddle, and the music, heard through the distance from these boats, was more sweet and animating than any I have ever heard since. When the boats stopped for the night at or near a settlement, a dance was got up, if possible, which all the boatmen would attend, leaving the cook to watch the boat, and woe betide him if he was not found watching when they returned. Those inhabitants who shunned their acquaintance or did not receive them with a hearty welcome, were sure to suffer for it either in person or property. Respectable families, therefore, who could not join in their revels and participate in their excesses, were careful not to settle where they would be exposed to their visits. The families on or near the banks of the river accessible to the boatmen, were generally the hardest of characters.

As the use of the pole required a much greater exercise of the muscles of the body than ordinary, or perhaps any other manual labor, these men acquired incredible strength and hardiness, which they sought opportunities of displaying. Fist-fighting was their pastime. The man who boasted that he had never been whipped, had attained to a dangerous eminence among his fellows, and was bound to give fight to whoever disputed his superiority. The keel-boatmen regarded the flat-boatmen and raftsmen with great contempt, and declared perpetual war against them. Wherever they met, a battle would ensue. They had their laws, which were strictly observed. If the crew of a flat-boat or of a raft were to be whipped, an equal number of keel-boatmen volunteered or were detailed for the service; and if they were worsted in the fight, none interfered for their relief. They were great sticklers for fair play. They often committed great excesses in the villages where their voyages terminated, breaking furniture, demolishing bars and taverns, and pulling down fences, sheds, and signs. One of their favorite amusements was sweeping the streets in dark evenings. This was done with a long rope extended across the street; a party of men having hold of each end moved forward quickly, tripping up and capsizing whatever happened to be within the scope of the rope. Men, women, children, horses, carts and cattle were overturned. The mischief accomplished, the actors would retreat to their boats and conceal their rope, while those of their comrades who had not engaged in the sweep remained behind to enjoy the sport.

The branches of the Ohio, such as the Cumberland, the Kentucky, the Scioto, etc., could be ascended only in the spring and fall, in consequence of low water; the freighting on these rivers was therefore limited to a short period, and this brought many hundreds of the boatmen together. These assemblages would sometimes set the civil authorities at defiance for days together. Their riotous and lawless conduct was carried to such a length that sober men began to regard them with apprehension, fearing that if their numbers increased with the increase of transportation on the western rivers, they would endanger the peace of the country. But intemperate, profane, and riotous as they were, they had some redeeming qualities. They were trustworthy. Money uncounted was safe in their hands, and if freight was damaged by accident or carelessness, they never hesitated to make full compensation for the damage. Although they would not hesitate to rob a hen-roost, yet they would expose themselves to any fatigue to preserve a cargo from injury, and would not pilfer an article connected with their freight. They always espoused the cause of the weaker party, and would take up the quarrels of an old man whether he was right or wrong.

Once the frolic in New Orleans had ended for the flatboatmen, they sold their boats for building material or firewood and began the long journey home by way of the Natchez Trace to Florence, then across the Tennessee River to Nashville and over the Louisville and Nashville boat road to Louisville and Lexington. In Louisiana they purchased horses which they either rode or loaded with fancy goods from the stores. These returning boatmen traveled in companies in order to avoid trouble with the Harpes, John Murrell, and other highwaymen who operated along the boat roads. For twenty years the land pirates enjoyed fat pickings by robbing Kentuckians returning from New Orleans. Through all the difficulties of transporting their goods to market, the Kentucky boatmen were gallant. They drifted to New Orleans aboard their clumsy craft, and walked home overland. They gambled, fought, loved, and struggled bravely with their long steering poles and stubborn side sweeps to land their cargoes in the southern market. These stanch, rugged Americans were vital agents in pushing the American frontier westward, and in sustaining the economic foundations of western commerce. Perhaps of almost equal importance was the fact that they made the term "Kentuckian" one to be physically respected. These early flatboatmen contributed to the American language many of its bold and colorful terms. They were the half-horse, half-alligators of American frontier literature who had the moral

fortitude to jump up and down and click their heels together and sing, when their boats were being churned
to pieces in the rocky falls of the Ohio River:

> Hail Columbia, Happy land.
> If I ain't ruined, I'll be damned.

Falls City II, one of the last of the Kentucky River boats, plied the river between Louisville and Valley View from 1898 through 1908. The crew consisted of a captain, two pilots, two engineers, chief clerk and assistant, first and second mates and the steward who was overseer of the culinary department.

One of the Kentucky River steamboats hauling passengers, freight and mail, the packet Royal made an average speed of 7 to 12 miles per hour upstream and 12 to 15 downstream. Overnight trips on the Royal from Frankfort to Louisville or Cincinnati cost the traveler $6.50. The Royal and the packet Richard Roe were the last vestige of the old-time river boats, running as late as 1920.

5

Kentucky Steamboats

Many steamers ran with the Kentucky's tide. Some of these boats, as proud as the Kentucky itself, puffed haughtily up and down the stream. They had a wide range of destinations. Some of them scrubbed their noses on the cobblestone front in faraway St. Paul. Many more rocked restlessly before the water fronts of Louisville, Cincinnati, Pittsburgh, and New Orleans. Lower decks of these boats were crammed with rich cargoes of Bluegrass products. Strolling through the main halls and around the texas decks were Kentucky gentlemen and ladies, and just plain Kentuckians. Some of these were giggling belles accompanied by their mothers, who were on their way to social gathering places in the lively old South. Others were politicians (among whom was the proud Clay himself) on their way to conventions or to congresses. There was the lean, gangling, hatchet-faced, red-horse Kentuckian leaning lazily on an elbow looking westward toward newer and cheaper lands. About him played and quarreled a vigorous progeny which was to become a vital part of western society. Sometimes there hovered in darkened corners of boiler decks a dusky band of poor human chattel traveling south to an uncertain destiny in the malaria-ridden cane, rice, and cotton fields.

From the beginning the Kentucky River was a part of the romantic steamboat drama of America. A new day had come in the Kentucky's rollicking history. Steamboats were marked improvements over the clumsy rafts which warped their way through the narrows and over the shoals to the Ohio. Both distance and time were shortened. Puffing little Kentucky River steamboats could make the run down to the great Louisiana market in twelve days if wood and tail winds held out. Coming back the craft required thirty-six days, a good head of steam, and considerable luck before they rounded to at Frankfort.

River navigation was not a new thing to the people of the Kentucky valley. For nearly half a century they were hearing about river navigation. Some of the yarns of those hardy men who had floated down to New Orleans and walked back rivaled the favorite tales of the old pioneers who had driven the Indians beyond the Ohio. Among these early navigators was the apt scholar, Jack Russell. Young Jack had back of him the best of Kentucky pioneer tradition. He and his folks had been the first of his line to cross the great Appalachian wall, mark out a land claim and plant a home upon it. He had heard the bloodcurdling screams of the Indian warrior. Too, the Russells had undergone all the hardships of a raw frontier country. When their fields produced more grain and hemp than the family could use the menfolks put off to New Orleans with the surplus loaded on flatboats.

"Roaring Jack," as the boy was soon called, drifted to market past snags and bandits and sold his family's goods, sewed the money securely in the pockets of his grimy pantaloons and walked home. The river was the boy's school. Floating leisurely down the Kentucky, the Ohio, and the Mississippi the bright-eyed Kentuckian was always conscious of his surroundings. Sand bars, snags, points, bends, and eddies were daily assignments in his process of education. He rubbed shoulders with hard-fisted men, and with boys who acted like men. They all knew about the pirates' dens, the wiles of the river cheats, and the dives which held on under the bluffs of the low country like half-drowned dogs to driftwood.

Physically, the Kentuckian was all that legend has made out his fellows of the state to be. He was tall, with a muscular system as tough and flexible as steel cables. Jack was without fear, and at the same time possessed the rugged sense of fairness and courtesy which was to mark the men of his community. When later he became one of the most famous steamboat captains between New Orleans and Frankfort, all these qualities were to stand out in his dealing with passengers and shippers.

The real career of Roaring Jack Russell was to begin soon after 1811. In that year an incident happened which was to outline his lifework for him. Nicholas Roosevelt took the famous old *New Orleans* for its trial run downstream from Pittsburgh to New Orleans. Perhaps this smoking, sputtering version of the clumsy keelboat passed the young captain somewhere downstream. At any rate, it ushered in a new era in river transportation, and the lanky Kentuckian was to become a vital factor in that era.

When the *New Orleans* tied up above the falls in Louisville to await sufficient rise to negotiate that treacherous stretch of water which divided the Ohio into parts, Kentuckians were much interested. Their interest, however, was not so great as it might have been. Local newspapers were conducting propagandizing campaigns against the British. Speeches of the vigorous young war hawks who were assaulting the frugal old guard in Washington were far more interesting to Kentuckians than the complete revolution in river transportation taking place before their very eyes. Away in Washington two Kentuckians, Richard M. Johnson and Henry Clay, were thundering away. Their cries were for war. They were creating a first-rate fear psychology, coupled with an avaricious desire among their constituents for land. Jack Russell was caught up in this war hysteria. He volunteered for militia service to avenge the disgraceful treatment of his fellow Kentuckians at the horrible River Raisin slaughter. Old raftsmen drilled up and down streets of Kentucky towns while their rafts rotted at river landings. Soon they marched away to war, and very soon the Americans were victorious. The war was over. Victory at the Thames was a great matter of Kentucky pride.

Tramping back through the woods of Michigan and Ohio many a Kentucky raftsman dreamed of taking up where he had left off in the river trade. Among these was Jack Russell. Jack was anxious to get back to his pike pole and the river's hazards. The boy was grown, and he was rugged and tough. Campaigning with Shelby and Harrison had matured him. He was of man's estate and the river held nothing but hope for him. Soon he was to win his spurs as the long-horned fighter of the bends. Down at New Orleans a crawfish-eating snapping turtle had proved especially irksome to the Kentucky boys. He had, in good frontier river vernacular, "put the bee on them." There were few things which could match a half-horse, half-alligator Kentucky boatman, and the low-country bully was one of them. It had now become a matter of saving state pride that a Kentuckian be found who could whip the rascal. A scrapper, or at least he said he was one, was taken down on one of the runs to win back the glory of Ol' Kaintuck. All the way down the big bruiser recited menacingly what he was going to do. His threats were awful, and his backers were overjoyed, but as is true with all shadow fighters, the big Kentuckian ran when he was confronted by the snorting Louisiana gouger. Kentucky pride was at stake. Roaring Jack Russell stepped into the breach. He snatched off his coat, rolled up his sleeves, and tangled with the puffing "crawfish eater." It was a fine frontier battle. Fists swung through the air as though they were miniature cannonballs on tough steel cables. Ribs were gouged, and knees and feet whirled into action. Never had the Kentucky boys, in all their days of conflict, seen such a fight. Russell teetered, stumbled, sagged back and forth until it seemed that he most certainly would fall under the crushing onslaught of his opponent. He remained, however, and the big bully was soundly thrashed, and limped from battle a humiliated and deflated braggart. In his place stood the young Kentuckian. His fame spread fast, and soon people were whispering behind his back, "there is Jack Russell, the best scrapper aboard a steamboat."

Truly Kentuckian, Jack Russell was fond of feminine company and of dancing. When on his boat he led many a fancy figure with the fairest maid aboard for a partner, and in New Orleans he was always an ardent patron of the dance halls. There was something in his Kentucky courtliness, however, which antagonized other men. On one occasion he was throwing himself into a dance with whole soul and body when he was tripped. At first he thought it was an accident, but in the crowd he spied a swarthy, thick-set, man distinctly of the Latin dandy type. On the dandy's breast was pinned a huge diamond brooch, his fingers were loaded with glittering rings, and his ear lobes drawn with gaudy bangles. Decorative chains hung in profusion from his clothing, and over this gear were strapped bowie knives and pistols. On a second swing around he tripped Jack Russell again. This was too much. The Kentuckian hit the dandy squarely between the eyes and landed him flat on his back. The crowd gasped. Did Jack Russell know that he had just hit the pirate Jean Lafitte? No man in all New Orleans would have dared touch the brigand, let alone knock him down.

Lafitte was said to be a brave man, but he had never exactly encountered a determined Kentuckian before. He rushed from the dance hall and assembled his henchmen for an assault on the place. Doors and windows were barred, and the occupants prepared themselves to stand off the seige. Battering rams were thrust against the doors, flails pounded at the windows, and blunderbus pistols were fired through the building. New Orleans policemen rushed to the scene, but they were driven back by the pirates. They hurried back to headquarters to report a second battle of New Orleans in process, and it was not until militiamen were marched to the scene of conflict that the pirates were beaten back and quiet once again established.

Among the excited defendants of the dance hall was hardy old Captain Holton, of Kentucky, who had been under heavy fire at the battle of the Thames. The old captain came out frightened, and he told bystanders in a quavering voice that Roaring Jack Russell's fight with the pirates was the worst experience of his life.

Jack Russell now was regarded as the chieftain of rivermen. He had proved his bravery by knocking Lafitte down, and he was again to prove his strength in a less belligerent manner. It is said that Cap'n Jack had lifted a 1,647-pound weight and on another occasion had carried a burden of 1,245 pounds all the way across the deck of a large steamboat. He literally was the personification of the famous Paul Bunyan.

Many times Jack Russell had swung around that wide-sweeping bend before Natchez. He knew Giles Bend and the city before it like a book, but he was even better acquainted with that wild hellhole underneath the great chalky cliff called Natchez-under-the-Hill. Jack Russell, like hundreds of other Kentuckians, was fascinated by the city's wickedness. Since early boyhood he had heard horror tales of what happened to innocent men and women who fell into the filthy clutches of its gamblers and prostitutes. For years he had really looked for an opportunity to give the lowdown rascals a dose of their own medicine out of a hot spoon. This opportunity came on one trip down when Jack had taken on board a native minister who had more money than common sense. When Captain Russell's proud *Empress* buried her nose deep in the murky gumbo mud before the Natchez hellhole, the minister strolled through the miry lane of the town to make a purchase. In his simple way he displayed several hundred dollars in paying his bill. This was money which he intended to use in the purchase of western lands. Seeing his roll of bills was manna from heaven for the light-fingered thieves who gathered around the stranger. He was lured inside another house on the promise that he could get a better article there for less money. It was a simple ruse to catch a simple man.

Limping back to the boat, the old minister, between sobs, related his experience to the hardy captain. This was the excuse Jack Russell had wanted for years. He could make an assault upon the dens of vice which lined the river. He would either have the minister's money and the culprit, or the gamblers and their house.

He searched several houses, but the cutthroats had barricaded themselves inside their den and would not come out. Efforts to smoke them out short of setting the whole town on fire failed. Captain Russell became impatient. He lost his temper to think that the scoundrels were about to defeat him. Jack swore he would drag the whole damned pack into the river or have the money. He pulled his powerful boat around into position and ran a large rope around the house preparatory to carrying out his threat. For the gamblers this was serious; they knew the enraged Kentuckian meant business. One of them grabbed an ax and rushed out and cut the rope.

Captain Jack had not looked for so bold a move on the part of his opponents, and for a moment he was halted in his plans. The rope-cutting effort only delayed the final outcome. He sent a crew of deckhands racing around the house with a stout chain, and set the boat hard to stern. The flimsy house groaned and careened, then jumped from its foundations. It was headed for the river with a roomful of thieves. They were on their way to be drowned like rats and they knew it. Their hands were played out. They knew the captain held all trumps and they begged for a parley. If Jack Russell would slack away on his chain they would meet his request. He had asked for the preacher's money and the culprit; both were delivered to him. When Captain Jack's boat backed out and headed for New Orleans it left a smashed house behind it, but a happy band of thieves in it.

Scores of legends survive this Kentucky riverman. They all have to do with his iron courage in the face of river trials. Fires, snags, explosions, and racing make up vigorous chapters in the Russell story. There was the heroic account of the explosion of the *General Brown* just opposite Helena. The *General Brown* was loaded with passengers, livestock, and gunpowder. Its captain was one of those vainglorious creatures who proved a constant threat to the general peace of mind. He couldn't bear for another boat to pass him, and disregarding responsibility for his cargo, he would take a chance in order to win a race. The *General Brown* was "holding its steam" for a race with Russell's boat when its stay bolts let go. Roaring Jack became a hero when he helped to rescue the injured passengers and crew, and prevented the fire from spreading to the shipment of gunpowder.

Later Captain Jack Russell quit the river trade and retired to his farm at Frankfort to become a Whig candidate for the state legislature. For four years he was a successful legislator and then went back to the soil to live out his life as a Kentucky gentleman.

There was a rapid succession of boats on the Kentucky River. The roster is almost as long as your arm. Captain John Armstrong put the *Argo* in the trade, and then the *John Armstrong*. Then came the *Argo II* and the *Ocean*. At Frankfort Captain Innes Todd put the *Blue Wing* in the trade, and went for a time as its master.

The *Blue Wing I, II,* and *III* were to become vital parts of Kentucky's steamboat history. *Blue Wing II* for years almost rivaled the beloved Congressman Clay for a place in the state's affection. It was a handsome boat, built especially for the Kentucky trade. Notices of its maiden run proudly announced that it was 152.5 feet long with 27-foot beam and a 5-foot hold. Its boilers were 42 inches in diameter and 22 feet long, and the cylinders of the engine were 17 inches in diameter and it had a 7-foot stroke. William French designed and built the hull, and Curry and Miller built the engines. The *Blue Wing's* cabins and decks were so elaborate that it looked like a birthday cake made by a baker who was hopelessly infatuated with the idea of using a confectioner's gun. The scrollwork and gingerbread were the last word in the carpenter's gaudy art. The makers had set themselves successfully to the task of creating a veritable floating valentine.

Samuel Deye supplied the upholstery, and prospective passengers were told that the *Blue Wing's* beds were the very best to be had on the river. The beautiful furniture had been selected from the distinctive stock of J. M. Monohan, and the thick soft carpets were the handiwork of Best and Duvall. All these were names which indicated that the new steamer's owners had gone the whole hog in creating their boat. It was truly a luxury vessel. Lady passengers were assured of perfect comfort in the cabins, and if they were accompanied by squirming youngsters there was a trundle under every bed. Restless males were tempted aboard with the information that the beds in the gentleman's cabin were very wide indeed.

This palatial steamer was under the command of Captain Todd, who learned about the river under the tutelage of Roaring Jack Russell. Like his old master, Captain Todd had come up through the ranks from a flatboat. He had run aboard the old *Empress* as a clerk, and he was aboard that boat the night it burned to the water's edge in Louisville where it was awaiting the arrival of Captain Russell and his bride. Thousands of dollars had gone into refurbishing the old veteran, and its main cabin was stacked high with wedding presents. It was then that Captain Todd had set out to become an independent operator.

Proud Captain Todd had the honor of bringing the georgeous *Blue Wing* into Frankfort on her maiden run. Crowds swarmed the river bank to see the fairy

puff box push by. At Frankfort droves of curious sightseers strolled aboard to walk on its plush carpet, and to
stare wild-eyed at themselves in its full-length gold-
framed plate-glass mirrors.

The captain was an aristocratic gentleman—the
grandson of Judge Harry Innes, a pioneer jurist, and
the stepson of the great compromiser, John Jordan Crittenden. Being a Kentucky gentleman of the first water,
he carried on the best traditions of the Bluegrass country. Captain Todd set a famous table aboard his boat;
there were fine hams, fried chicken that was as crisp as
a spinster's temper, fine haunches of mutton, huge
roasts of beef, and luscious vegetables. It was said that
there was such a camaraderie between the captain and
his generous farmerfolk patrons along the river that on
each run they came bearing bounteous gifts of prize
farm products. In order to use all his gifts, the boat's
master carried hoards of visitors to whom he fed the
surplus food.

The succession of *Blue Wing* boats was a rich chapter in the kaleidoscopic social and economic history of
Kentucky. These boats ran from above Shakertown to
Louisville and Cincinnati on regular schedules for almost
a half century. Their passenger lists were rolls of Kentucky and the South's first citizens. Henry Clay was a
favorite with all steamboat men, but especially with the
old Kentucky masters, Russell, Todd, John Holton, and
Sam Sanders. Lean dignified John Crittenden went and
came on the Kentucky River steamers. Tradition has it
that he found complete relaxation in their cabins. Gruff
but humorous old Bob Letcher—governor of Kentucky
—was always welcomed in the seat of honor at the captain's table. Fire-eating but witty George D. Prentice
went aboard the boats on his journeys to the state capital and to the mineral springs.

Hundreds of legislative fledglings drifted into Frankfort for their first time to clutter up the state's legislative mill with their ill-conceived bills. For three months every year the steamboat cabins were jammed with politicians plotting and scheming to get what they wanted at the statehouse. One upriver shyster referred to the *Blue Wing* in his uncertain recollections of a winter in Frankfort at the state's expenses. He introduced his rambling speech of self-emulation with the assurance that, "arter you elected me I went down to Frankfort on the *Blue Wing* and as we wended our winding sinuosities amidst its lab'rynthian meanderings, the birdlets, the batlets, and the owlets flew outen their secret hidin' places and cried out to me in loud voices: sail on, Mullins, thou proud defender of thy country's liberties."

There were other, and gayer passengers. Parties of young men and women crowded aboard the Kentucky River boats on their way to popular Drennon Springs, or to the mineral springs at Harrodsburg where Dr. Christopher Columbus Graham was a generous host.

With such a precious and tempting cargo aboard, the cabins of the saucy *Blue Wing,* or the fast *Ocean* or *Dove* became happy hunting grounds for ambitious beaux and belles. A swashbuckling Bluegrass militia captain could find a soft-spoken Mississippi belle to become mistress of his estate. Or, perhaps, a rugged low-country planter formed a lucrative alliance with an independent and witty belle of the rich Bluegrass. The river and its direct connections with the cotton country tied the two sections together into a close knot of kinship.

On almost every steamer traveling the Kentucky River there stood out against the background of gaiety a somber little band of passengers who went into and returned from a world of material values. These were the Shakers from Pleasant Hill. On the periphery of the throng of belles and beaux traveled Shakers, dressed in their flat wide-brimmed hats, gray simple-patterned jeans, and coarse shoes. They were agents of the colony who were on their way "to the world" to sell fruit and vegetable seeds, brooms, chairs, cloth, blankets, and tool handles, or to dispose of fat livestock, meat, and grain. Or, on occasions, an anxious Shaker elder watched over a family of restless orphan children whom he was taking home to become converts of his socioreligious community. They were on their way to exchange membership in the order for keep during their dependent years.

It was with a genuine touch of affection that meticulous Shaker clerks recorded the arrival and departure of the river steamers. Their stern discipline was graciously lax in the matter of visiting, and there was an astounding amount of traveling back and forth of members from the various communities of the faith.

During the spring months the bulk of the fashionable passengers were bound downstream. They were on their way to the race courses of the lower South. Beginning with the races held at Vicksburg, the Kentuckians would move on to the tracks at Natchez and then to New Orleans. The grand climax of the season came at the fashionable Metaire Course, where the best racing blood in the country was entered in the contests.

Kentucky boats going south were loaded also with spindley-legged scions of noble Kentucky, Virginia, and English blood. Kentuckians early proved their horses' mettle, and usually the shouts at the rail around Metaire were from Kentuckians drowning out all the rest of race-horse creation. Cabins of the steamers thronged with owners, their wives, sons, and daughters. Trainers and jockeys intermingled with the high society of employers. The boiler decks were made into straw-packed stalls for the spirited thoroughbreds. Talk aboard was to one end and on one subject—horses. Blood lines, time, training, and racing incidents were threshed out time and time again. Kentucky was on its way to show the rest of the world its heels.

Among some of the most famous horses to reach the Metaire by steamer were the wonder horses Lexington, Arrow, Grey Medoc, Miss Foote, and Reube. In 1853 Lexington went to the southern tracks with an exciting reputation as a crack starter on the Association Track at Lexington. The "cracks" at Lexington were sure that their horse would do the same thing under the dreamy skies of southern Louisiana, and they took their rent money along to prove their confidence.

These were the days on which one is tempted to look back and call romantic. Underneath the fanfare and romance of the texas, however, a realistic worldly Kentucky was plying its everyday trade. Steamboats were money-makers, and they hauled millions of dollars' worth of hempen bagging and bale rope, tobacco, wheat and flour, corn and meats to the South. To Kentuckians and their downriver customers this was important—this was slavery's lifeline. The Kentucky's green waters and its busy little steamers were vital cogs in the ante-bellum cotton economy and the old southern way of life.

A defamer found his way to the pleasant Kentucky Valley during the decade before the war. Perhaps, after all, he may not have been as defacing in his witticisms as he was clumsy in his humor. This stranger was Philander Q. Doesticks, or Mortimer Thomson, who went about writing humor, which, "like Hodge's razors, was 'made to sell.'" Where other travelers were overwhelmed by the natural beauty of the Kentucky, he found it only a river "of sharp bends." The *Blue Wing,* he said, was "much the shape of a Michigan country-made sausage, and is built with a hinge in the middle to go around the sharp bends in the river, and is manned by two captains, four mates, sixteen darkies, two stewards, a small boy, a big dog, an opossum, two pair of grey squirrels, one clock and a cream-colored chambermaid." In this vein he goes on and on making humor to sell to Yankee editors at the expense of the little Kentucky "floating palace."

Before the end of its days *Blue Wing II* was to play a part in a fine upriver comedy. Occasionally the water got high enough for the Frankfort boats to run up to Irvine and sometimes they went up to the "three forks" at Beattyville. This was so seldom that the "coming of the steamboat" was almost as much a part of local folklore "as the year the pigeons came." Some of those bearded natives who rambled through the virgin forest with long hog rifles resting in the crooks of their arms had never seen a steamboat. That was the case of one of these on the morning of March 15, 1846, when the *Blue Wing* got through on a high tide to near Irvine. The banks of the river were lined with excited people waving and shouting to the captain and the crew. One mountainman was attracted by the puffing and rustling of the waters and rushed toward the banks, his rifle loaded with an overcharge to shoot the varmint. There it came, some strange antediluvian monster which had pulled itself free from the mud of the river's bottom. Its horns pointed straight up, and they spouted fire and smoke. If it was not stopped it would devour the mountain country. The old hunter rested his gun and drew a bead, dead center between the horns, if the varmint had brains that was where they should be. A more worldly-wise neighbor happened up before the old hunter pressed the trigger and knocked his gun barrel off the aim. When the would be protector of the mountains was informed that he was about to shoot a steamboat, he snorted: "Do you call that a steamboat? Well, she stood a smart chance of getting shot; I was going to give it to her 'tween the horns!"

War and railroads ruined the river trade. Kentucky steamers wore out and were never replaced. Only once since the big day of the boats has there been excitement over river navigation. In the early decade of the present century the Frankfort Chamber of Commerce became excited over a revival of trade. Columns of the *State Journal* contain the exciting news that within a few years rival companies would be fighting for trade, and piling freight high as the old turnpike bridge in Frankfort. But somehow this scheme, like many others, proved to be a fabrication of an overactive secretary's imagination, one who hoped to boost his city's importance as a market.

Occasionally a little steamer shoves a load of sand and gravel before it, or a showboat or pleasure barge for a one-night stand, but the real steamboat days remain only as a happy memory. There are no more fine steamers, and palatial accommodations on the river. The last famous Kentucky boat to carry on the competition with the railroads for freight and passengers was the *Falls City*. Once and awhile this boat had passengers but, except for a skylarking excursion party, its passenger list was shabby. Its captain was interested primarily in revenue-bearing freight, and accommodations for passengers were exceedingly meager. It was said that a fastidious patron protested that the boat's towel was filthy. This angered the captain, and unlike his genteel predecessors, he shouted, "Damn you, a hundred men have wiped their faces and hands on that towel, and you ain't no better than they were."

6

Bluegrass Kentuckian

A TRAVELER in the eighteen-thirties wrote a line that would even yet describe much of Bluegrass Kentucky. As this observant visitor was jostled along in a stagecoach over the rolling hills of the plateau country, which nestles in the giant curved arm of the Kentucky, he was much interested in the land spread out before him. He was favorably impressed with what he called the champaign country. It billowed before him like a huge static green wave of the sea. The rugged land waves were broken only by long lines of trees which followed fence lines out of sight or were eddied about trees gathered in pleasing clusters over the surface of the pasture land. Some of the richest land in the United States is to be found in Bluegrass Kentucky. Like the huge oaks that spread their long sinewy arms far out from their great trunks, the land has stamina.

Philosophizing as the clumsy coach jolted its way up and down hill at the heels of an alert team, James Hall observed: "It is seldom that the eye of the traveler is delighted with so pleasing a combination of rural beauty and tasteful embellishment. The dwellings are commodious and comfortable; most of them are very superior to those usually inhabited by farmers, while

many are the elegant mansions of the opulent and refined. These are surrounded by gardens and pleasure
grounds, adorned with trees and shrubs, tastefully disposed. There is something substantial, as well as great
industry, in its productions." This philosophical observer described one of the things which have attracted
the attention of hundreds of visitors to the Bluegrass.
"The woodland pastures," he wrote, "which are remarkably beautiful, [give] to its extensive farms an unusual
degree of elegance, and to the whole character of the
scenery an originality, which attracts the attention of
the most casual observer, while it fills a genuine admirer
of nature with the most pleasurable emotions."

This was one of the features of the country which
first attracted the ambitious American pioneers who
trudged through the friendly gap in the steep eastern
wall into Kentucky. Among this trailworn throng was
many a lusty pioneer who stopped and stared with
open-mouthed wonderment at the vast plateau spread
out before him to the north of the Kentucky River.
These westward-moving Americans rushed up through
the narrow gorges from the fording places in the deeply
embedded river to search for a claim, or they poled
their way up the Kentucky from the Ohio to the Elkhorn country as did Hancock Taylor in 1774 with his
surveying party.

Many an enthusiastic land hunter dropped to his
knees, in what he called the "Great Kentucky Prairie,"
to dip up double handfuls of its mahogany loam soil to
admire its rich waxy fertility. What a joyous sight it
was to the eyes of a man who had grown weary staring
at the thin red clay or monotonous pale-brown sandy
soil east of the mountains. It was largely to escape the
certain economic enslavement which such land promised that many of them had mustered enough courage

to make the hazardous journey west. As these new frontiersmen strode westward, wiry pea vines sawed across their bony shins at each step. These vines were matted in the young and tender trim cane, and they even grew under the shade of the spreading elm, post oak, black cherry, walnut, and sugar maple.

Here was a country where grass would grow under trees and that was a sight few of the Easterners had ever seen. The future of this land was writ large on its very surface. Long and deeply worn trails penetrated to the heart of the region. Herds of buffalo, deer, and elk swam the Ohio and wandered deep into the great primitive pea and cane grazing land of the Kentucky valley. Pioneer hunters followed in the wake of the herds of buffalo, elk, and deer, as did the Indian warriors and hunters before them. These pioneers plodded along through the wilderness and through the savanna lands where the Indians had kept the country burned off in order to enhance its grazing possibilities, and they knew that someday the country would be famous for its livestock. Whether they were conscious of their important role in manifest destiny or not is open to serious doubt. Perhaps this term was coined by political apologists who wished to justify their various large territorial grabs. There can be no doubt, however, but what the first pioneers in central Kentucky dreamed of the great days of livestock grazing which were to come. People who loved livestock measured the desirability of the land in terms of grass and water. In this respect the Kentucky Bluegrass became an extravagant answer to even the most pleasant dreams of a grazier.

In his later jocular moments, the central Kentucky pioneer boasted that the potato hills on his land looked like cedar stumps. His corn patch, to hear him tell it, produced an astounding number of bushels, even under the most adverse conditions. He complained in mock seriousness that his pumpkin vines grew so fast that they grabbed hold of him and threw him down and had him hog-tied with runners before he could escape the field. Sometimes he varied the story with the complaint that he never got any pumpkins because the vines grew so fast they wore the little pumpkins to pieces dragging them on the ground. He joked that he planted nails and harvested crowbars. With a merry twinkle of satisfaction the Bluegrass Kentuckian has looked for a century and a half out over his rolling acres of gracious fresh land with its copses of trees. In such moments when he has gloated over his country, the Kentuckian has pitied heaven because of its shabby comparison. At other times, and in moments of unusual humility, he has called the Bluegrass "God's Footstool."

It was this wide rolling plateau which was to give Kentucky its nickname, and likewise to characterize the state to the rest of the nation. Poets of every degree of excellence and poetic jubilization have poured out a sizable stream of laudatory verse. More than a half a hundred poems have been written to eulogize the Bluegrass alone, and many of those entitled "Kentucky" are confined to the central region. Their authors have fallen under some one of the Bluegrass's many moods, and they have suspended these permanently in their writings. Novelists have ever found the Bluegrass a thrilling source of color and character. In the immediate ante-bellum decades, the popular American sentimentalist, Mary J. Holmes, moved from New England to the Elkhorn Creek in Woodford County. Around her home near Midway she gathered enough color to lend a touch of regionalism to all her novels. One of these, *Tempest and Sunshine,* was Bluegrass in ink. Even the characters were easily identified by local and contemporary readers.

Years later James Lane Allen, a sensitive son of the rich Kentucky plateau, distinguished himself in the American school of postwar local colorists. His short stories, published in 1892 under the title of *The Blue Grass Region of Kentucky,* are reminiscent of a Kentucky which Allen believed had been. Perhaps he hoped this Kentucky would be again. He placed about the region a cloak of romance which hovers over it even yet in this realistic, material age. Allen's other novels helped to develop this spirit. *The Kentucky Cardinal, The Mettle of the Pasture, The Bride and the Mistletoe,* and the others entertained a large reading circle at a time when both central Kentucky and the nation were trying to overcome the unhappy effects of reconstruction. So confused did James Lane Allen become in this unpredictable age that he made much of his writing an earnest fictional apologia for the change which had come over the Bluegrass. Scores of other writers of both fiction and history have found inspiration and factual materials for their literary efforts in this country. Today, perhaps the great Kentucky novel is to be written from the rich material lying dormant awaiting the genial touch of an industrious imaginative writer who has both energy and perspective.

In all the writings on Bluegrass Kentucky, no one has clearly answered one question for the outsider. Thousands of expectant and sentimental visitors have asked, "Is the bluegrass blue or not?" It becomes nothing short of an act of brute heartlessness to answer, "No." For a brief interval only a bluish haze hangs over the fields of bluegrass. This is that brief moment when the heads go through an advanced stage of pollination. Even then a fair degree of imagination is necessary to see the blue. The history of this grass in America is exceedingly vague. It is of English origin, but no one seems to have explained with any degree of complete satisfaction how it reached Kentucky. Nevertheless, it is the luscious growth of this grass which gives the Bluegrass region the appearance of being a thick natural emerald carpet.

Like the delicate bluish haze that lingers over the sprawling Bluegrass meadowland is the courtly tradition of Kentucky gentility. Large pillared mansions or substantial farmhouses have come to symbolize the land. Such of these as were seen by James Hall, Timothy Flint, and other early visitors to the Bluegrass have served as stage properties in this romance. When rugged buckskinned pioneers led their families across the mountains to conquer the wilderness, there were intermingled with them a fair sprinkling of eastern tidewater and piedmont gentry. Among these were John Brown, George Nicholas, Caleb Wallace, General William Russell, Thomas and Humphrey Marshall, Thomas and Nathaniel Hart, and David Meade. In instances some of these genteel immigrants sent slaves and overseers ahead to prepare homes for their families and fields for their support. They brought their families west, not to a land of uncertainties, but rather to one whose possibilities were already known, and where they knew they could enjoy most of the comforts of their eastern homes.

Bluegrass Kentucky proved to be an ideal place where romantic and imaginative gentry could play at the gentle art of being English lords of the manor in frontier America. Among the small group of patricians was David Meade, who brought to Kentucky an air of good living that was to set a social standard for many years to come. In fact, some elements of the good life are still alive to give the region a shading of romantic culture.

David Meade was educated in England at Dalfton and Fuller's academies. On July 4, 1796, after he had already built up a considerable estate in Virginia, the colonel landed at Maysville, Kentucky, with his family to begin life anew in the virgin land of Kentucky. They had traveled down the Ohio by flatboat, and from Maysville they journeyed by horseback. Pack horses brought in their household furnishings and fineries. The colonel had already located an ideal spot for his future home on the bank of Jessamine Creek, and here it was that he was to build his famous estate, "Chaumiere des Prairies." Almost immediately upon his arrival in Kentucky, Colonel Meade was to become the common denominator of Kentucky gentility. He and his family brought west with them a fused social philosophy of England and Virginia, both of which became acceptable to central Kentuckians.

Chaumiere became a noble blend of all of the Meade family's background plus the freshness of frontier Kentucky. The grounds, with their ancient sugar maples, black walnuts, cherries, spreading elms, and white oaks, were an idyllic spot in the virginal western forest. Colonel Meade's house was a strange building which ran almost the whole scale of prevalent architectural styles. It represented the gradual stages of the family's adaptation to its new surroundings. For a better name contemporaries called it a "villa." A villa, in the eighteenth century American sense of the word, was a rambling house which sprawled out in all directions. Chaumiere had rooms constructed of native stone, of brick, of wood, and one of mud. A large octagonal brick living room formed the central part of the house. Back of this chamber was a spacious dining room paneled in black Kentucky walnut. There were many other passages, alcoves, and corners. The central part of the structure had two stories. Back of all this was the large kitchen with a wide fireplace lined with jacks and cranes, with a battery of bake ovens opening in the sides. Chaumiere des Prairies had a gracious reputation for its well-cooked foods before the end of the eighteenth century.

Contemporaries who came to Kentucky during the early eighteen hundreds were impressed with the talk around Lexington of Chaumiere and the Meades. In fact, Colonel Meade's became a sort of community institution for receiving distinguished visitors. A pretty good clue that a visitor was accepted socially was the fact that his host took him out to Chaumiere for a call. Many of these callers have left interesting descriptions of their experiences at the famous estate. Horace Holley, president of Transylvania University during its happy days of expansion in the twenties, journeyed, along with other Kentucky gentlemen, out to Colonel Meade's. After his first trip Holley wrote that the party was met at the gate to the estate by the seventy-year-old master himself. He was dressed in the meticulous style of the colonial tidewater gentleman. He wore a square coat and great cuffs, a court vest, short breeches, and white form-fitting stockings. Madame Meade was dressed in the same period and style as her husband. She wore a long-waisted dress, a white apron, stays, ruffles about the elbow, and a white colonial house-cap.

As the party was seated in the great brick octagonal room, the observant New England Yankee, Horace Holley, had an opportunity to appraise his host. The Yankee's eyes searched out every line of Colonel Meade's face, and stared at his general profile, and then he resorted to the shrewd eastern pastime of personal comparison. The new president of Transylvania believed that the Lord of Chaumiere looked like Timothy Pickering. This was a distinct mark of favor, for what New Englander was not proud of Colonel Pickering?

Horace Holley was far more impressed with Colonel Meade when he learned that the colonel made no pretense of engaging in any gainful occupation. Colonel Meade explained that he had come to Kentucky to live the life of a country gentleman, and that he had succeeded. The Easterner looked upon his host, perhaps, with more wonderment because of his genteel idleness than he would have if he had boasted that he daily violated all the Ten Commandments. One other bit of the colonel's eccentricity impressed President Holley. The colonel maintained that he never wanted a visitor to warn him of his approaching visit. It made no matter to him how large a company called at his gate, for his slaves always had dinner enough for them.

In the linen closet at Chaumiere were very fine tablecloths and linen, and hanging in the cupboard was enough glass and chinaware to serve a hundred guests. The solid silver service was brought from England to Virginia in the seventeenth century, and it was for a time the finest service in Kentucky. In keeping with the fine table equipment was the well-stocked larder. Turning on the spits in the rambling kitchen were choice meats of the region, and delicious vegetables and pastries were available in large quantities.

On another occasion President Holley and nineteen of his Lexington neighbors and visitors drew up before the gate of Chaumiere without warning. At dinner they were given a banquet of choice meats and delicious pastries. There were always enough carefully trained slaves to meet any request for entertainment of the guests of Chaumiere. When the meal was finished, Colonel Meade always insisted that his guests take a stroll through his carefully landscaped grounds. One strolled through a Kentucky forest on a rich carpet of bluegrass. To this natural setting there had been added a curious mixture of miniature ornamental Chinese temples and classic garden houses. There was a lake, the center of which was an island adorned by a Grecian temple, which was a shrine to the classic spirit of the artificial lake.

Seven years after Horace Holley had driven out for the first time to Chaumiere, Dr. Craik, rector of Christ's Church in Louisville, wrote an account of his visit to the estate. He believed there was nothing else like it in America. With his taste for the English way of life, the Episcopal rector wrote a glowing account of this pleasant place. He found that by 1825 Colonel Meade's hospitality had become so great that he had to reserve two days a week for public entertainments. Even years later Dr. Craik remembered Chaumiere, and in his recollections he compared its grounds with those of Central Park in New York City.

Every famous visitor who came to the Bluegrass, and who could spare the time, was driven out to Chaumiere. In a score of years many distinguished travelers enjoyed its hospitality. Most exciting of all this long string of distinguished callers was Colonel Aaron Burr, of New York. During his early days in Kentucky he visited with the Meades as a pleasant house guest. When the evil days came near and Joseph Hamilton Daviess, federal district attorney, had him arrested on a charge of treason, Burr was given over to young David Meade for safekeeping. Already the ex-vice-president was a favorite with the family. At the table, however, he had an eccentric habit which attracted attention. Before he would eat bread, he picked it up and smelled of it carefully. He explained to his hostess that he did it because he had "a very peculiar stomach, and could not eat a morsel of bread that was the least sour." Harmon Blennerhassett sometimes visited Chaumiere with his friend Burr, and his name became connected with the estate.

Colonel Meade lived to be ninety-four years of age, and during the major portion of his life he was an active man. His wife lived to be almost as old as he. He was a direct link between tidewater Virginia and the prosperous Bluegrass Kentucky. At the time the colonel died Bluegrass Kentucky had reached the stage in its culture when it was building pompous Greek revival houses. Rich lands in the region were producing thousands of tons of hemp and tobacco, and the Bluegrass farmers were becoming prosperous. He even lived to see the peculiar change which came over much of the Bluegrass because his neighbors became infatuated with Scott's Waverley Novels. At Lexington, Colonel Joseph Bruen and John McMurtry were to carry Colonel Meade's dream of an Anglicized Bluegrass one step further by building Tudor cottages and castles.

Colonel Meade's story was not to have a happy ending. His idyllic dream of living life through as a gentleman of leisure was to end as he had planned it, but his sons were unable to keep the estate. His fine china, glass and silverware, which had been set before hundreds of guests, was scattered among relatives in Kentucky and Virginia. The Joshua Reynolds paintings fell into unappreciative hands. One of them, said Colonel Meade's grandson, William Lightfoot Thompson, was used by his uncle to cover a meat barrel until the paint was scrubbed off the canvas. Dissolution of the estate was complete. Chaumiere was sold to a practical farmer, and in time what had been a carefully tended park became a farmsite with its rugged utilitarian appearance. Once it was said that Colonel Meade ordered a slave to bring a wheelbarrow to pick up a chew of tobacco which his Nicholasville neighbor, Congressman Samuel Woodson, had spat on the grass. Congressman Woodson, out of spite, ordered the slave to wait until he could finish with another chew. This was all gone, and where there had been a fine lawn, there was now a heap.

Wherever in America the land has been fertile enough to create and to support well-to-do families, there have nearly always been unhappy stories of dissolution. Sons of capable fathers have shown a woeful lack of ability, or they have become dissolute and wasted the substance of the land. Bluegrass Kentucky has had its full chapter in this human story. Sons of famous Bluegrass gentlemen have not always been able to follow in their fathers' footsteps.

There is another chapter in the story. Bluegrass families have disappeared because of the failure of their daughters to make satisfactory marriages or to make any marriages at all. There have been numerous reasons why this is true. Outstanding is the daughter's unhappy failure to find a prospective husband who possessed both a satisfactory economic and social status to meet her family's demands. Many times a daughter of a well-established family has refused to descend the social scale and "marry beneath herself." It is one of the tragedies of the Bluegrass that much of its virile pioneer stock has ceased to exist in the state because of the failure of its daughters to marry. Many a proud maiden lady has remained at home and clung steadfastly to the family portraits, the homestead, and the family papers as a last stand against the ravages of the sons of more prolific but less proud Kentucky women.

Inside the Bluegrass there was the early beginning of a culture which has enriched its history. There were doctors, lawyers and other professional men who brought honor to the region. Among the doctors was Dr. Samuel Brown, who before the turn of the century had introduced to the American frontier the art of immunization against smallpox. Across the river at Danville, in 1809, Dr. Ephraim McDowell focused the attention of the medical world upon his pioneering work. He performed courageous yeoman medical service for suffering womankind in his ovarian operation upon Jane Todd Crawford.

Among the legal philosophers who brought distinction to the Bluegrass were George Nicholas, Caleb Wallace, Joseph Hamilton Daviess, John Breckinridge, and Henry Clay. Nicholas in 1792 was the leading influence in the drafting of the state's constitution. Likewise he led a militant assault against the encroachment upon individual and states' rights by the federalistic government of John Adams. Joseph Hamilton Daviess was chief accuser of Aaron Burr and caused whatever nefarious scheme the New Yorker had planned to be delayed and then to fail. John Breckinridge was the guiding force behind the Kentucky resolutions offered as protests against the denial of fundamental democratic rights in the famous Alien and Sedition Laws. Henry Clay, of course, became an American political institution. His first notable political speech was made on the bank of the Town Fork of the South Elkhorn Creek. Following George Nicholas in his bold attack upon the federalistic laws, which Breckinridge's resolutions attacked, the young Virginia lawyer proved himself an aggressive orator. Many other Bluegrass lawyers have distinguished themselves before the American bar. Kentucky lawyers have enjoyed a happy distinction in the nation's legal history.

Miles of whitewashed fences around horse farms in central Kentucky tell a story of an interest in horse breeding and racing. This, however, is only one side of the interest of the Bluegrass's recreational history. Kentucky people have always had a sporting side to their culture. In the early days, travelers through the region were impressed by handbills nailed to tavern walls which advertised bear baitings or rifle shootings. Occasionally one of these contemporary accounts tells of the practice of gander pulling. This sport was that of the poor man playing at knighthood in a modest but somewhat heartless manner. Back east of the mountains the landed gentry of the Virginia and Carolina tidewater sought entertainment in the ring tournaments instead of by torturing a defenseless greasy gander suspended head down.

Sporting in Kentucky took many forms. Almost from the beginning there were race paths where proud contestants matched their nags against those of their neighbors. Where there was no path, horsemen raced their entries up and down the main streets of Bluegrass villages or up and down the public highways. Early town minutes, and acts of the Kentucky legislature, contain restrictive legislation against such sport. Even the charters of turnpike companies contained clauses which forbade horse racing down a public road.

By 1805, John Bradford began to issue a special spring supplement to the *Kentucky Gazette* publicizing stud horses. Records of Bluegrass horses were advertised, and some of them, like the famous stud Dare Devil, had astounding records. His owner claimed that he had been ridden from Frankfort to Lexington in the

Overleaf: Racing at the Old Kentucky Association Track around 1886, sixty years after the track was founded.

morning and run in a four-heat, four-mile race in the afternoon. In making a sharp turn in the track the stud had jumped a high board fence with his 200-pound rider, and had been jumped back onto the path and brought home the winner.

Down near the Kentucky River in Jessamine County, the famous old pioneer soldier Colonel Benjamin Netherland offered a $50 prize for the best one-mile heat "free to anything with four legs and hair on." This was a challenge to the rollicking Irishman Michael Arnspiger. He pretended to take Colonel Netherland's offer literally and proceeded to train a bull to run in the race. On the day of the great contest Arnspiger appeared at the race path astride his bull. His equipment was outlandish enough to frighten every horse in the country. Across his long-horned charger's back was thrown a dried bull's hide which gave him a hideous appearance. Arnspiger carried a tin horn and wore long sharp-pointed spurs. Every time he dug the spurs into the bull's side, the animal sent up a bloodcurdling bellow. The horsemen gathered around the post with their nervous mounts to challenge the right of the eccentric Arnspiger to enter the race, but the judges ruled that it was "free to anything with four legs and hair on." When at last the flag was dropped and the jockeys headed down the path, the devilish Michael dug his spurs in the bull's side, blew his horn and set forth. The bull bellowed like Gabriel's trumpet, the horses took to the woods, and Arnspiger trotted home astride the bull —winner of the purse.

If it was not running a horse race with a bull entry, it was something else. Always Bluegrass Kentucky has been a sporting land. Horse racing has been only a part of the story. There is an old pastime in the Bluegrass which has been practiced from the time the first settlement was made. Cooped up in many of the panniers which rocked back and forth from the sides of pack horses were gamecocks and hens. Old Virginia bloodstock was being brought across the mountains to entertain the Kentuckians in their moments of relaxation from the fight against the raw frontier environment. Since "cocking" is a bloody business, it made a ready appeal to the vigorous frontiersman. Likewise its gory aspects have caused it to be under a ban from certain elements in the Bluegrass. Its written history in the Kentucky River valley is exceedingly spotted. Once and awhile a traveler referred to it or a sporting magazine carried an article in the abstract about this sport. Frequently there were articles about cocking in the *Turf Register,* but these were written about procedure in breeding and training rather than as descriptive of the contemporary state of the art. Always, it seems, cocking has been an illicit consort of horse breeding and racing. In 1845 the sport was well developed in Bluegrass Kentucky. William Porter included a note in his miscellaneous column in the *Spirit of the Times.* He wrote: "Yesterday, and today were 'some' at Memphis, Tennessee. Shy and Means of Kentucky and Colonel Abingdon, of Tennessee, were each to show twenty-one cocks [a main], and $100 on each fight. If 'General Jim' heels for Old Kentuck, I should like to back him for a small smile."

Today there are many cockfighters in Bluegrass Kentucky. They do not shout their identity from housetops, but within the clan this fact is well known. In the winter and early spring, the sport goes on with a boom. Down a lonesome tree-lined country lane, a highway signal lamp burns in a farm gateway. This is the sign of the cockpit, and in the community, perhaps at the top of the nearest hill, a yellow light flickers dimly through the chinked cracks of an innocent-appearing tobacco barn. The visitor pulls his automobile up in line with the others parked in a semicircle. A group of men speaking in subdued tones stands about the door. Just inside the vestibule a ticket salesman asks a dollar for admission to the pit. Once inside the door, the visitor sees before him a strange row of lattice-work cages extending almost up to the ceiling across one end of the barn. In a hasty glance, these clumsily constructed enclosures have somewhat an Oriental appearance. From deep in the block of cages comes a lusty crow from a long-legged cock who is ready for the fight before him. In front of the coops are tables and racks where the cocks are prepared for the pit. A sweating man works away vigorously with a sharp pocketknife, fitting collars to the stubby shanks of a rooster. Another holds the bird's feet in position to receive the gaffs. These are long slender steel instruments with needle-sharp points. The collars of the shanks are thrust down tightly over the collars of the muted natural spurs and are tied on with leather thongs. A few minutes later the cock will be placed in the ring to cut, hack, and pick at an opponent until one or both of them are dead. One of the cocks jumps up; a leg flashes past his opponent; the gaff goes home; and his victim is "rattled." A bead of telltale blood bubbles on the end of the injured cock's beak, and the referee shouts "handle your birds" to the managers. The injured cock is gathered up in the handler's arms. The handler places the bird's head in his mouth and draws off the strangling ooze of blood. Next he bites the comb and blows on its back. Again the cocks are in the ring to fight until one or the other is dead or victorious.

Around the ring, loud jovial betters shout "two on

the red," "five on the black," or banter with robust badinage, reflecting upon the fighting capacities of the combatants in the ring. A wave, a nod, a wink, raised fingers make and accept bets. There is no centralized betting organization. A bet is a gentleman's obligation, and the loser is obligated to hunt up the winner and pay off.

Two cocks are released in the ring, and a wave of excitement runs through the crowd. Enthusiastic cockers crowd up to the ringside and talk in knowing professional lingo about the fight in process. Back in the crowd docile farm women nurse babes at breast and watch every hack and pick made by the bloodthirsty gamecocks. A bird is down; his wings and legs give one ghastly shudder and then quiver to a dead stop. He is dead; a gaff has touched a vital spot. But before the opposing cock can claim the victory, he has to hack or pick at the dead bird once within twenty minutes or the fight is a draw.

Cockfighting has given rise to a strange lingo. A "dunghill" fowl is a coward who flies the pit and runs from a fight. His doom is sealed because his owner wrings his neck in disgust. A "huckster" is a sharp chicken trader, dealing usually in mongrel stock. Then there are the descriptive fighting qualities of cocks. They are "game," "close hitters," "bloody heelers," "ready fighters" with "good mouths," and are "quick to come to point." For months before a cock is pitted in combat he goes through an intricate series of maneuvers. He is "flirted," or tossed into the air, to develop his wings. He is held by his thighs and "fluttered" to strengthen his legs and wings. Before a fight the cocks are "dried out" by careful rationing of water; and when the season is over they are "put on the walks" to run wild in natural surroundings. Under a year of age, cocks are stags. They are in the height of fighting form if they live to be three; and at four they are ready for retirement. Cocks are fought in "hacks" or in single fights, in "mains" of fifteen to twenty-one cocks of one owner pitted against a similar number of another. They are fought in tournaments and derbies on terms agreed to between owners.

Cockfighting is sometimes called the poor man's sport in the Bluegrass, but actually many of its most ardent patrons are wealthy people. The clan is tight-lipped where the sport is in danger of being prohibited. It is quite possible that hundreds of people have lived long lives in the Bluegrass without ever having heard of the cockpits in the region or having seen a cockfight. Yet along a country road a game cock flies across the road ahead of a speeding automobile, and a flock of timid hens take cover from the approaching machine under the tall grass in the ditch. Sometimes it has occurred that an enthusiastic cocker's family has not even known of his interest. An old-time fighter in the Bluegrass stood with one foot on the side of the ring and laughed heartily at the mess his wife got into with their preacher. She had cooked one of his gamecocks for dinner, but it had been rubbed with oil of peppermint, and the meat was ruined. It struck the old-timer as high comedy to see the preacher being offered gamecock for dinner.

This silent sport, hidden away behind the beckoning highway signal flare and the chinked walls of a tobacco barn with its improvised amphitheater about the pits, goes on with vigorous support. To stir up the Humane Society and the women's clubs would be bad business. Yet the Blue Grass Kentuckian of today has not undergone a tremendous change from the day when the cantankerous English travelers in the region spent much of their time reading the vigorous announcements of sport-to-be from the handbills tacked to tavern walls.

In the final analysis Bluegrass Kentucky is more than a region which can be definitely located by a geologist or a geographer upon a soulless map. It is not alone a matter of geographical tangibility, but it is likewise a state of mind, a matter of great community pride, and, so far as a region can be, a satisfactory way of life. The Kentucky mountaineer displays anxiety that the outsider will not look with favor upon his land. It is the same with the native of the Bluegrass. In some of the early travelers' accounts, visitors to the region have mentioned the fact that the natives of the Bluegrass were anxious for a favorable comment upon the countryside. The Honorable Charles Augustus Murray, an English traveler, sensed this characteristic very well when he described its rolling fields, which he mistakingly called level. He wrote: "On this account it is called the garden of Kentucky, and its inhabitants make very heavy demands upon the admiration of the visitor." If Charles Augustus Murray were making the journey in the middle twentieth century, the same demands would be made of him. Immediately upon being introduced to a visitor the Bluegrass Kentuckian asks the traditional question, "How do you like Kentucky?"

There are few communities in the United States which stand out so boldly above the others as does the Bluegrass. Its miles of rolling green hills pierced by the narrow winding lanes, lined with native cherry, walnut, and locust trees, give the whole land a happy appearance. It is this happy character of the land which makes the native son say, "I have traveled around a lot in my lifetime, but there is only one place where I can live and be happy, and that is right here in the Bluegrass." The Bluegrass of Kentucky is one of the rural areas in the United States where the community value of the land often is the equal of its intrinsic value.

7

Kentuckian, Mountaineer

WHEN the traveler goes east from Lexington, he passes through Winchester, and then turns right on the highway which some sentimental promoter has called the "Trail of the Lonesome Pine." Before he has gone far he begins to sense that the road is winding between and over knobs and down into their succeeding valleys. Then the knobs lift up, and far ahead the traveler catches the first sight of the Appalachian Range rolling out before him. This is an exciting land. Its ridges do not reach up into the clouds, except in certain places, nor are there any snow-capped peaks to top off the rugged topography. Before our traveler is a land as strange within its geographical limitations as is China, India or Africa. Through its deep folds the Kentucky River and its tributaries have plowed their deep beds. Like some great subterranean animal the river has searched for floodwaters in every corner, and in its search it has left a deep impression upon the land. The river has played an important part in creating the interest and the strangeness which hover over the long blue line of mountains sprawling across the Trail of the Lonesome Pine.

As one rides toward the Appalachians along the Trail of the Lonesome Pine, he begins to discover that

121

they are more than colorful splotches made by soil experts and geologists on inanimate maps. Before him lies a region filled with many and highly varied human resources. Perhaps already our traveler has heard the popular stories that the people of these hills are Anglo-Saxons, and that because of this they are given to quick fits of temper which lead to creekbank killings and interminable family feuds. If he has listened to his radio on Saturday nights he has heard wild hillbillys raising the rafters with their boisterous wit and music. Then there are the well-known theories of Elizabethan survivals which set the mountaineers of the Kentucky River valley apart from other people of the state. Actually the visitor will find few or none of these specific types in the flesh. The Kentucky mountain people, it is true, are difficult to understand, just as all rural and isolated people are difficult to know. Because of this fact, this region becomes a veritable kaleidoscope of social patterns when it is examined both through the eyes of the agents of social adjustment and through those of the exploiters who have looked upon the mountains only as a source of material wealth. Before one can begin to understand this strange up-river country and its people there are many common everyday experiences of the people which it is necessary to examine. All these things comprise a pattern, which at times appears to be without discernible reason.

Seldom in this Appalachian country, where the ridges hover over the tributaries of the Kentucky, is one far away from a mountain stream tumbling restlessly and unceasingly over its rock-strewn bed to the main forks of the river. These tiny creeks have exerted a tremendous influence upon the lives of the people who live along them. They have been a utilitarian part of the natural surroundings of the country. The constant gurgling of the current as it has eddied and swirled in these myriad highland rivulets is a musical sound which the mountaineer never forgets. He may live much of his lifetime away from the highlands, but his memory is always recalling the creeks of his home country. These rapid streams have ever been sources of supply of drinking water, of power with which to turn tiny corn mills, and as highways leading to the great and confusing world on the "outside."

As the blue ridges draw nearer, and one begins to discern the outline in detail, there are many sharp ridges which run up high behind cabins, and the many breaks in the broad general contour which appeared as tiny lines on the huge blue canvas now become ravines and creek beds. Around the first sharp bend in the mountain road, the outsider has crossed a line of sharp regional demarcation which is to be a distinguishing characteristic of major social importance. For one thing, readily noticeable to the stranger, is the fact that he is in a land of genuine hospitality where he can rest assured that he will be treated with kindness and generosity. Where materialistic industrialism has not burrowed too deeply into the hearts of the people, the "stranger within the gate" philosophy still prevails.

There is an old story that has been bandied about the Bluegress by stodgy after-dinner speakers which does the hillman more credit than most of the tellers realize. It is said that a stranger went into the mountains for a visit, and stopped by a mountaineer's cabin for dinner. He arrived, unfortunately for the host, at a most inopportune moment. Food was scarce, and the best the old lady could scrape up was a mess of baked potatoes. When the company sat down at the honored place at the head of the table, the master of the household was a bit flustered, but come what might he was going to be hospitable. He picked up the pan of potatoes and extended them toward the guest with the invitation, "Stranger, take a tater. Take damn' near all the taters."

This is, of course, a hackneyed story. But the fact is that mountain hospitality is absolute. No man ever went away from a mountain cabin without being offered food and a place to sleep. The meals might be different from those served in a metropolitan hotel, and perhaps the peach tree limb, which is used to keep the flies away, swishes actively above his head. He might even begin to wonder if the limb was active enough before he reached the table, but his skepticism never goes so far as to question the genuineness of his welcome. At night he may have to bed down in the room with a half dozen more people, and perhaps sleep with two or three of them, but that is no reflection on the hillman's willingness to share what he has with the stranger within his gate. Even the mountain idiom reflects this hospitality. When a man says men are intimate friends, he says, "They are as thick as four in a bed."

It took years to build highways and railways into the land-bound hill country about the Kentucky's headwaters. Not until late in this century was this important improvement in transportation facilities made. So here it was in America that the primitive culture of the European and English background of the settlers of the valley was fused with that of the backwoods and preserved in a pleasing degree of virginal freshness. Almost every Kentucky mountainman today speaks a dialect reminiscent of earlier Anglo-American speech. He still carries *pokes* of corn meal home with him from the mill, or, like his pioneer forefathers who threaded their way through the eastern mountain wall,

he has *hearn* of *hit,* or he has *heared* the bad news
a'ready. He has *sot* on a split-log bench in the school-
house while his dinner *spiled thar agin* the wall. A different social class of people from his own or the people
of another community are often spoken of as "that
generation of people." In his speech the mountainman's voice is sharper, and there is a bit of a lingering
telltale overtone which gives evidence of his place of
origin. It is difficult for the hillman to add "*s*" to the
ends of his words. To him it is never a thousand years
ago, but "a thousand year ago." All this may go to
show that the Kentucky mountaineer's speech is Elizabethan. Perhaps some of it is. Many folklore scholars
say that this is so, but they hunt diligently for ex-
ceptional words to prove their points of contention.
The Kentucky mountain speech is that of the American frontier. A few characteristics of speech are general wherever there are southern highlanders, but more
often speech characteristics are localized in relatively
small areas.

A good illustration of the "old-time" mountaineer's speech and power of homely description is that
of "Dock" Pratt, of Hindman. In the characteristic
language of his home community, the old mountaineer
tells the story of the great swarms of wild pigeons
which once flew through the eastern Kentucky woods.
"I just tell what I allus was taught from my forefathers," says Dock Pratt. "I used to set fer hours and
listen to my daddy. . . . No one ever knew what
caused hit. He said the elements'd be darkened fer half
a day when they'd be passin' over. Well, I've been in
pigeon roosties myself. The pigeons roosted thar like
a swarm of bees, until the timber'd break down. Some'd
root up; some'd break down. And he said you could go
next mornin' whar them pigeons roosted and pick up

a sackful whar they'd get crippled whar the timber'd fall. Just with a stick you could kill a sackful. (Would you like to live back then? More pleasure in life.) Them pigeons would light in a beech grove whar they were scratchin' fer beechnuts, you know. You couldn't see the pigeons fer the leaves a-flyin'.

"They went on and on and went to the waters and undertook to cross the sea and hit was stated in the papers they sunk some ships, as they were tryin' to cross the sea. They (people) couldn't hardly beat them off. They lay on them ships like on the timber and sunk them. Some old people say they must have thought there was better food across the waters. Hit was, I believe, a favor from the good Lord above. Why, they'd eat a field of grain up in a little while. They gathered like the locusts in the days of Pharaoh and then they went, just like them. From that day to this the country has never been bothered with them pigeons agin."

Occasionally the mountaineer has been quite philosophical in the adjustments of life which he has had to make since he forced his way up the narrow Kentucky creek valleys. His home from the time of his first penetration of the frontier has been in most instances the log cabin. A painting of a crude log cabin sitting off on a narrow perch above a rapidly flowing clear creek with a rugged mountainside towering up behind it could easily become a highland symbol. As mountain families have grown, room after room has been added onto the one room beginning. The big room with the fireplace was for pa and ma and the little'uns; the open hall was a trot for the dogs; the shed room for the kitchen; and the annexes for the bigger children and the wayfaring stranger. The homely wise and philosophical Dock Pratt on the "Left" Fork of Troublesome made the clever architectural observation on the practice of crude cabin ventilation. "Did you ever hear of a generation that didn't know how to take care of itself?" asked the old philosopher. "In the old days they built their homes without any windows, but they put in two doors—one where the first rays of the sun would come and the other where it would get the last rays at night. Then the sun in hits travels would sarch out all the dark corners and purify them." Even today in the narrow coves which dig back into the rocky highlands, the log cabin sits astride the creek, or perches on the side of the ridge above the stream, the fireplace is at one end, and one door opens to the east and another to the west so that "the sun in hits travels may sarch out all the dark corners and purify them."

Other homely philosophers have been as ingenious as have mountain architects in ferreting out satisfactory solutions to their people's problems. Illness has ever been one of man's outstanding worries. It has always stalked after him on his adventures into new lands. It was so in the case of the Kentucky mountaineers who moved into the land ahead of the general advance of knowledge of major medical discoveries in Europe and along the Atlantic seaboard. Trudging through Cumberland, Pound, and Big Stone gaps in the late eighteenth and early nineteenth centuries, the mountain immigrant put himself upon his own therapeutical ingenuity. In time to come he was either to concoct or to utilize folk remedies brought into the land with him for the treatment of all his diseases. There are thousands of these remedies still extant, and still used by many of the descendants of the pioneers. A baby strangled with the thrash can be cured quickly by being given water from a stranger's right shoe, or by having the breath of a posthumous child blown down its throat. The orphan must not, however, accept pay for his services.

A pregnant woman carries the responsibility of her child on her shoulders. If she hungers for a certain type of food and that hunger is never satisfied, the baby will likewise hunger for the same food, and he will cry continuously until his hunger is satisfied. When a woman is heavy with pregnancy, she should never become excited; and if she does, she should never touch her body with her hands because she will mark the child at a corresponding place on its body at which she touches her own. There are still those who believe that women who see horrible sights will bear deformed children. A snake will mark a child; sight of an open wound will cause the child to be born with an open sore. In travail a woman should hold salt clinched in her hands to ease the pains. An ax placed under the bed with the bit turned upward will help to make delivery easier. After the child is born, the doctor or "granny woman" should place his or her shoes on the mother and have her walk around a bit to drain the womb of the afterbirth. Then to stop bleeding the mother should don the attending aide's hat and wear it. The number of balls upon the umbilical cord of the first-born child denotes the number of children the mother is to have.

Lucky is the child who is born on Christmas Day, for to him is given the power of understanding the speech of animals. If, however, a child has the misfortune to be taken downhill before he has been carried up, he will go downward all his life. As the child grows older, the first louse discovered in its head should be cracked on the bottom of a tin cup, and he will become a good singer. Never allow a child to go under a bed on its ninth birthday, for to do so is to stop its growth. To test a mother's love the child should blow the fluff from the head of a dandelion. If the fluff is blown off in one puff, then it is a well-loved child; two puffs, not so good; three puffs, the mother is too indifferent to care.

Unsightly marks and warts can be removed by simple formulas. Rub a wart with the skin of a chicken gizzard, and bury the gizzard under a stone at the "leak of the house"; and when it is rotted, the wart will disappear. Birthmarks will disappear if they are rubbed with the hands of a corpse. Cut as many notches as you have warts on a sassafras root and plant it. If it lives, the warts will go away.

There is practically no end to the brews concocted from herbaceous plants. Black star, yellow and black snakeroots are all valuable herbs for the brewing of "home" remedies. Tea made of "Bamdilla" buds will cure a cold; resin from several trees will cure boils; and wild-cherry bark tea will cure ailing children. Ginseng has played an active role in American history. It was used in the early China trade, and at one time it was the only commodity in Kentucky which could be counted upon to pay a profit in the overland trade from Kentucky back over the mountains. It likewise finds its way into folk medicines. Plantains, mullein, pokeberry, bluetop stickweed, burr vine, and hundreds of other common weeds and herbs are collected into the mountain granny women's herbariums. Grease is always a prime necessity for the treatment of diseases where external applications are necessary. And, of course, corn liquor adds a rejuvenating touch to all the primitive concoctions.

There is a complete field of folk preventive medicine, which, I believe, has not heretofore been set off specifically in a classification by itself. If one would prevent rheumatism, the bane of man's existence in a primitive community, he should carry a buckeye in his pocket. A bit more fantastic, but equally effective, is to sleep with a dog, and you'll never have rheumatism. The dog will draw off the tension which causes the ailment. Wash your hands in the first snow, and they will not chap all winter. A hog's tooth worn about the neck will prevent toothache. Never think too much of a child or it will die. Pass contaminated water over nine pebbles, and it will be purified. A pine knot placed in drinking water will prevent typhoid fever. Wear earrings, and you will never go blind. If a person sleeps with his heart toward the fire, he will become ill. Sometimes a horseshoe nail fashioned into a ring will prevent many diseases. A lock of hair cut from the head of a victim of asthma and pegged in a hole in a tree at the height of the victim's head will prevent a further outbreak of the disease. Man in the mountains has gone on from one generation to another fighting off ailments. He has made himself ridiculous at times in doing so, but all his simple preventions have had some remotely reasonable basis to support them.

It is only a short step from the realm of folk-medieval medicine into that of superstition. The Kentucky mountaineer is bound down by restrictive superstitions which would require a voluminous catalogue to list them. Likewise it is difficult to tell which are highland superstitions and which are a part of Kentucky folklore generally. Anyway, if you sleep under a new quilt, what you dream that night will surely come true; or eat the inside of a chicken gizzard, and you will marry rich. Put a sand rock in the fire, and it will keep the hawks away from your chickens.

Never have two clocks running in the house at the

same time; and if you drop your dishrag, kiss it, and your sweetheart will come to see you. "Wash and wipe together; you'll be good friends forever" or "Wash and wipe together; live and love forever." If you leave the coffee cup out of the saucer after a meal, you will have bad luck. Throw a shoe after a man when he starts on an errand, and he will succeed in his purpose; but burn the wood of a tree which has been struck by lightning in your fireplace, and there will be a death in the family. Drop a line in a quilt when you are making it, and a member of the family will die. Take a rabbit's foot and scratch someone with it, and you can make him do whatever you please. When you sleep with a stranger, tie your toes together, and the one who gets the shortest piece of string will marry first. A snake gliding across your path is a sign that you have an enemy. If you go to bed thirsty, your soul will wander, and it will drink from filthy mud puddles.

The third son always gets the brains of the family. If a girl builds a good fire, her sweetheart loves her; and if a mother cuts a baby's fingernails too short, he will turn out to be a thief. Never walk with one shoe on and one shoe off or twirl a chair on one leg, for both these acts will bring misfortune. And above all never plant a cedar tree. When it gets big enough to shade a grave, you will die. In the mining regions up the Kentucky River there is a superstition that no woman must be allowed to enter a coal mine. If it is known that a woman has gone into a shaft, it is doubtful that miners can ever again be coaxed into going into the mine. The folk mind of the highland of the Three Forks country is not characterized alone by its endless folk remedies and superstitions which crop out on the slightest provocation but by many other folk beliefs.

Ghost stories are not so numerous as are the superstitions, but they are a factor in the upriver culture. Sometimes natural phenomena will form the basis for a community legend. One of the best stories along the Kentucky is that of "the phantom dog" of Lots Creek. The gentle little black dog toddles in and out of the cabins along the creek. He comes in for food when he is hungry, or he just comes in for a friendly visit. He trots in and out with the regular scratching cadence of a pet dog toddling over the floor. There he is as plain as daylight, but he is physically intangible. He runs in and out among the legs of frightened mountainmen and women. He jumps out windows, scratches at doors, and trots up and down the trails. He has never been known to bite anyone or to become fretful. Time and again frightened mountaineers whose aim is deadly have shot at the phantom, but their bullets pass right through him without effect. The little dog keeps up his visits, and every year he adds to the string of witnesses who have seen him.

As to the physical quality of the mountain people themselves, there is an old argument which continues to hang fire like a badly loaded and primed muzzle-loading rifle. Many have asked if the mountain people were of virile stock or if their forebears were shiftless men who failed to keep up the folk movement westward. One group of sociological students has said they were shiftless, unambitious people. They have held that the more virile of the pioneer settlers moved westward to find better land, and neither accident nor incident steered them aside. It is the old linchpin theory that stimulates this point of view. A wagon broke down, or a horse broke one of its legs, or a member of the party became ill and died, and the family stopped to bury him and never moved on to their primary destination.

This theory has crept into much of the writing

on the mountains. John Fox, Jr. rambled over all the
Kentucky River valley. He combed the region with
a fine-tooth comb looking for material out of which
to construct his novels. He believed in the linchpin ex-
planation of much of the population of eastern Kentucky. At least, Bluegrass man that he was, he was
always conscious of a difference between the mountains upriver and the Bluegrass downstream. He built
two of his best-known books about this thesis. One of
these, *The Little Shepherd of Kingdom Come,* is a perfect maze of sociological contentions and sectional confusion. The author's best-beloved character, out of all
the strong mountain characters which he created, was
little Chad Buford. John Fox and his favorite mountaineer, Chad, argued by the hour over their sectional
differences of opinion. John did attempt to dignify
Chad by digging up his great-grandfather from an un-
marked grave near Cumberland Gap and relating him
by blood to Colonel Buford of Lexington. But even in
the matter of the Civil War the two could not agree.
Fox's sister recalls the afternoon when Chad suddenly
announced, *"I'm going into the Union Army."* Her
brother had argued with the headstrong mountain boy
that he should remain neutral or join the Confederate
Army, but the mountaineer loved the Union. He prevailed stoutly against all his creator's arguments and
held steadfastly to the mountaineer's belief that his government came first. In this, John Fox, Jr. showed an
acute knowledge of his mountain people.

Again in the *Heart of the Hills,* Fox built a story
on the differences between the Bluegrass and the hill
country. Already Fox's old teacher and friend, James
Lane Allen, had built a paper Bluegrass in his famous
"local color" short stories and novels. The ground was
prepared for the mountain portrayer to produce many

fruitful novels. John Fox, Jr. mixed his colors in the *Heart of the Hills,* but he was never able to blend them. He was ever conscious of the geographical and sentimental differences between the two sections of Kentucky. Several sociologists have held to the same theories. They have all been honest enough, but seldom have they been well enough informed on all the ramifications of folk origins to speak with final authority.

The Kentucky mountaineer really originated beyond Kentucky, and perhaps even beyond America. Racially he is a blend of Scotch, Irish, English, and German with an occasional dash of other national influences. There was the old Scotch patriarch, John Combs, who came to America in 1770, and like so many other Scotchmen he moved across the American frontier in good pioneer style. John Combs was a Revolutionary War soldier, and after the war was over he and eight of his ten sons moved west to Kentucky. In 1798 the Combses came through Pound Gap and settled on the North Fork of the Kentucky River along Carr Creek. From this beginning, which the present generation calls "the nine," a very large family has come into existence. It would be a safe bet in certain communities along the North Fork of the Kentucky for even the most patronizing candidate seeking office to greet a stranger with "Good morning, Mr. Combs," and be almost certain of getting the man's name right. In time there came to be so many Combses, and there was such a limited number of suitable given names in the family, that their names were doubled with homely characteristics descriptive of the individual. There was Nicholas "Danger," Nicholas "Birdseye," "Tight" Jerry, "Loose" Jerry, "Free" Jerry, "Round" Jerry, "Slow" Jerry, "Chunky" Jerry, "Short" Jerry, and "Beet Nose" Jerry.

This custom of distinguishing individual members of a family with homely prefixes and suffixes still prevails in the mountains. There are today Vince Sloane and "Kitten Eye" Vince, "Hopping" Shade Combs and "Blanky" Shade, "Big" George Dobson and "Little" George, "Cedar Head" Sam and "Pot Head" Sam Combs. Likewise there are "Smoker" Bill Stacy and "Blossom Eye" Bill, "Red" John Combs, "Blue" John, "Sorrel" John, and "Silly Captain" Jack. Scores of other names are prominent in the Kentucky mountains, and sometimes an individual who is intimately acquainted with the region can tell a man where he lives by his family name. Among these are the Bachs, Pigmans, Sloanes, Hargises, Cockrills, Turners, Amburgys, Napiers, Allens, Stewarts, Halls, Days, Eversoles, Stampers and Farmers. There is an old tradition which clings to the name Napier, pronounced "Napper." It is said that the name was originally Reynolds but that one of the clan fought so bravely on the field of battle that a Scotch king changed it to "No Peer" or "N'Peer," and since it has been changed to "Napier."

Next to the Combs family in the mountains, the Bachs are perhaps the second most important from the standpoint of cohesiveness, multiplicity, and accomplishments. This family is of German origin. Joseph Bach, a cousin of Johann Sebastian, came to America in 1770 because of religious persecutions in Germany. In 1798 he moved his family to Kentucky, and from Joseph and Elizabeth Huffman Bach have come thousands of descendants. Most of these have lived along the North Fork. This family has supplied much of the leadership in their home communities. At Jackson, Dr. Wilgus Bach became a good Samaritan among his people. In his heavy medical practice, in a land where medical service was indeed meager, he became an outstanding authority in the treatment of gunshot wounds. He took much pride in his family's American background, and he compiled a voluminous family record which cuts across the whole mountain population.

8

"All Hands Up and Circle Left"

WHEN American pioneers fought their way with vigor and courage through the narrow mountain passes which penetrated the long and frowning Appalachian wall, or pushed their way on clumsy "push" boats upstream from the Bluegrass, they brought with them a sense of neighborly co-operation. Neighbor joined neighbor in helping a man to build a cabin, to deaden trees, to shuck his corn, or to marry off his daughters. Women came in to help the wife with her cooking, spinning, weaving, canning, and quilting. Men worked hard all day to help their neighbors with their heavy work, but after all it was not exactly drudgery. Common work became a sort of relaxation. Always during these workings the bottle was passed freely on its round of gaiety and good cheer. After the hand sticks and axes were put away, or the eave logs of a cabin laid, there was a frolic. No man could give a working and ignore the entertainment. Usually the party, if it followed the building of a cabin, was a bran dance. Corn bran was sprinkled on the new floor, and the shuffling dancers helped to polish it with their feet. Here is perhaps the great American folk typographical error, or so it seems, the hillbilly rabble on the radio would have it. Pioneers never gave a "barn" dance, but they were forever publicizing the "bran" dances. So it was in the mountains. These Kentucky-mountain folk gatherings have helped to preserve for America much of its rich and early culture. Foremost of all forms of entertainment, then as now, was the square dance. There are numerous types of the dance called by the simple description of "square." It is impossible here to go into the details of the steps, but while gay dancers whirl to and fro keeping time with the musicians strumming away on banjos and guitars or sawing on fiddles, they all keep apace with the caller. He shouts:

> All hands up and circle left.
> Swing your partner and the one you meet.
> That's what makes the swing so sweet.
>   (First couple lead out.)
> Lady 'round the lady and the gents go slow.
> Lady 'round gents and gents don't go.
>   (Meet in the center and swing.)
> Ladies change and gents the same.
> Right hands cross and "How do you do?"
> Opposites swing, and don't forget your
>   honey in the center of the ring.
>   (Second couple lead out.)

Another formation leads out with a somewhat more rapid stride. The caller shouts:

> All hands up and circle left.
> Swing your opposite and then your own.
> Get your girl and promenade home.
>   (First couple leads out.)
> Swing your partner, swing Ma, swing Pa.
> Swing the girl from Arkansas.
> Four right here on the corner.
> Opposite turn, and swing your own.

There is the famous "Old Tucker" formation, a really beautiful running dance set. "Old Tucker" is an odd man in the ring who becomes a potential robber of every man's girl, and a butt of the caller's ad libitum jokes. When the set breaks, the Tucker tries to grab a girl and put another man in the center of the ring. Likewise every time the set breaks, one dancer, alternating between men and women, drops out. There are nearly twenty calls in this dance. It begins:

> All hands up and circle left.
> All the way 'round.
> Half way 'n back.
> Dance, Tucker, dance.
> Swing your partner once on the corner.
>   (All hands up and circle left.)
> All way 'round.
> Half way 'n back.
> Come on, Tucker, give us one.
> Swing your partner on the corner.
> Left hand lady don't you slight.
> All hands up and circle right;
> All way 'round.

These dances, fortunately for lovers of the primitive dance, are still popular in the upper Kentucky Valley. I have seen rural schoolhouses almost rocking on their foundations to the rhythmic swing of a rollicking dance. Young mountaineers seem to be born with the ability to go through a running set of a square dance with astounding grace and ease.

From dancing to playing games is but a slight figurative step, and folk games in the highlands have survived in their original forms during the changes of many generations. There are many; perhaps no one can name them. An exceedingly intelligent native woman who has charge of one of the important social agencies which are anxious to maintain as much of the indigenous culture as possible, has said that only by eternal vigilance and constant association with mountain people can one hope to discover much of their lingering and traditional background. On the school grounds a group of young children gather in a circle to play a game, and immediately the careful observer discovers that they have dragged out of the history of their ancestors a rare folk game.

It has ever been true in the mountains, as well as elsewhere, that kissing is the real excuse for most party games. A boy breaks the ice of timidity and for the first time kisses his blushing girl when he would not dare do so otherwise. Hanging onto the Doorknob is just such a game. A boy grasps the doorknob with his right hand, extends his left arm across his chest over his right shoulder and asks the girl of his choice to hang on with her right hand. She in turn crosses her left arm over her right shoulder and asks a boy to hang on. Thus they go until everybody in the room is "hanging onto the doorknob." The first girl kisses the boy, turns and kisses the boy behind her, and the kiss is passed down the line and returned to the first boy who stoops and kisses the knob.

Pleased or Displeased is always a comic favorite. A leader begins by asking a member of the party if he is pleased or displeased. Of course, it is the game for him to be displeased, and the solicitous leader is anxious to have him pleased. The displeased player is asked to state what his pleasure is, and he answers "to see Joe and Fannie measure ten yards of ribbon." Joe and Fannie come to the middle of the room and face each other. The boy takes one of the girl's hands in each of his, and they stretch out their arms to form a cross. First they lower their right hands toward the floor, and when they reach the lowest point, they kiss. This is repeated until they have lowered and raised their arms ten times. The game goes around the circle until everyone present has contributed an antic to the happiness of the party.

When Pleased or Displeased loses its humor, there are always other games which will pep up the party. Picking Grapes is a favorite. A boy and a girl are chosen, and a strong homemade hickory chair is placed between them. They catch hands and begin to climb up into the seat of the chair, a rung at a time. Each time the couple balances itself on a new rung, the boy reaches over and kisses the girl; and when they at last stand in the seat of the chair, they hug and kiss. Going down rung by rung the romantic "grape pickers" exchange smacks.

For sheer intimacy, Hooping the Wheel has no equal. All the players at the party get down on all fours in a circle. The leader places a dime in his lips and presents it to the lips of the female player on his right. She in turn offers the dime to the lips of the boy on her right, and from one set of lips to another the dime passes until it reaches the starting point, and the wheel is hooped. If, however, a clumsy player drops the coin, it is necessary to start all over again.

Digging a Well is an exciting pastime if your partner is an appealing young woman. The boy selects a girl and announces that he is going to dig a well four or six feet deep. If it is to be six feet deep, the couple gets down on all fours, and six persons lock hands over their heads. As the couple digging the well attempts to kiss, the six persons who have locked hands over their heads try to force them apart. These are all good bean stringing, "stir off," and Saturday night party games.

Another community social which has eddied traditionally in the upriver country is the box supper. Girls prepare fancy boxes of food and offer them at public auction at a party. Mountaineers can work up a tremendous amount of rivalry and excitement over the sale of these boxes. Those who are running the party are usually seeking funds for a community enterprise, and they are clever enough to bring about the collection of a nice sum of money from the audience. There are the elections of the prettiest girl and the ugliest man at a penny a vote. No boy can ever afford to let his sweetheart go down in disgraceful defeat, and to be gallant he has to nominate her as a contestant. He puts her name on the list and then fights for her election as long as his pennies hold out. The ugliest man is usually some comic figure of the community or some dignified soul whose feelings are ruffled at receiving the questionable honor. In the selection of this important honor the candidates are marched before the crowd to display their lack of manly beauty and to tolerate the catcalls and sassy remarks of their backers. It is all a fine bit of community comedy which is nearly always worth the price of the pennies spent on the votes.

When the fancy-colored crepe-covered boxes of food are offered for sale at public auction, the bidding becomes rampant. Boys often co-operate to run the prices of certain boxes up on the girl's sweetheart. If they can force him to lose the bid, they are so much the merrier. In fact, courtships have been broken off because of the inability of a boy to buy his girl's box. Nearly always there is a bit of minor social tragedy and unhappiness connected with a box supper. Some pale, bucktoothed girl has her shabby little box offered for sale with the hope that she will catch a beau. When her pitiful little box is sold, its blushing owner steps forward, proud of the fact that it really found a buyer.

On top of all the superstitions, dances, and games

are the mountain songs. Like the moods of highland life, these songs run the whole scale of human emotions. The hills are the American stronghold of the English ballad forms, and in their stories they set forth accounts of tragedies and of happy events. There are all sorts of songs and all sorts of ballad singers. Perhaps the greatest argument, which goes on continuously between the jealous-hearted song catchers of today, is that between the purely Elizabethan scholars and those who take their ballads as they find them without regard to their ancient folk origin. The technical song catcher who goes into the mountains to find only versions of those songs which are listed in the famous Child Collection is about as thorough as the man who wishes to study the peculiar impressions made by pigs' feet in a country lane by studying only the tracks of red pigs. There are too many folk songs in the Kentucky hill country which are not in the Child list for the ballad hunter to go into such a blind alley. The art of ballad making is a live one, so alive, in fact, that even the WPA has appeared in song. Deep in the Kentucky country a shrill, nasal balladier sings of William Bluett, a combination of local and English themes:

There was a woman lived in Hampshire,
She had one only son, and him she loved most dear;
She had no other child but he,
She brought him up in pomp and vanitee.

When this youth grew up in his estate,
He run through with it all, although it was very great;
There was nothing left undone that he could do the worst,
Of sin, theft and murder, too.

When he was bound in the prison so strong,
His mother came there to see her son;

Cassius M. Clay posed in front of White Hall for a Lexington photographer, Captain Isaac Jenks on the occasion of his marriage at the age of 84 to Dora Richardson, a 15 year old Kentucky River orphan.

But, poor soul, she was not permitted to go in,
So she walked up to the bars and spoke to him.

Then the poor mother did get to see her son, and to
remind him that he might "a-lived some pleasure for to
see, but to your dear old mother you are a miseree."
The boy talked back and told her that he hated the sight
of her. His mother kissed his lips "ten thousand times or
more" and went away in sorrow. The end came:

> When he was on the gallows so high,
> He prayed to the Lord for mercy,
> Saying, "Pity, Lord, the only son,
> Or my soul is forever left undone."

They hanged the boy, and:

> When he had hung till he was almost dead,
> There came a dove and hovered his head three times,
> Then ascended to the sky
> Which put the people in sad disprise.

Many a highland dance has moved off to the tune
of the sad, sad "Daemon Lover" who forsook "gold
crowns, and it's all for the sake of thee." Through thir-
teen verses the mountain troubadour tells the sorrowful
story of the wife of the house carpenter who ran away
with the faithless demon lover to gain possession of his
"seven ships sailing on the sea." He sang:

> "Well met, well met, my own true love,
> Well met, well met," said he,
> "I've just returned from the old salt sea,
> And it's all for the love of thee."

Then the demon boasts:

> "I could have married a king's daughter there,
> I could have married her," cried he,
> "But I have forsaken these golden crowns,
> And it's all for the sake of thee."

He begs the maid to go away with him, to receive what he was unwilling to give the king's daughter:

> "Oh will you forsake your house-carpenter,
> Oh, will you forsake him," cried he.
> "Oh, will you forsake your sweet little babe,
> And go along with me?"

His persuasion was complete, and the house carpenter's wife made a heartless decision:

> She laid her baby on its downy bed,
> And kisses she gave it three,
> "Lie there, lie there, my sweet little babe,
> Bear your father companye."

But too late the sinful mother discovered that she had run away with an adventurer who had none of the things of which he boasted, and she was left stranded. She was drowned, and her ghost lamented:

> "What hills, what hills, my own true love,
> What hills as white as snow.
> That is the hills of heaven, my love,
> Where you and I can't go!"

Not all the highland ballads, by any means, are of English origin. Local tragedies and remarkable community incidents have ever inspired the simple poet to make new compositions. Poor Goens, a community

character, fell a victim to murderers, and a poet tells his
sad story:

> Come all ye people who live far and near,
> I'll tell you of a murder done on Black Spur,
> They surrounded poor Goens, but Goens got away
> And went to Eli Boggs's, and there he did stay.

> Old Eli's son, Huey, his life did betray,
> By telling him he'd go with him to show him the nigh way;
> When they saw him coming, they lay very still,
> Saying, "It's money we're after, and Goens we'll kill."

> They fired on poor Goens, which made his horse run;
> The shot failed to kill him; George struck him with a gun;
> "Sweet heaven! Sweet heaven!" poor Goens did cry,
> "To think of my companion when I have to die!"

> And when they had killed him, with him they wouldn't stay,
> They drank up his whisky and then rode away;
> They sent for Mis' Goens; she made no delay,
> And when she was coming, she saw his grave on the way.

> I wish you could have been there and a-heard her poor moan,
> Saying, "Here lays his poor body, but where's his poor soul?"

Bad men often became the subjects of the primitive
songs along the North Fork and up and down its major
branches. Up Troublesome and on Carr Creek, Talt
Hall and Claib Jones carried on their famous war. Talt
was a bad actor who had killed more than twenty men.
In the end, however, he was hanged for one of his
crimes, and he became a hero of sorts in a song. It was
a characteristic recital of highland meanness. The singer
invites his hearers:

> Come all you fathers and mothers,
>   And brothers and sisters all,

I'll relate to you the history
Concerning old Talt Hall.

He shot and killed Frank Salyers,
The starter of it all;
He's breaking up our country,
He's trying to kill us all.

They arrested him in Tennessee,
And placed him in Gladeville jail;
He had no friends nor relations,
No one to go his bail.

He heard the train a-coming,
Got up, put on his boots;
They're taking him to Richmond
To wear the striped suits.

He heard the train a-coming,
He heard those Negroes' yells;
They're taking him to Richmond,
To hear the Richmond bells.

He wrote his brother a letter,
To his own home country,
Says, "See your satisfaction, brother,
Wherever you may be."

He wrote another letter,
Saying, "Brother, now farewell";
Says, "See your satisfaction, brother,
Or send your soul to hell."

He got upon the platform,
He wrung his hands and cried,
Says, "If I had not a-killed Frank Salyers,
I would not have had to died."

From one sad recital to another the ballad singer goes his way. He calls upon fathers and mothers not to let their sons and daughters go their errant way. The poet-reformer reaches a low stage of despondency in "The Drunkard's Hell." He recites his own experience in trying to reform all Kentucky.

'Twas on a dark and stormy night,
I heard and saw an awful sight,
The lightning flashed, the thunder roared
Around my dark benighted soul.

I saw a gulf far down below
Where all poor dying drunkards go.
My awful thoughts no tongue can tell.
Is this my doom the drunkard's hell.

I saw another weeping crowd
With bloodshot eyes and voices loud.
"Come in, young man, we'll find you room.
This is the whisky seller's doom."

I started on, got there at last.
I thought I'd take one spiritual glass.
But every time I viewed it well,
I thought about the drunkard's hell.

I dashed it down and left that place
And went to seek redeeming grace.
I thought of all who once did pray
Because God washed my sins away.

I started back to change my life
And see my long-neglected wife.
I found her weeping by her bed
Because her darling babe was dead.

I told her not to mourn and weep.
Her darling babe had gone to sleep.
Its little soul had fled away
To dwell with God through endless day.

I took her by the lily-white hand.
She was so weak she could not stand.
I laid her down and prayed a prayer
That God might bless and save us there.

My drinking days have passed away,
Since first I knelt on my knees to pray.
And now I live a sober life
With a happy home and a loving wife.

If all the boys in this town
Would pass a law throughout the land,
The whisky shops would have to flee
And leave the State of Kentucky free.

As with all other aspects of mountain life, industrialism has exerted an influence upon the ballad maker. Coal mining has appealed to the doleful singer, and the tragedies of this industry have furnished fruitful themes for dolorous songs. Perhaps the best evidence that ballad making goes on year after year, and that the ballad maker is sensitive to the changing scene about him, is this humble effort bemoaning the fate of "George, the Miner":

All ye miners come and listen
To a story that is true.
George got killed while at the tipple
Never to return back home again.

We may never meet again,
We may never meet again,

Be prepared for death and judgment,
We may never meet again.

George's wife packed his bucket
As she had oft times done before,
But she'll never, no, no never,
Pack poor George's lunch any more.

George had kissed his wife and children
As he left his own home door,
But he will never, no, never
Kiss them any more.

Look up yonder at the crowd of miners
As they stand 'round George's door,
Longing in their hearts to see him
Just as they had done before,
But they'll never, no never,
See Poor George's face any more.

Always, the mountain scene is an interesting one. Many social remnants have remained intact. Even in this modern day when there has been an invasion by the *"juke box"* and the "jenny barns," a type of bundling still prevails. A boy in one of the isolated communities goes to call on his sweetheart; her family goes off to bed. The meager supply of firewood is burned before the boy is ready to go home, and the courting couple lies down across the bed and covers up to keep warm. In the mountains this custom is called "laying across the bed." Once I visited a home along the Middle Fork, and the boys of the family went courting. Early the next morning they came home and explained that they had gone to sleep while "laying across the bed" with their girls. This custom perhaps will rapidly pass out of existence with the development of better roads.

A certain sign of change in the hill country is the willingness of women to eat at the table with their menfolks. In an earlier day the women of the mountain household waited until the men had finished eating before they sat down at the table. Woman up the Kentucky River was never placed on a pedestal. She took her lord and master in all seriousness. Even today there is a curious barrier between sexes in the rural communities of the mountains. A polite rural man is extremely cautious in opening a conversation with a strange woman. I know of one young Bluegrass woman who engaged a miller and his neighbor in conversation while waiting to have some corn meal ground. Another neighbor stood by and listened for a time, and then turned to the old miller and asked, "Do you know this woman?"

Woman in the mountains had her work planned for her in the very beginning of settlement in that country. Her duty has been to bear children. The land was thinly populated, and it needed, as did the American frontier generally, men to help settle it. A mountainman's respect for a woman in many instances rose and fell in proportion to the children she had or had not borne. Many of the pioneer patriarchs were the fathers of fifteen to twenty-five children. Dr. Wilgus Bach recorded in his journal several instances of a man becoming the father of more than twenty children. However, it is significant that under each of these patriarchs' names appear the names of at least three wives. At one time ten children was such a small family that the father was somewhat apologetic, and twenty were fine company and a source of pride to the fertile head of it. It is yet somewhat a matter of pride that the mountainman takes in the attitude that "the country needs good men."

There are many sides to the culture of the Kentucky highland. Perhaps no one will ever be ingenious enough to compress the whole story between the covers of a single volume. It is a difficult task, alone, to run down the various folk leads. Aspects of mountain life and customs bob up like native sons in the laurel thickets. The popular conception of the mountaineer is that he is a walking bit of picturesque folk lore, on one hand, and a feudsman, on the other. In reality he is neither, except in some isolated instances. In his relationship to his environment the hillman, like all rural people, is not tremendously boisterous. Long ago he cultivated the habit of silence, partly because his forefathers have handed down to him the practice of moving through the woods as quietly as possible. Often Kentucky newspapers report killings from ambush in the mountain countries.

To one who has tramped through the rugged country, the ease with which this method of committing a crime is carried out can be easily understood. I stood on the bank of Laurel Creek and watched several men pull an automobile from the stream bed with a truck. When the machine was pulled about halfway across the creek, the chain broke; and while a new connection was being formed, a man offered a suggestion from the laurel thicket at my side. I was startled to know that I was standing so close to a man of whose presence I was completely ignorant. He explained that he had come up the creek when he heard the roar of the truck to see what was going on. In that long easy gait which the highlander uses going up and down hill, he had made his way along the steep bank without either making a noticeable sound or exhausting his energy.

It is with this same startling quietness of manner that the Kentucky mountaineer exposes significant bits of his culture. His customs and ways of life appear on the surface when one least expects them. The truth of the matter is that not many of the upriver people are conscious of their interesting folk institutions. Likewise, it is true that not every mountainman is endowed with a rich Elizabethan folk background. Perhaps a very small percentage know and can sing the early English ballads, or have heard them sung for years. These ballads, in their original forms, however, are to be found. A blind guitar picker lolling in the door of the courthouse on county court day, or when the circuit court meets, can rap off "Barbara Allen," "Lord Lovel," or "Fair Eleanor" on his battered guitar, or an old-timer can recall the words to a score of these songs. Too, many young people can sing the old songs, and occasionally they add new verses or lines to a traditional composition to make a new version.

It is not the ballad in its truest form that is significant in the folk culture of the Kentucky mountains along the headwaters of the rivers. Rather, it is the influence they have had upon the musical taste of the region. These melancholic and boisterous songs which were "fetched" in by the earliest pioneers appealed to the taste of the rugged people. They cut a groove of appreciation which has endured the ravages of the changing times. In the early days it was impossible to transport heavy musical instruments such as the organ and piano into the Appalachian coves. Consequently, the guitar, banjo, dulcimer, and fiddle were used as instrumental accompaniments to the singing of the primitive songs. This being true, the taste for music has always been, through a necessity, one of robust vigor.

In 1846 a company of two hundred hardy sons from the Three Forks country marched into Lexington with hog rifles slung over their shoulders. They had come to go to war. News had reached the hills that the

United States and Mexico were at war; and if their country was in a fight, they did not propose to stand by and see their fellow countrymen participate in the fray without their assistance. They had no idea of where Mexico was or what the war was about. They were not interested in knowing any more than that the United States was in a scrap. When they arrived in Lexington, all their leader asked was, "Whereabouts is Matamoros?"

Fifteen years after this, late in September of 1861, Captain T. J. Wright and Captain R. Winburn traveled up the Kentucky River seeking volunteers for the Union Army. Beside the river at the Willis farm in Owsley County, a three-piece band hissed and pounded through a patriotic air, and then the two recruiting officers made eloquent appeals for recruits. As the notes of "Sally Is the Gal fer Me" died away following the eloquent oratory of the two strangers, thirty sturdy South Fork boys stepped forward to offer their services to the Union cause. Not only were Captains Wright and Winburn seeking men, they were seeking guns. If a man could not go to war, he could at least send his gun. To ask a mountainman to part with his gun, however, was almost like asking him to get along without his respiratory system. One old-timer reluctantly handed over his rifle with the tearful admonition, "Capt., take care of her, fur she cost me twenty-five dollars, and I split rails at fifty cents a hundred to pay most of it."

Years later when the United States needed volunteers for the World War, the boys from up the river, came trooping down to offer their services. Those counties along the river had perhaps the highest number of volunteers in proportion to the population of any group of counties in the United States. Breathitt citizens boast proudly even yet that not a single man was drafted from the county. From Devil-Jump Branch at Hell-fer-

Sartain up the Middle Fork came an outstanding hero, Willie Sandlin. Today the younger generation keeps the tradition alive, and the upriver country has sent thousands of volunteers into military service.

The people who live along the Kentucky's headstreams are proud of their land. They are, however, at once its greatest boosters and its greatest enemies. The anxiety for an outsider's good opinion often becomes pathetic. So often have they been made the unhappy butt of rude jokes or they have been handicapped for lack of economic opportunity that they have been forced into an embarrassing defensive position. It is with ancient Scotch clannishness that they stand shoulder to shoulder in bold defense of their homeland. Yet they will mislead the stranger by pointing out to him the spots where highland murders have occurred, or where, as they say, "trouble took place." They forget to tell that the killing occurred fifty years ago, for the mountaineer's inherent sense of time, where news is not geared to the speed of the daily paper, is based upon a long-time scale. I think the same startling notion of the fierceness of a community could be built up quickly in Louisville or Lexington if every visitor were conducted from place to place and told that on this spot we had trouble and a killing. Unfortunately many writers, who had neither the proper perspective nor the facts for what they wrote, have written of this country. Also, it is possible that many observers have been the innocent victims of "stuffing." After all, the mountaineer, despite much of his morbidity at funerals and in his folk songs, has a keen sense of humor. He has keen enough insight, usually, to tell a greenhorn writer what he wants to hear.

Kentucky mountain society is simple in its structure, yet, paradoxically, in its very simplicity it becomes complex. Here in America the modern and ancient forms of life are being blended, and it is rapidly becoming difficult to identify one or the other. But fortunately there are yet deep coves which push back from the river where primitive life may be examined in its natural state behind the log walls of a cabin. In this country there are yet hundreds of rural Americans who get keen enjoyment from the same games, dances, and music which entertained their great-great-grandfathers. They are still trying to solve their problems and cure their illnesses with the same nostrums which were brought into the land from across the mountains.

9

A Land in Which to Dream

IN THE year 1796 a strange young man of foreign appearance rode along the steep Kentucky River bank. He was carefully picking his way close to where Hickman Creek cuts its bed boldly between towering limestone banks to pour its floodwaters into the larger stream. Jean Jacques DuFour, Swiss immigrant and happy dreamer, was searching for a plot of good land. Back in his native Vevay, Switzerland, he had spent long hours poring over a map of the world. He was especially interested in America. Many times the young man had heard stories of the great democratic nation which had come into existence across the Atlantic. Perhaps this new country held a fortune for a youthful adventurer. On the map before him he discovered that Kentucky was on an approximate parallel with Switzerland, and without stopping to ask questions about soil and climatic variations he jumped to the conclusion that the American frontier would be the land in which to materialize his dreams of prosperity. As he jogged along on his horse that day in '96 he dreamed of barrels of rich beady Kentucky port, sherry, Madeira, and sauterne being loaded onto Kentucky River flatboats bound for the private cellars of American winebibbers. A glance at his map told him that he was near the point where the Kentucky dug deepest into the rich blue limestone plateau. Here the palisades were steep, and they closed in near to the stream's edge. As though it had suddenly changed its mind, the river turns back sharply to assume the general northwestward course it has followed down the mountains.

Cutting back to its normal course, the river is met by proud little Hickman Creek which flows in swiftly through the fertile Bluegrass lands all the way from Lexington. This creek for centuries has borne a rich burden of Bluegrass soil in its current. Just before it loses itself in the larger stream it drops most of the rich soil it has snatched up in its mad race through the rolling green meadowlands along its course. At the same place, the Kentucky, weary from carrying such a heavy load of mountain soil, likewise drops much of it. This sprawling shelf where Bluegrass and mountain alluvium are fused is a rich garden plot of bottom land. As he sat astride his horse and looked over this fertile tongue slanting down to the river's edge, DuFour must have murmured what a glorious piece of land for a man to have to experiment with a new type of agriculture. A homesick Swiss immigrant could settle down underneath the sheer cliffs of the palisades and feel perfectly at home. The beautiful river tossing between its deep tree-crowned banks brought a sense of romance to the sentimental newcomer.

Jean Jacques DuFour was an active promoter. Soon word was passed around in Kentucky that a vineyard society was to be organized, and that an experienced Swiss wine maker had already come to the state to begin the venture. He had located a site for the vineyard, and within a short time Kentucky wine would please the American palate. America was to learn to drink wine with a keen relish. At Lexington, Editor

John Bradford was interested. Frequently in the *Kentucky Gazette* he gave notice that members of the vineyard committee were meeting at Postlethwaite's Tavern. They were perfecting plans for the organization of the exciting new industry. In 1799, seven hundred and fifty acres of land "lying in the big bend of the Kentucky river near the mouth of Hickman creek," were bought. Enthusiastic supporters of the project boasted extravagantly that "in less than four years, wine may be drunk on the banks of the Kentucky, produced from European stock." Kentucky was to become in the wine trade as important a factor as it already was in the making and selling of whisky.

Jean DuFour was happy. His dream was coming true. Kentucky capitalists were giving his scheme financial backing, and soon he would become America's great vintner. He planned to go to France to secure fine European cuttings with which to plant the rich Hickman Creek bottoms and hills, but he was unable to leave New York because of the naval war then in progress. DuFour needed vine cuttings if he was to make good the Kentucky boast that in four years his wine was to be on the American market. He bought roots of as many different varieties of grapes as he could find in Philadelphia and New York gardens. From North Carolina he imported the famous Catawba grape. He returned to Kentucky and planted his vineyard. Two varieties were to furnish the main stock for the big wine industry. They were to be, said M. DuFour, American Madeira and Burgundy grapes.

The Kentucky vineyard was off to a happy start. Many other Swiss immigrants came to the great bend of the river to assist in making the Kentucky Vineyard Association's abundant crops of grapes into fine bubbling wine.

In Kentucky, on the rich river-borne alluvial soil, the grapevines grew luxuriantly. The vineyard gave great promise of being a success. Under careful supervision of the mastergardener the vines were trained to run up trellises. Buds put out, and rich healthy green bunches of young grapes took form. Each morning young DuFour went to his vineyard to see his dream maturing before his eyes. He handled the luscious bunches of tender young grapes with the fondness of a young mother inspecting the plump dimpled hand of her baby. Soon he would have an abundance of beautiful ripe fruit which he would crush and make into sparkling wine. Here on the bank of the Kentucky River would be a sort of happy France in America.

François Michaux, a Frenchman, came to visit Kentucky on his botanical tour, and everybody at Lexington was talking of the promising vineyard down on the river. This was exciting news indeed to a man who was visiting America as unofficial observer for his country. If Kentucky was to become a wine-making community, then France certainly would want to know about it. Michaux saddled his horse and rode out from Lexington to Nicholasville and then to the river to visit with Jean DuFour and to inspect his vineyard. One gathers from Michaux's account of his journey down to the "Mouth of Hickman" that he was afraid he would find DuFour succeeding in his venture. If he was, it would be bad news for France. This anxiety, however, turned to pity. But DuFour was not succeeding. What had been a grand vision of success was rapidly becoming a heartbreaking nightmare of failure. Many of the beautiful green vines were barren. They had put on a heavy crop of young grapes, but as these reached maturity they shriveled and dropped to the ground. Where the fruit remained on the vine it was of poor quality. Another surprising handicap faced the Swiss dreamer. Out of the Kentucky woods came swarms of birds to devour his precious grapes. Here was a difficulty which no amount of map study could have revealed. These birds, like a plague of grasshoppers, were sealing DuFour's doom.

What had promised to be such a fine undertaking in 1796 was a gross failure in 1802. Jean DuFour had failed to realize his ambition to make Kentucky a center of vine culture in America. His vines refused to produce, or if they did, the birds destroyed the fruit before it was ripe. One sees the immigrant farmer failing pitifully in his attempt to make a living on the bank of the Kentucky. In 1802 he advertised in the *Kentucky Gazette* that he had rice for sale, rice which he had imported from New Orleans. Later he warned his neighbors that he had patented a process for drying grain, and that they must not infringe upon his rights. All this, however, was a sad end to a happy scheme which DuFour had planned so carefully. Once his name had meant possible riches for Kentucky, but now it symbolized grandiose failure.

Out of failure, however, came a generous amount of success for DuFour. One variety of grape which he had secured in Philadelphia promised success under more favorable conditions. Out of the garden of Governor William Penn during the early years of Pennsylvania colony had come a hardy grape that produced a luscious fruit. It had been improved and adapted to American soil by the governor's gardener, Alexander. The variety was called Cape of Good Hope in honor of its place of origin. Swiss settlers at the Good Hope colony of Constantia had discovered this grape, and with knowledge of this hardy variety of vine in his mind, DuFour again set forth to find an ideal plot of ground for a vineyard. He journeyed down the Kentucky River, and above its mouth on the opposite bank of the Ohio, in Indiana Territory, he located a fertile tract which gave promise of adaptability to vine culture. There was founded the colony of Vevay, and in years to come the finest wine in America came from the immigrants' presses. Where the "Mouth of Hickman" vineyard had failed, Vevay colony succeeded.

Cape of Good Hope cuttings were productive even on the banks of the Kentucky. An interesting semipolitical situation grew out of the experiment with vine culture in Kentucky. Perhaps all the facts will never be known. When Jean DuFour and his fellow countrymen were in Kentucky they formed a friendship with the rising politician Henry Clay. Clay had come out to Kentucky from Virginia the year after DuFour rode down the Kentucky River bluff to locate his vineyard at the mouth of Hickman Creek. The two men were to enter the struggle of establishing themselves in Kentucky at the same time. In his frequent trips to Lexington between 1797 and 1803, the foreign vintner saw the Virginia lawyer on the streets of the town. Clay was attracting much attention. He had delivered his famous speech condemning the damnable federalistic Alien and Sedition Laws at the Maxwell Springs, and he got himself elected to the legislature in 1803. All this J. DuFour knew and, partly out of admiration for the young politician and partly for subtle purposes of advertising, he sent Clay four bottles of native Constantia wine made from Cape of Good Hope grapes.

Henry Clay drank three bottles of the wine, and the fourth he saved. When he was appointed United States senator in 1806 he carried the remaining bottle of Kentucky wine to Washington with him as a gift to President Jefferson. President Jefferson opened Clay's fine bottle of Constantia wine at a dinner party, but when he passed it around those who drank of it made wry faces. They even made sour remarks about its vile taste. To the sensitive Kentuckian these remarks were intolerable. He asked a good friend what he thought of the wine, and he got the disheartening answer that it tasted like raw corn whisky. It was raw whisky. Some member of the Clay household, as the master was to discover later, had drunk the wine and refilled the bottle with whisky.

The fact that he had been made the laughingstock at President Jefferson's table bore heavily upon Senator Clay's sensitive conscience. In a letter to President James Madison in 1811 he undertook to clear the matter, and to redeem the reputation of native American wine:

H. Clay presents his respects to Mr. Madison & sends him a bottle of wine made from the grape of the Island of Madeira, which has been cultivated in Kentucky. He regrets that the specimen is not more ample, but it is all that he could have conveniently brought in his carriage.

H. Clay had the mortification to have been present some years ago at the exhibition at Mr. Jefferson's table of some Kentucky wine which having been injured in the process of fermentation was of the most wretched quality. The sample now sent will he flatters himself restore in some degree the credit of the wine of that state.

Henry Clay, perhaps, restored the virtue of Kentucky so far as James Madison was concerned, but Jean DuFour had failed to make his venture come true in the state. Kentucky soil was adapted to the production of grass, tobacco, hemp, and grain, but not to the vine. DuFour was just one of many who dreamed of success on the banks of the Kentucky River or on one of its tributaries only to wind up in failure.

While the European Vinegrower was digging away at the soil of the fertile Hickman Creek bottom, another Kentucky dreamer, Edward West, at Lexington, was waiting upon customers who came to buy watches, clocks, and silverware, and in his spare moments was inventing many useful mechanical devices. As he stood over his silversmith's anvil and hammered out slender coin silver spoons, graceful knives and forks and ladles, or as he built clocks and repaired watches, he conceived a cure for rheumatism, the frontiersman's worst malady. This disease could be cured by a process of metallic attraction. Rheumatism, it was said, was attracted by iron, and West thought that all that was necessary to cure it was to invent iron bands to go around the ankles and wrists. Soon he was advertising that he had perfected such therapeutic equipment and had it for sale in his shop.

Edward West had an imaginative mind, and he was not satisfied with a single accomplishment. He was anxious to lighten the lot of his fellow man. Blacksmiths for centuries had stood long hours over hot forges and anvils fashioning crude bits of iron into nails. It was a tedious process to cut off pieces of coarse metal and then to hammer them into blunt nails. Again West applied his scientific mind to an ancient problem of humanity, and in a short time introduced a machine which simplified the process of making nails, and soon the supply of nails had increased a thousandfold. So successful was his idea that before the end of the eighteenth century Lexington merchants were selling cut nails to carpenters who were building the important frontier cities of Pittsburgh, Louisville, and Cincinnati. A promoter paid him $10,000 for his invention. But Edward

West, here deep on the American frontier, kept the honor of being father of the nail industry.

From one idea to another, the young inventor's mind wandered. He read the *Gazette* and listened to the gossip which went on about him. Western America was growing. People were coming from everywhere, and they were producing enormous amounts of valuable goods which had to be shipped down the river to market. But few of the boats which went downstream would return. It was a simple matter to send goods to New Orleans, and the boatmen who lay sprawled out on the sunny decks of their drifting flatboats, or who wrestled diligently with a stubborn oar, wished for some type of self-propelled boat. To men with shrewd business foresight, it seemed that all the people along the Kentucky River needed was a mechanical boat that could travel upstream against a stiff current. This idea fascinated Edward West.

With all the precision of the scientific scholar, West went to work to invent a steamboat. In his little shop he tinkered with tiny cylinders, connecting rods, springs, and balances. After hammering away at cutting and fitting a small hull, the inventor was ready in 1793 to give a public demonstration of his steamboat. Six years earlier John Fitch had tried out the idea of a steamboat on the Delaware River, but his experiment had failed. Later, James Rumsey in Virginia met the same sad fate with his boat. It was an exciting day in Lexington when it was known that the local watch tinkerer was to give a public demonstration of his wonderful machine. Perhaps this was the day on which Westerners would be set free from their transportation handicaps. With top hats bobbing up and down on the banks of the tiny town fork of the South Elkhorn Creek the local dignitaries congregated to see Mr. West show off his boat. Town fork had been dammed up so as to create a pool of sufficient width and depth to float the boat.

West got up steam in his miniature boiler, and when he opened the throttle of his little boat it set off across the rising pool. It worked! At last a steamboat was a reality, and doubtless many of those present locked their arms underneath their long-tailed coats, cocked their heads, and speculated on what this moment meant to their state's future. They already knew what the river commerce was worth to Kentucky. If Edward West could speed up this trade he would make his name immortal. It was a happy day, indeed, for the state. Soon, the inventor hoped, the steep banks of the Kentucky River would reverberate with the loud hissing of self-propelled boats.

Edward West was a dreamer, and he lacked the ability to transfer his idea from the miniature to a practical working craft. He did not know how to cast the parts on a larger pattern, and he lacked capital backing to undertake such a visionary scheme. His job was completed, the task which remained was up to a "practical" individual who could take other men's ideas and make them work. Men with money were interested in West's idea, but they doubted that the boat would go in rough water. Could a steamboat make headway against the stiff current of a river? This was a question which the inventor unfortunately could not answer to the satisfaction of potential supporters.

For twenty-three years Edward West's miniature steamboat gathered dust. His idea of steam navigation was neglected, and what promised to be a major American invention failed for the lack of confidence on the part of a practical man with money. The original model of West's steamboat was destroyed by the British when they burned the government buildings in Washington in 1814. A model of the engine was placed on display in the Eastern Kentucky Lunatic Asylum. It was, perhaps, not an unfeeling implication that the handiwork of Lexington's mechanical genius was put in such an unusual place for public display. Kentucky, as a matter of fact, took great pride in its son's invention, but West failed to realize his dream of revolutionizing western American commerce for lack of confidence on the part of his unimaginative and overcautious fellows.

In 1811, Captain Nicholas Roosevelt came down the Ohio aboard the *New Orleans,* and revived once again an interest in the West in steam navigation. By 1816 a steamboat company was organized in Lexington, and it acquired West's patent rights. A steamboat was built, and on April 28, 1816, it departed for New Orleans from the mouth of Hickman Creek. This event was not at all exciting; already western Americans were becoming familiar with the steamboat. On every hand definite plans were under way to increase the number of vessels plowing through the western waters. The Kentucky inventor lived to see his idea succeed in other hands, and to feel the deadening influence of it upon the little inland town which native sons had so proudly given the name "Athens of the West." When West died in 1827, Louisville had robbed Lexington of much of its commercial glory.

These two dreamers, Jean Jacques DuFour and Edward West, promoted their dreams and then failed. DuFour moved on to succeed elsewhere, and West rested on his laurels of being an excellent silversmith, and of having invented a cure for rheumatism and a nail-making machine. It was something, however, that by failure at the mouth of Hickman Creek the Swiss vintner learned to succeed at Vevay. Likewise, it was distinctly to the credit of Edward West that he conceived the idea of the steamboat, even if he did fail in making it a practical machine. It was not West who failed; rather, it was his "practical-minded" neighbors, who lacked the foresight to back him with both money and faith. Yet Edward West went to his grave a famous man. He had given to America one of its commonest, yet most useful instruments, a cheap well-pointed nail.

10

Shakers

ANGIER MARSH, writing from Bourbon County, Kentucky, in 1802, wound up a letter to a friend in the East by saying: "I am on my way to one of the greatest meetings of the kind ever known: it is on a sacramental occasion. Religion has got to such a height here, that people attend from a great distance; on this occasion I doubt not but there will be 10,000 people and perhaps 500 wagons. The people encamp on the ground and continue praising God day and night, for one whole week before they break up." Perhaps when Marsh rode on to the grounds at Cane Ridge he saw a huddle of people struggling with friends who had the jerks. One literate observer saw two men rush out with a charging young boy between them, and he heard the child cry out in anguish: "Thus, O sinner! shall you drop into hell unless you forsake your sins and turn to the Lord." "At that moment," said the traveler, "some fell like those who are shot in battle, and the work spread in a manner that human language cannot describe."

Kentucky frontiersmen became confident at the turn of the eighteenth century that the country for which they had striven so bravely would be theirs. At last the Indian menace was at an end. Filthy and crowded forts were long ago deserted, and where there had been virgin wood in the great Kentucky valley there were now rich fields of grain, fine pasture lands and comfortable homes. Kentuckians collectively could enjoy the new-found freedom and prosperity. Frontiersmen were stolid in their religious beliefs and expressions just as they had been silent and forbearing in suffering and galling hardship. But the years at the turn of the century were years of emotional upset and of vigorous religious expression. The spiritual soil was extremely fertile, and the season was propitious for a religious idea to take in Kentucky.

From 1800 to 1805 a community outpouring of the spirit occurred at Cane Ridge, which, true to prediction in Angier Marsh's letter, perhaps has never been equaled in the annals of American religious history. The preaching was fervent, and the electric power of the exhortations was startling. Years later the pioneer Methodist preacher, J. B. Finley, described the experience at Cane Ridge which led to his conversion. "I stepped upon a log," confided Brother Finley in his autobiography, "where I could have a better view of the surging sea of humanity. The scene that then presented itself to my mind was indescribable. At one time I saw at least five hundred swept down in a moment, as if a battery of a thousand guns had been opened upon them, and then immediately followed shrieks and shouts that rent the very heavens. My hair rose up on my head, my whole frame trembled, the blood ran cold in my veins, and I fled to the world for a second time, and wished I had stayed at home." This was a communal breaking of emotional bonds. Men who throughout their lives had been calm creatures now clawed and barked up trees like dogs at the devil, or crawled on the floor playing marbles and other childish games in humble obedience to the Scriptures that "except ye be converted and become as little children ye cannot enter the Kingdom of Heaven." Others danced about the altars. Some ran back and forth, while others got the jerks and fell forward in deathlike feints. A horrified and orthodox Presbyterian minister wrote a friend that, "the bodily exercise had assumed such a variety of shapes as to render it a truly Herculean task to give an intelligent statement of it to any person who has never seen it."

This great western revival at Cane Ridge was a crucible into which denominations were poured with the grave possibility that they would suffer material change if not complete extinction. Man as an individual was dignified in the sight of his God. Here was waged another of the age-old fights for man's right to appear as an individual before God. The question arose as to whether the man or the presbytery was to be welcomed into the divine presence. Cane Ridge preachers stoutly maintained the independence and dignity of man, and denounced as false the hopeless contention of man the depraved being. Five Calvinists defied the authority of the presbytery and held out for the individuality of the soul. These five, Richard M'Nemar, Robert Marshall, Barton W. Stone, John Dunlavy, and John Thompson, were tried by the synod of Springfield, Ohio. They ridiculed the accusation of waywardness placed against them, and in their Garden of Gethsemane they formulated a classic document in the history of American freedom of worship and religious toleration known as the "Last Will and Testament." It set forth a bill of rights for the free man who respected and loved his God. Religion, to the signers of the "Last Will and Testament," was a matter of simplicity. There was God, the Father; Christ, the Son; the Bible, a fundamental rule of faith; and the people, the subjects. A confession of faith, a cardinal tenet of the church, was man-made and artificial, said the five recalcitrant ministers. Here in Bourbon County in 1805 was rank heresy—the heresy of Luther, of Zwingli, of Calvin, of Knox, of Roger Williams, and that of Lewis Craig who "could not meet a man on the road but he rammed a text down his throat." From this break with the presbytery came the Church of the Christian Disciples, a truly American institution. It was into this state of fervent religious and ministerial revolution in the American backwoods that the idea of Shakerism was poured. News of the great frontier revival had spread far and wide, and naturally it reached the ears of the communal sect at Watervliet, New York. Kentucky seemed to the elders to be a land of spiritual promise for an expansion of the order which called itself "The United Society of Believers in Christ's Second Appearing." Thus armed with the authority of the New York elders and the spiritual blessing of Mother Ann Lee herself, three stanch Believers in Christ's Second Appearing set forth to the western country to prospect among the excited people at Concord and neighboring Cane Ridge. This trio, Benjamin Young, Issacher Bates, and John Meacham, in 1805 wandered westward, guarding the precious document which they bore to the fervent revivalists in the Kentucky valley. This general epistle of the church, entitled *The Church of Christ, Unto a People in Kentucky and Adjacent States Sendeth Greetings,* was to be read before the New Lights by Benjamin Young. Blundering through the woods with their equipment saddled on a pack horse, the messengers, from the "Land of Canaan unto the people of Kentucky and adjacent states," lost their way. Early in March of that year they found themselves at Paint Lick on Paint Creek, a branch of the Kentucky River. Perhaps it was this mistake in routing that two years later was to see the establishment of a Shaker colony on the banks of the river.

The Shakers might have been blind to Kentucky's brand of common everyday horse sense and elemental biology, but they had a practical eye for good land and desirability of location. When they reached Cane Ridge, the three apostles of the Believers in Christ's Second Appearing found the time ripe to strike for an organization in Kentucky. Two disgruntled Presbyterians, Richard M'Nemar and Benjamin Worley, were interested in this new communal doctrine and went with the elders to the newly established Union Village in Ohio. Here they were told the full story of the new order. It was a story centered around the spiritual teachings of a female Christ. She, like so many other fervent apostles of a new faith, had fled the persecutions in England and had landed at New York in 1774. She had planted her spiritual utopia first at Watervliet and then at New Lebanon.

Mother Ann's theory of religious worship and of religious life, from the viewpoint of Kentucky pioneers at any rate, was a bit unusual. There was some confusion in her major contention. Mother Ann claimed to be either the spiritual daughter of God or the female embodiment of Christ. The whole question was bound up with the complicated issue of sex, or the neutrality of sex, and in the end the unlearned layman came to conceive of the order as being somewhat a theological hermaphrodite. Throughout a maze of higher Shaker criticism one wanders—speculating whether the text before him is Scripture or the currently revealed word of God. There were, however, certain points which Young, Bates, and Meacham could make clear. The disciples of Christ's Second Appearing believed in divine healing, spiritualism, testimony, tongues, sanctification, revelations, prophecy, dreams, celibacy, and vision. Some of these points appealed to the romance in the backwoodsman's soul, but such a promise as divine healing, where suffering had been intense, was especially attractive. Dreams, revelations, and visions fitted in nicely with the superstitions of the people.

To people who listened to long-winded Hard-Shell Baptist preachers, or to the stern offerings of Presbyterian ministers, all the promises of Shakerism seemed easily within the realm of possibility. A literal-minded people was ready to accept every point of Mother Ann's belief without serious question, with only two exceptions. Common ownership of property and celibacy were open to debate. Despite the celibacy of Christ, the pioneers of Kentucky believed wholeheartedly in marriage and in large families. The western country was pleading for a population increase, and there was a strong patriarchal pride in large broods.

It was to face the rigorous task of converting the Kentuckians that Benjamin Young, Richard M'Nemar, a recent convert, and Malcolm Worley left Union Village in 1805 to join John Dunlavy. They were again headed for Concord and Cane Ridge, where the camp meeting had become unusually rampant. They were on their way to compete in their preaching with such vivid imagists as James McReady, who delivered torrid blasts at sinners. In rasping and accusing tones McReady growled in his famous sermon, "The Character, History, and End of the Fool": "He died accursed of God when his soul was separated from his body and the black flaming vultures of hell began to encircle him on every side. Then all the horrid crimes of his past life stared him in his face in all their glowing colors; then the remembrance of misimproved sermons and sacramental oc-

casions flashed like streams of forked lightning through
his tortured soul; then the reflection that he had
slighted the mercy and blood of the Son of God—that
he had despised and rejected him—was like a poisoned
arrow piercing his heart. When the fiends of hell dragged
him into the eternal."

The Shaker elders proposed to offer their plan of
salvation along with that of the Kentucky denominations. But even in a meeting such as that in Bourbon
County, where brotherly love and the spirit of the Lord
prevailed, there were prejudice and intolerance. The
elders ran amuck. They were refused permission to
speak and were threatened with prosecution for disturbing public worship. Barton W. Stone and Robert
Marshall were appointed to hear the elders' pleas and to
pass on the question of allowing them to preach.

Before Stone, himself a rebel, and Marshall could
examine the elders, thousands of people were sneering
at them. An outraged brother in a storm of righteous
indignation, shouted "Go to Hell!" to Issacher Bates.
Others cried out, "They are Liars! They are Liars! They
are Liars! According to fable 'a liar is not to be believed, even when he speaks the truth.' " No one could
expect a fair hearing under such circumstances, but the
cause was not lost. Any religious group could have
found supporters among the excited thousands who
milled about the grounds at Cane Ridge. Elisha Thomas
and Sam Banta were there from Mercer County on the
Kentucky River, and they were interested in what the
Shakers had to say. The elders were taken aside to a
private house, and there the foundation was laid for
what was to become the order at Pleasant Hill.

Near where the gentle little Shawnee Run Creek
flows from the bluegrass savanna through a heavily
wooded ravine to the Kentucky River was located the

140-acre farm of Elisha Thomas. He gave this farm to the disciple of the holy Mother Ann as a communal beginning in Kentucky. It was here that a small band of converts, subscribing to the true principles of almsgiving as set forth in the Biblical commandment "To sell all thou hast and give it to the poor," in the belief that "Give and it shall be given unto you," signed the first family pact. True to Biblical prophecy, the order increased rapidly in numbers, and in material well-being. Soon there were three thousand acres of fertile land where there had been only the small Thomas farm.

As the order grew in both communicants and riches, it was moved up the riverbank to the noble promontory overlooking miles of gently rolling Bluegrass country. Near this spot the Dick's River joins the Kentucky in a deep-cut narrow valley. Before the communal site, the main river wound its way in and out of what was a huge geological wrinkle in the face of the jovial countryside. Here was as noble a place as man could have found to give expression to a simple idyllic hope for a happy life. Here the Shakers were to build a strange but prosperous institution in the heart of a new and realistic frontier land. Long before the dreams of Fourier, Robert Owen, John Humphrey Noyes, and the transcendentalist at Brook Farm were to stir the American peace of mind, the Shakers were operating a prosperous community on the banks of the Kentucky.

Pleasant Hill might well have appeared on the map of the Kentucky valley as a large, dark, and unexplored circle. It was a spot unknown to most outsiders, and the strange sensational things said to have gone on there were beyond the pale of normal human reason and understanding. Strange tales filtered to the outside, and often the "worldly" community was aroused to the point of threatening a hanging. Because of their state of celibacy there was gossip that all the males were castrated, and, paradoxically, that the Shakers, divested of all modesty and clothing, danced themselves into sexual orgies. Further, it was said that children were born of such debauchery and that they were hidden under the dark covers of infanticide. These stories excited both the popular imagination and the savage natures of the Shakers' Kentucky neighbors. During the early years there was constant antagonism between the Shakers and the people of the community. In 1811 the Kentucky legislature was faced with the question of accepting or rejecting a law proposed by a Shaker enemy which would have violated the freedom of worship clause of the Constitution. The next year a law was passed by the general assembly which was intended either to force pacifist Shaker men into the ranks of the state militia or to confiscate the sect's property. Feeling in central Kentucky ran high when the Shakers refused to go to war. Several of the brothers were drafted into the militia and they hired substitutes, and when these faithless hirelings failed to go to the army Shaker property was seized, but later returned.

Pleasant Hill community was well organized. There were four families, East, Center, West, and North, and over each of these presided an elder and an elderess, a deacon and a deaconess, and a board of trustees. Elders and elderesses were responsible for the family's spiritual affairs, while the deacons and deaconesses, along with the trustees, served the temporal man as stewards. In their religious ceremonies astounding things occurred. There were the holy dances in which sin was shaken from the body. Males in a group danced anticlockwise, while the females passed them going clockwise. To scoffing and profane outsiders the dance had only an amusement value and they could not under-

stand how such a practice could rid the soul of its burden of sin. Shakers looked on the practice as obedience
to the Scriptures. David had danced with might and
vigor before the Ark of the Lord. Likewise the women
had followed fair Miriam with timbrels and had danced
in their moments of spiritual bliss.

To be truly spiritual the dance had to be vigorous,
and the body had to be thrown about with grace and
limberness. When the ceremony gave the appearance of
becoming a perfunctory performance of the ritual, the
community scribe was vexed. He feared the order was
becoming too formal to receive the prophecy of the Divine recorder, the Lord appeared saying "Such proud,
delicate motions I cannot accept, so ye must limber up
your bodies as the limber willows." A group of angels
appeared unto the congregation and presented four
trees as emblems of suppleness to be planted at the four
corners of the meetinghouse.

Strange and frequent visitations are recorded in the
"Spiritual Journal" over the span of years from 1807 to
1875. Had the unsympathetic observer been permitted
to read the daily recordings of the inspired scribe his
attitude would have indeed been violently skeptical.
This was the Shaker's secret from the world. He did not
shout news from his communal housetop of spiritual
visitations. Even yet it seems strange to read in bold
handwriting that Father Job spent a day on the banks
of the Kentucky, or that angels in droves came bearing
switches for the communicants to take up and drive
away evil from Pleasant Hill. Abraham, Isaac, the angel
Vicalen, Ruth, and Mother Ann Lee all appeared from
time to time. The "Great Teacher," or Mother Ann,
came bearing little bags with the mighty power of God
contained within them. There were gift balls of liberty,

and at times the meetinghouse was literally overrun with balls of fire, which were gathered up by the faithful.

Of a more contemporary nature were the famous American visitors. Among these spiritual callers, of course, was General George Washington. Likewise Benjamin Franklin came to Pleasant Hill and so did other prominent Americans who were long since dead. The noble savage was always on hand. It is not a matter of record whether Washington and his friend Franklin were present with Chiefs Cornstalk and Tecumseh, but these savage dignitaries did visit Pleasant Hill. It was with childish enthusiasm that the Believers received their red friends. At times the savages came in throngs, and they ran and leaped with joy. They came often in anguish, and begged to have their tortured souls saved from damnation. On top of these outlandish visitations, one last account must be added. Records tell of happy individuals floating about through the air. Women became so wrought up in outdoor meetings that they were wafted back to their rooms. These were strange accounts indeed to come from the banks of the realistic Kentucky River.

Down through the series of Shaker communities came word in the early forties that the Lord wished each order to select a holy place for special worship. At Pleasant Hill the temple of sancitity was located out of doors and was called the Holy Plain of Sinai. This undertaking was kept a secret from the world because few persons in Kentucky would have been sympathetic with the notion of this outdoor shrine or holy of holies.

Inspired elders located the Holy Plain of Sinai in September, 1844, and industriously the brothers cleared and graded the land. In less than a month the sacred garden had received the finishing touches and was sowed with Kentucky bluegrass. Sinai's Holy Plain was in an idyllic spot. Amidst beautiful farm lands, with lovely meadows rolling away to the rear and the deep river gorge in front, it was a place where a man could be uplifted even without the potent support of Shaker spiritualism.

It was with a note of both pride and triumph that the laboring elder wrote in his scrawling hand the entry for Thansksgiving Day of that year. "This day," he wrote, "appointed by Governor R. P. Letcher, Governor of Kentucky, to be kept as a day of prayer, praise and thanksgiving, was observed accordingly. Meeting was held for the first time on the Holy Sinai's Plain." About this sacred place of the Lord centered the whole story of spiritual mysticism in the order. Shakerism kept pace with fermenting America, and just as the thirties and forties were stirring years for a worldly and spiritually perverse generation so they were for the devout Believers.

The whole impetus for Sinai's sanctified plain came from New Lebanon, and entry after entry in the Shaker journals tell of this phenomena. Philemon Stewart, of the New York community, received in 1843, *A Holy, Sacred and Divine Roll from the Lord God of Heaven to the Inhabitants of Earth*. This was a volume of divine revelations compiled by angels and prophets among whom were Jeremiah, Peter, John, Ann Lee, and the angel of God, Merah Vakua Sina Jah. Unfortunately for the Believers, the *Divine Roll* became an unhappy revelation to worldly as well as to devout, and soon it proved a liability in the hands of skeptical and intolerant worldlings. Efforts were made to suppress it, but the devout at Pleasant Hill seemed to have been indifferent to the orders from the hierarchy and they kept their copies, thereby preventing its total destruction. Angels and other divine emissaries came to the

Holy Plain of Sinai at Pleasant Hill. They lighted the altar fire, delivered divine proclamations, and exhibited numerous other spiritual manifestations.

There were so many supernatural revelations and visitations that one can never hope to work his way through the whole maze of spiritualism. To the Shakers themselves they were vital—they were manifestations of their faith and of eternal hope and generous charity. For the worldlings in the green Kentucky country more tangible values came from Pleasant Hill. This communistic sect presented a fine example of the powers of thorough organization and discipline of energy, coupled with a genuine pride in workmanship. Shaker buildings, standing today with their "celibate" doorways where the females entered those on the right hand and the men passed through those on the left, are splendid examples of simple, sturdy Kentucky architecture. Architects for the community had a feeling for their surroundings, and they harmonized their structural lines with this environmental sensitivity. Walls, two and three feet thick, and mortar lines, a little thicker than the blade of a trowel, bear testimony of capable workmen doing a proud job for a community of ideals. Stone buildings intermingle with those of brick to indicate the discovery of a rich storehouse of native building materials along the Kentucky River palisades.

Internally there was a satisfactory division of labor in the community. Men engaged in agricultural and associated industries, while the females employed themselves in the processing of the farm's products. There was a water-driven mill, and a communicant millmaster who ground thousands of bushels of plump grain into flour and meal to be baked into fragrant loaves of bread at the communal ovens, or to be sent downstream in flat- and steamboats to a rapidly expanding southern cotton planter market. There were sturdy smiths who kept the farm implements in condition, and between seasons they turned their inventive wits to the creation of new gadgets. The Shakers were gadget lovers. They were forever developing new tools and devices. For instance, their novel candleholders and racks, dump wagons, buzz saws and many other labor saving tools were mechanical wonders of the time. Ingenious mechanics devised a water system for the community, and through the use of clumsy homemade leaden pipes they enjoyed the luxury of running water.

The men engaged in other trades. They made broad "Shaker" brooms, a household necessity far up and down the Kentucky River. They made chairs, furniture, cooperware, paper, baskets, and they tanned leather and made shoes and harness. Likewise they dried fruit and sweet corn, and fermented an excellent type of cheese.

Shaker women rivaled their brethren in pride of craft. From their boiling kettles they dipped excellent preserves, jellies, and pickles. Even today many Kentuckians like to recall the excellency of Shaker jellies and preserves. They become so eloquent in their descriptions of these delicacies that one wonders if the golden jelly was not, like the *Divine Roll,* itself an inspired creation. Occasionally a story comes to light of a family hoarding a jar of Shaker preserves or jelly as a culinary documentation of a high standard of both Kentucky cooking and power of preservation. When the women were not engaged in the processing of a superabundance of fine products from the farm, they were busy with cards, wheels, and looms.

In all their affairs of life, save one, there was a certain gaiety about the Shakers. Even the inspirational visitors were never in a neutral mood; they were in a mood of either anger or jolly laughter and joy. More often it was the latter. Such stern and officious clerks as Vicalen and Merah Vakua Sina Jah, and even Father Job, seemed to have come in fairly jovial moods. Yet in dress the Shakers gave expression to a soul-stifling drabness. Not a bit of color, except that of the necktie, appeared in the Shaker costume.

Their scribe records from time to time the fact that the women were producing yards of drab natural-colored woolen cloth out of which to make coats and trousers. Bolt after bolt of mixed gray linsey-woolsey (then a mixture of cotton and wool) rolled from the looms to make heavy formless dresses, jackets, and face-concealing stave bonnets for the women and children.

Farming at Pleasant Hill was more than a prosaic matter of producing a return from the land, it was likewise a fulfillment of the cardinal Shaker command to "give and it shall be given unto you." By their very thoroughness and ingenuity they were giving intangible alms to their worldly Kentucky neighbors. Pleasant Hill became a sort of semiagricultural experiment station with a bit of the agricultural and mechanical college thrown in. They bred and produced fine strains of beef and dairy cattle. At a time when the farmers of Kentucky were purchasing and producing shorthorns, the Shakers bought, partly through the influence of Henry Clay, shorthorn bulls and heifers and developed the "wild-eyed" strain. They refused, however, to breed mules—an animal which had made the Kentucky River grazing country famous in the South. In the eyes of the Believers the mule was a sin in the sight of God. He was a devitalized creation of man.

Each spring and fall Shaker brethren loaded their community's products on Kentucky River boats and set out for the southern markets. Frequent entries in the Journal record the departures and arrivals of the Shaker tradesmen. With a touch of dire foreboding, but with a hopeless ignorance of geography, the clerk recorded that "Micajah Burnet started with some hogs and cattle to Port Gibson, [Mississippi] away to the wilds of the west among the Indians." Again, "Four brothers set out for the South with cattle, hogs, and garden seed." Brothers "Abram White and Jacob Varis went forth with pigs and garden seed." "Brother Amos took passage in the Steamer *Ocean* for New Orleans." That same day David French, Benjamin Bryan, and Elkhanah Scott started down to the lower country with cattle, hogs, and garden seed.

Shaker men went throughout Kentucky and the South with garden and grape seeds for sale. In their rich soil, and with Shaker determination, they decried matrimony and mule breeding, but improved the breed of cattle, hogs, and sheep, and dabbled in the breeding of field crops and garden vegetables. They were the first to visit the southern country with tiny packets of virile seed for sale. Throughout the daily records, seed salesmen come and go. "Abram White and L. Varis took passage on the *Blue Wing* at Mundy's Ferry with garden seed for the lower country." Just before this Brother Abram had been to Nashville with grape seed. Scarcely a steamer left the upriver landing without a respectable company of gray-clad brethren on their way to sell excellent products to the "world."

Throughout almost a century of history of the utopian village at Pleasant Hill two personal forces stand out: the leadership of John Dunlavy, and the indomitable personalities of the scribes. John Dunlavy was a rugged and intelligent leader who was largely responsible for planting the community on the banks of the Kentucky and for making it thrive. His hand of leadership shows on the surface in many places.

Shaker discipline included the keeping of numerous journal records, which were divided between spiritual and mundane affairs. Without identifying themselves as individuals, the journalists covered the daily activities of the families, and no occurrence was too trivial to receive their attention. Whether recording an outlandish service, in which Cornstalk, Tecumseh, and their subjects create quite a disturbance with their heathenish supplications, or the rise and fall of the temperature, the scribes were ever sensible of their obligations. For hours at a time the journalists recorded the happenings around them. They kept an excellent record of the weather, for weather to their farming community was a matter of vital concern. To the residents of Pleasant Hill, the river was a kindred spirit. They loved its beautiful green current, and its deep swale. It was an active partner in their dream of perfectionist living. On its current valuable cargoes of farm products were shipped to market, and useful building timber was brought downstream. The river was the connecting link between the Shaker in his realm of spirituality and the "world" which he in reality loved.

Time after time the landings and departures of river boats were recorded in the Journal. Shakers were fond of travel, and they loved the boats which transported them on their frequent journeyings. With joyous affection the scribe noted the arrival of the *Dove* or the departure of the *Blue Wing,* or the fact that the *Buckeye* was behind time. Here intermingled with the record of a thousand trivial occurrences in communal life is a chapter in the story of Kentucky River navigation.

Reading the Shaker Journal is somewhat like get-

ting a surreptitious peep at the records of St. Peter. "Winter Shakers," reprobates, profligates, and lovelorn communicants kept the weary scribe laboring at his tedious duties. His recordings ever bear the stamp of pontifical judgment in which he was free with his own personal opinions. At times he yawns behind his hand at some trying and uninspired ceremony or digs his pen deep into the paper in a temperamental outburst at some faithless act. After a day of sacrifice, the clerk frankly confides to his book: "I was very glad when the day was past and gone." But quickly he rose up and smote an obstreperous sister in this: "Friday morning between 2 and 4 o'clock Katherine McCullough left the center family and took the broad road to destruction!" Then dipping his pen in vinegar he literally shouted on paper at her: "REPROBATED CREATURE! AWFUL! AWFUL!" It was within the same tone of judgment that he recorded in heavily inked letters "EXPELLED!" after many names. Often a terse note such as that telling of the wayward Lucy Lemon found its place in the record. "Lucy Lemon," wrote the scribe, "was kindly invited to go to the world. She went!"

Entries in December indicated a rapidly growing belief in the faith, but in the following April and May with the appearance of warm weather there was a wholesale returning to the "world." The community was victimized by bums who professed to be converts for the purpose of spending a comfortable winter where the board and lodging was good. Women more frequently than men "went to the world." Occasionally a woman and a man, who perhaps had paid too frequent visits to the "kissing bridge," went forth together.

One can easily imagine the excitement within the general community and the state of mind of the journalist on that morning of September 29, 1849, when

Facing: The double front doors of the East House are typical of the Shaker architecture.

an excommunicant came back to claim the man she loved. "Caroline Whittemore, the harlot of Harrodsburg," he wrote, "who had been brought from Lincoln County when a child and stayed till she was driven off in consequence of her wicked ways; came back here today with one or two of her associate prostitutes under the influence of liquor called to see Brother James. She, in violation of the order, sought and found him at the East Wash House where she grappled with him and bore him off, she carrying a large horse pistol in her hand and swearing vengeance to those who dared interfere. James made no resistance but walked willing along with her."

One sees the outside world reflected in the Journal —as though the diarist peeped at it from an ivory tower. First there was slavery, which the order abhorred but toward which it did not take an abolitionist attitude. Negroes were bought from time to time and were converted and freed. "Today," wrote the recorder, "we purchased James Crutcher a colored man who had been a believer about nineteen years. We kept him hired here while his owner retained him a slave. We have bought him to prevent his being sold South. He was accepted on equal terms." Other Negroes found their way into the order, and eventually to freedom.

When the clouds of disunion hovered over the nation, the Shakers were quick to sense the impending crisis. They held prayer meetings in which they begged for the maintenance of the Union. The Believers were pacifists, and talk of civil war meant for them more unhappy persecution. Then came the war. Kentucky remained neutral, but it was invaded despite its neutrality. Troops of both sides advanced upon the Kentucky River valley. In 1862, Union troops galloped across the river to Pleasant Hill and demanded foodstuff. Then came John Hunt Morgan and his hard-riding men. It has been said many times that the Shakers and Morgan were friends, but secreted away from the turmoil about him, the clerk has left a clear record on this score. "Morgan's men," said he, "called for supper which we furnished—and camped in our office stable lot, and threw out pickets on all roads." Later two horses were stolen, and then the entry that they had fed, against their will, four hundred Confederates, and had nearly worked the sisters to death cooking for them. They kept their horses hidden away, but even taking this precaution, a telltale entry says they had to buy four horses to replace those stolen by the soldiers.

When Kentucky was caught up in the throes of reconstruction, Pleasant Hill was not to go unmolested. Brigands robbed and stole from the Shakers. Unscrupulous blackmailers, using the guise of the Ku-Klux Klan, undertook to extort money from them. A note was addressed to the elders demanding that they send $200 to E. J. Rees of Oxford, Ohio, but they were not to mention the fact to a soul; if they did, every elder in the village would be killed and the village itself would be burned.

Dissolution set in with the war. Prayers offered for the safety of the Union should likewise have included a plea for the community. Shaker membership began to decline after 1865, and the elders made frantic efforts to proselyte for new additions.

It was a cold and uncompromising age of materialism that followed the Civil War. The days of antebellum religious fervor and social experimentation were now history. This was as true in that land along the Kentucky River as elsewhere in the United States. On page after page of the Shaker record the signs of deterioration become progressively noticeable. The meticulous handwriting of the scribe becomes exceedingly shaky, and the content of the entries is less significant. Then comes failure of leadership, old age, debt, and then desolation.

Through the eyes of critical fellow communicants we see Pleasant Hill community failing. An entry in the Journal of the South Union community in Ohio tells the story of the approaching end. "The ministry," writes the recorder, "return from Pleasant Hill. We found things in a very broken state. The people had almost lost all sight of our gospel orders and discipline. They were holding no meetings for spiritual gain. What a pity it is that souls will in their old age loose [sic] most all the gospel travel they have gained in a long life." Then with a discerning eye the critical visitor from South Union writes: "Pleasant Hill must have been a beautiful place in its early days. Everything denotes there was once a flourishing people here. The land is good as any in the state and the crops look well." In 1923 the last Shaker from Pleasant Hill died, and the land passed into other hands. A dream came to an end, and Pleasant Hill with its sturdy buildings now stands as a monument to an ideal that dissolved itself in stringent materialism. An age of realistic religion supplanted the emotional era of Cane Ridge.

No longer do Lot, Abraham, Isaac, Jacob, Tecumseh, and Cornstalk visit in the community. Below the village the Kentucky River still flows on, but the steamboats which the Shakers loved so dearly are gone. But behind both has lingered the knowledge that they stood for honesty and services well rendered. The Shakers doubtless were sensational and even ridiculous at times in their spiritual mysticism, but they made up for this shortcoming in their genuine charity and neighborliness and in honorable craftmanship. At this late date in Kentucky the hallmark "Shaker-made" carries with it a significant connotation which many contemporary dreamers have tried to recapture.

11

Hard-Shells

WINDING its way around knobs, under steep
points and rocky ledges, the three forks of the Kentucky River pass many a scene of human activity, but
none so rampant as the Saturday and Sunday meetings
of the Hard-Shell Baptist Church. Somewhere, back in
its very beginning, the upper Kentucky country became the battle ground of the Hard-Shell faith. These
Separatist Baptists followed the traveling congregations
over the mountains, and at Gilbert's Creek, on the
Dick's River after Lewis Craig's congregation had
moved on, they founded the first branch of the church,
and from there they moved upstream. It is American
frontier individualism institutionalized. It has had its
feet washed, it has pulled off its jewelry, given up
swearing, dancing and gambling, and it has required
that its women keep their hair and dresses good and
long. Gathering up the remnants of belief of many
other churches and sects it hands down in its rules of
faith a rigid belief in divine, or faith, healing, visions,
sensational and emotional conversions, and public testimony of salvation. Rules, however, are constantly subjected to individual interpretation and observation by
the Hard-Shell brothers.

Along the trails and roads deep in the mountainous

region of the Kentucky River valley, knots of people gather monthly outside of crude little church houses to discuss the provincial affairs of everyday life. They talk about killin's, birthin's, flirtin's, dyin's, and the growin' of hillside corn. The men squat around in circles, digging tiny trenches with sharp-pointed pocketknives, carving bizarre figures from scrap pieces of wood and bark, or just sitting and spitting an occasional fine liquid dart at an imaginary target as a social preface to the meeting of the church. Then comes the bold announcement that church is "to take up." Lean, gaunt men, browned from long days of exposure to a boiling mountain sun, or blown brown by fickle currents of cold air which pour over sheltering ridges, stretch themselves upright, close their pocketknives, spit out their chaws, pull their overall suspenders in place or tighten worn belts around their shrunken middles, and stroll nonchalantly to their seats of honor and male dignity at the right hand of the crude pulpit. Women, browned by the same sun which has burned its way deeply into the skins of their men, drawn from the burden of having too many children and from washing and ironing grimy clothes and cooking and helping with the crops, are in their places to the left of the pulpit. They are there with suckling children tugging at their breasts or with crawling babies who are constantly winding their way among their mothers' calloused feet. There are preachers enough to serve a dozen such churches, and all of them have come to deliver a sermon and to dispute bitterly with their colleagues' interpretation of the Scriptures. God's servants, say the Hard-Shells, should not accept pay, and an education is unnecessary preparation for the ministry. If a man were paid he would be thinking too much about money and not enough about salvation. All a preacher needs in the way of education is a call to preach.

Lack of education has always been somewhat a mark of pride with the Primitive Baptist ministers. It has given them a democratic feeling and has placed them on an earthly level with their followers, an advantage they have treasured. Many of them have boasted in their sermons: "Now, my brethering, as I have told you, I am an oneddicated man, and know nothing about grammar talk and collidge highfalutin', but I am a plane unlarnt preacher of the gospil, what's been foreordaned and called to prepare a pervarse generashun for the day of wrath-ah!" This is a characteristic "opening" for the vigorous and faithful up the Kentucky River. Some weary old servants have labored in the cause of the primitive faith in that country. Pious "Raccoon John" Smith preached throughout the hill country, following the valley of the North Fork eastward. He rode and walked from cabin to cabin telling the backwoods people of the rugged beliefs of the Hard-Shells. "Raccoon John" literally blazed a trail of separatism which paralleled the course of the river. This old soldier of the cause was the mountain people's guidepost in spiritual matters until he became confused and joined the Campbellites. Following in John Smith's footsteps was an army of individualistic preachers who farmed scrawny hillsides during the week and worked even more diligently in the Lord's vineyard on Saturdays and Sundays. These ministers went forth, dressed in the coarse work clothes of farm laborers, and it was seldom possible to tell the shepherd from the flock.

There is the story of shrewd Brother Mason Williams who combined farming, preaching, and "politicking" with happy results in all three callings. Brother

Mason had raised his voice in defense of local legislation at the state capital for four years as a state senator. Down the river at Frankfort he had learned a new style of dress. The senator-preacher was on one occasion directed to a Hard-Shell deacon's home to spend the night, and he arrived there ahead of the master of the house. He was dressed in his store clothes, and his manner was that of a polished "outsider." When he dismounted before his host's gate he announced to the womenfolk that he was there to preach next day. Before long the travel-weary parson sprawled out on the porch floor and was asleep, and the women began to speculate on what kind of preacher he was. He was dressed well enough to be a Presbyterian, yet he might be a Mormon elder. It was finally suggested that they examine his hymnbook to determine his denomination. The women opened his saddlebags, and when one of them ran a hand in to get the hymnbook she encountered a bottle of liquor. She held up her evidence and exclaimed, "Oh, he's an old Hard-Shell Baptist! Here is his bottle of whisky!"

There were eccentric brethren who did unusual things in the name of the individualistic Hard-Shell church. There was the prophet Jeremiah, who, in order to keep the records straight, and to prevent confusion with the Hebrew prophet of the same name, added the surname Lovelace. Prophet Jeremiah of the Kentucky valley professed the miraculous powers of making the blind to see, of healing the sick, of relieving pain, and of walking on water. His neighbors believed that Brother Jeremiah's faith-healing powers might be real, but they were openly cynical when it came to the question of his strolling on the surface of the Kentucky River. The prophet was challenged by a doubting Thomas to perform his miraculous feat. Jeremiah ac-

cepted the challenge, but just in case his spiritual buoy-
ancy should play an unkind trick on him, he took the
precaution to lay a trestle about eight inches under the
surface of the water which would hold him up as he
walked to midstream. A skeptical joker discovered the
planks and removed one of them where the water was
deepest, and awaited the water-walking Jeremiah's appearance. At dusk the solemn prophet appeared on the
bank of the Kentucky in a flowing white robe, and at
the water's edge he stopped to offer a prayer. Then he
asked the audience to sing as he performed his miracle,
and as the songsters closed the first verse of their song
Jeremiah reached the end of the first plank. The next
moment Brother Lovelace stepped head over heels into
the river, and his saintly robe dragged him down. In
panic he screamed, "Bretheren, save me or I perish!"
and as he gasped for breath and floundered in the
treacherous current, a hardened realist answered back,
"Can't give you any assistance—all damned fools like
you ought to drown." This was an extreme case of
miracle performing. But still there are faith healers.
Uncle Shade Combs, up the Troublesome Fork, en-
joys the patronage of a large clientele who seek health
through an act of faith.

The Bible is the rule of faith and every word is
divine law, and the Hard-Shell accepts it literally. His
communion service follows with strict decorum the
practice of washing his neighbor's feet. Too, his whole
conception of religious life is a literal imitation of the
Biblical pattern.

At his services, the Hard-Shell preacher stammers
and flounders in his sermon until he is caught up in
a rising crescendo of warm autointoxication which
comes from the sound of his own voice. Soon he is in
a state where his emotions are ungoverned, and the

mountainsides ring with a monotonous shouting of in-
coherent sentences brought to abrupt closes by gasp-
ing, ineffective "ah's." These sermons are crammed with
homely idiomatic vernacular and backwoods analogies.
They are always warped into arguments to support the
Hard-Shell rule of religious faith. A verbatim example
of this emotional type of sermon is this vigorous outpouring: "An' wen the ole hoss sees hit he stops-ah,"
thunders the excited brother in begging his neighbors
to turn back from sin, "an' his yurs pints right straight
at the stump-ah! An' every har on his back pints right
straight at his yurs-ah! an' he says: there hit is-ah!
Thar's the booger-ah! Oh! he'll ruin me-ah! An' thar he
stans-ah! with his laigs stiff lack fence rails-ah! an' you
cain't get him apast that ole stump-ah! But ef you've
got a good strong bridle-ah! yer kin git him *fernent*
hit-ah! an! then he gives a great snort, so—boo-ooh! an'
he goes by hit with a jump-ah! and twarnt nothin' but
a stump-ah! Now, brethering, they hain't no more
harm in the doctrings of the ole Hardshell Baptist
church-ah! than they is in thet ole stump-ah!"

Then the brother rises high in his pleading, and
he gets into an emotional state which is called by the
Hard-Shells the "short-rows" of preaching. He launches
into a plea for the Hard-Shell right side up or down by
appealing to Hebrew history, found as he says, "Somers
in the Bible, an' I hain't agoin' ter tell yer whar; but
hit's thar." Raking perspiration from his foaming brow
and pulling open his shirt collar, he sets off again, this
time into a personal confession. "But oh!" shouts the
foaming preacher as his brethren respond with loud
Amens, and give him hearty handshakes, "my brethering-ah! How well I remember-ah! jis' lack hit war
yistidy-ah! the time wen I found the Lord-ah! a heap
o' people sez they cain't tell the time-ah! nur the place-

ah! Wull, I reckon they cain't-ah! Kase they hain't never aben no time an' place-ah! If a man's hed peace spoke to his never-dyin' soul, he kin mighty soon tell the time 'n' place-ah! Oh! I remember hit well-ah! I war twenty-one an' agoin' on twenty-two years of age-ah! An' I went ter meeting-ah! an' I went home afeelin' mighty bad, kase some o' the gals hed slighted me-ah! kase I war lame-ah! An' I felt bad thet they wouldn't show me as much 'tention as t'other young men thet war cumridges o' mine-ah! An' agoin' hum-ah! I rode off by myself-ah! ter go hum by a round-about way-ah! O my brethering-ah! I reckon I war afeeling sorter lack poor ole Joner-ah! Lack I'd love to go off in the ships of Tarshish-ah! An' I felt just lack I wouldn't akeered p'ticular ef hit hed aben the whale's belly-ah!

"Wull I got out on the mounting-ah, an' 'peared lack I couldn't go home-ah. An' I got off my hoss an' sot down under a hick'ry tree-ah, afeelin' lack 'Lijah wen he sot under the juniper tree-ah, awishing he cud die-ah. An' awhilst I war thar, they come up a powerful big storm-ah, an' my nag got loose an' I couldn't ketch her, an' off she went fur home-ah! aleavin' me on the mounting-ah. Oh! my brethering, how hit thundered-ah! An' peared lack the hull sky war one streak o' lightenin'-ah. An' the limbs commenced ablowin' off'n the trees-ah! An' the trees began abendin'-ah! An' the warter come down in sheets-ah, an' wet me to the skin-ah! Now, I jist want to tell you I got over wantin' to die, mighty soon-ah! Oh! then I begun to realize thet they's somethin' comes after death-ah! An' I warn't ready fur hit-ah! Oh, my brethering, I thought I'd prayed before-ah, but I found thet night I hadn't never done it before-ah! I prayed an' prayed, an' every streak o' lightnin' I thought I could see an angry God above me, an' a yawnin' hell below me-ah! But right wile the storm war aragin'-ah, an' the lightnin' war aflashin'-ah, an' the thunder war acrackin'-ah, the Lord spoke peace to my never-dyin' soul-ah! I seed the lightnin' but hit didn't skeer me. I heerd the thunder, but I warn't afeard no more. I felt the rain soakin' me, but peared lack hit didn't wet me then. I jist felt lack singin' an' I sung an' prayed an' shouted thar all night, an' they found me in the mornin' an' I kin jis shet my eyes an' see the place whar I foun' the Lord. I cud go to thet ole hick'ry tree the darkest night the Lord ever made. An' wen they axed wut church I'd jine, I sez, sez I, 'Lemme jine the Baptist,' sez I; 'not the Missionary Baptist, nor the reglar Baptist, but the ole, Two-seed, Iron-Jacket, Predestination Hardshell Baptist-ah! For on this rock I will build my church, and the gates of hell shall not prevail against hit-ah!"

Sins included in the Hard-Shell category are many, but most cardinal of them, perhaps, is that of dancing. One brother condemned it in ringing criticism. "Thar dancin', and thar foolin', and thar drinkin', and thar gamblin'," said he, "does the devil's work hyar." This prohibition of dancing outlawed the instrument of the dance—the fiddle, and hatred of this was transferred to other musical instruments. Hard-Shell songs are sung without instrumental accompaniment. They are dragged out a line at a time, and these after the lead of the "liner." This perhaps is the most primitive music sung by the white man in America today. It is sung in an elemental key, and in a remarkably slow time. These songs all have gloomy themes. They plead for a better world to come; in one of them the congregation drags on in melancholic meter, and in doleful supplication they cry:

Guide me, O Thou Great Jehovah,
  Pilgrim through this barren land;
I am weak, but Thou art mighty,
  Hold me with Thou powerful hand.
    Bread of Heaven,
Feed me till I want no more.

Physical man asks in his simple songs that he be
given food to maintain his body without having to
make the terrific physical fight for it which has been
necessary for him to do in the Appalachian highlands.
In dolorous strains, the Hard-Shell congregations along
the river pour forth their sad plaints proclaiming a
positive faith in "Jerusalem, My Happy Home" or
"I'm not Ashamed to Own My Lord," or in tearful
despondency they wail, "I Am Alone in This World"
or "I'm Glad I Was Born to Die." What joy these primitive, simple people find in their musical moralizing over
their earthly troubles. With their faces wreathed in
sadness, suffering an eternal despair they drag through
line after line as though they were pulling their physical systems apart, sinew by sinew.

Before transitory and depraved man can claim conversion, it is necessary that he have a vision signifying
divine acceptance and that he repeat it publicly to
his brethren. There was the case of Nannie Everidge,
who had wandered deep into the dark recesses of sin and
then had tried to turn aside. Poor Nannie tried hard
to have a vision, and to slip the heavy burden of sinful
misery and woe from off her weary shoulders. In her
sleep she heard Brother Elam Hale preaching, and then
she saw a stream composed of balls of fire falling past
her bedside. Her body was racked with pain, and fear
of eternal damnation piled up daily until she went to
bed an agonized sick wretch. Her hopes were for a life

of plenty—a life where worldly goods which she had always been denied would be given her freely. The vision began to unfold itself. It was of a country store stacked high with the good things of life. Even faithful Brother Elam came by Nannie's visionary house with a sack of fine foods, and the sack burst and Nannie was supplied with the goods of this earth. These were the things which freed an imprisoned soul from a torturous burden of worldly sins. This was the vision which signalized a complete spiritual rebirth for Nannie Everidge. But where this favored convert was able to come through her vale of tears, and to enter into a new life free of balls of fire drifting by her bedside, and bestowed with the bountiful spiritual treasures of a well-stocked country store, many another bedeviled mortal has had to sit without the pale of the church because of the failure to have a vision.

In rigorous observation of Christ's example of humility, a cardinal rule of Hard-Shell faith is that of washing of feet. "We believe," say the rules, "that the Lord's Supper is the command of the Saviour, and that by the use of bread and wine and feet washing, it should be kept up until His second coming by His believers." It is man's humble sacramental tribute to the cause of Christianity that he wash his neighbor's feet. Along the Kentucky River he keeps the faith literally; the Hard-Shell communicant strips off his shoes and socks and plunges his feet into a tin dishpan to be scrubbed and dried by a neighbor. The neighbor comes with a towel girded about his loins, and in literal obedience to the Scriptures he washes and dries his fellow's feet and the service progresses from member to member. It is a meek ceremony of neighborly reciprocation.

Promise of future life is the eternal hope of the faithful, and the worldly life is only a single link in a chain of predetermined events. Death is the final earthly transformation. Through this grim portal, mortal man marches to his reward, be it an eternal life of happiness or one of worldly miseries compounded. The faithful Hard-Shell looks forward to death in his preaching, and likewise in his songs. He sings, paradoxically enough, in tones of deepest grief, "I'm Glad that I Was Born to Die." Death is ever uppermost in his mind, and in its sober ceremonies he has developed a sentimental folk custom which ties modern America to an earlier age of primitive American pioneering.

12

Funeralizing

DEATH is a grim thing in the mountains of Kentucky. Man in this isolated corner of America is a great respecter of its fearful powers. He has paid frequent tribute to its ghastly visits to his neighborhood. High above the Kentucky valley there are scores of green knobs crowned with shining whitewashed gravestones. There above the mountain home is the graveyard, so placed that every time the mountainman looks up he sees it and remembers to be sad. The lonely hillman misses a member of his family far more than if he lived in a community where life moved on at a more exciting pace. As in every other aspect of his rural life, he has even institutionalized, in his own simple way, the stern reality of dying.

When the rural mountainman dies, sympathetic neighbors come in to build a crude triangular coffin or to deliver a cheap "deal" box bought from a hardware store. Sorrowing friends wrap the box in white cloth and prepare the body for the long climb to the "point" of the knob. In the modern age when cameras are common, numerous pictures of the corpse surrounded by the family are taken and they are displayed for years to come with an air of sorrow intermingled with pride. In earlier days when the body of a loved one, or a faithful servant of the community, was consigned to the earthly bosom of the hill country a grave house was erected over the mound. These little houses protected the grave from both the elements and that fiendish ghoul, the "grave robber." Many Kentucky mountain people still believe that there is an animal, resembling, so it is said, a cross between a slender weasel and an anteater. This thieving varmint, according to highland legend, digs into the grave and destroys the body. Likewise, the grave house is a mark of profound respect and enduring love. Often an obliging Samaritan has been generously thanked for a favor by having it said to him, "You ought to have a pretty grave house when you die."

Many grave houses stand out against a rugged mountain background as drab sentinels of the death watch atop the burial ridges which overlook the Kentucky River and its numerous branches. The old ones were of logs covered over with hand-riven boards, and the new ones are of planks, covered with tin. At El Bethel, near Indian Old Fields, there are several of these tiny houses. One especially is interesting. It shelters a collection of sentimental trinkets and a large photograph of the deceased. Tireless hands have kept this homely shrine of memory in immaculate order. Outside of Hazard in the community graveyard, along the bank of the North Fork of the Kentucky, there are several houses. The one which shelters the grave of Everett Combs causes the visitor to pause in wonderment. A grief-stricken mother has spent many tender hours in decorating it. On the glass side of the house is pasted a long and mournful Appalachian highland ballad which pours out a tearful story of love and adoration. Within, the little shrine is decorated for childhood's happiest experience—Christmas. There is an artificial evergreen tree, a Christmas wreath, paper flowers, a tiny package on the doll table, two large pictures of the dead child, a lithograph of Christ on the mountain, and placards of "Suffer Little Children to Come unto Me" and "I Am the Resurrection and the Life." To a mother this is a tender remembrance of a child who had been a joy in a home, but to an indifferent world which passes the cemetery gate in a monotonous workaday procession it is a weird hang-over from another day.

On Saturdays and Sundays in midsummer and early fall, the roads near the mountain graveyards are crowded with processions of people. Groups of women and children mope along bearing bunches of paper flowers, rolls of bright-colored crepe-paper streamers, and bundles of white cloth. Behind them come knots of silent men. Those in front are old and morose, they bear upon their faces the imprint of sanctimony, a mark which indicates they are preachers and deacons. It is true they are on their way to a "funeralizing" but there will be no rough "deal" coffin housing its pallid tenant. Long before, perhaps many years before, the morning of the memorial ceremony this ghostly freight has been transported up the ridge. It is even possible that already numerous ceremonies have been held over the grave. For the bereaved family the delayed funeral is a moment of grievous social triumph. These days have been planned in advance by the family for nearly a year. Those stooped, sad-eyed, and heavy-bonneted women in black funeral dress have spent long hours laboring over a hot cooking stove preparing for the company which will stop by their houses after the preaching. The family directly interested in the services has put forth their best efforts at preparing a bounteous meal because the preachers will, out of pastoral respect, return home with them for dinner.

At the graveyard the brethren have already erected in the open a preaching stand and seats. A series of rough log benches have been placed before the platform, but the stand itself is a pale of communication. Within its sacred confines only the mourners and the converted are allowed to sit. At the grave, careful hands have traced the outline of the eroded and bare clay mound with whitewashed stones, and the mildewed headstone has been cleaned. Bright-colored paper streamers are stretched in a crude triangular pattern from head to foot, and bright curled paper flowers top off the decorations. Nearly always a photograph of the dead one leans forlornly against the headstone. Indeed, death is made a continuously morbid affair on those ridges which tower above the narrow valleys of the Kentucky.

Services are opened at the grave by the reading of an obituary of the departed member. Here is the militant Hard-Shell's opportunity to make a fervent plea for the salvation of the living members of the family. In hushed tones, the memorialist drags out the life history of the one buried beneath his feet. But it is with special pleading that he drawls out the last words of the dying. There was Clell Collins, deputy sheriff, who was killed while raiding a moonshine still at the head of Carr Creek. Clell was one of the faithful, and late in August of the next year his family had his funeral preached. The committee on resolutions wrote: "When he called for his children and told them to pray, Jesus had come and he had to go home with him. We will not write all the sweet words that he left but we feel shure [sic] that the Lord did come and took him home." Then emphatically the brethren sermonized: "So we would say to the children not to forget the council that father gave them to pray and meet him in heaven." Clell's memorial was morbid indeed, for the family had brought a framed photograph of him as he lay a corpse and this was passed about among the congregation.

Hundreds of such obituaries, as the one written for Clell Collins, each year end in pleas for the conversion of the living and for the primitive faith. Hard-Shell brethren long ago realized that at no time was man more susceptible to conversion than in the presence of death. At no time could the faith hope to recruit new membership with more ease than underneath the spreading branches of mountain beeches in the family graveyard.

In the procedure of memorial services three specific objectives are kept in view. The service is held primarily to pay respects to the dead, but likewise it is to convert the living and to warm over the converts who have grown cold. Preachers are placed on the agenda according to their fetching powers and in degree of friendship for the family. With shirt collars agape, and baggy trousers hanging heavy at the end of ancient suspenders, the first soldier of the cause takes to the field before his fellow ministers. In his initial moments on foot he mumbles and seesaws verbally back and forth, offering the hackneyed excuse that he is not prepared and that really he should not be there. But it is imperious duty that has called him, and the Lord, he hopes, will blaze the way. Soon, he is positive, the Lord will inspire him and he will be able to warm up to a sermon. Only by divine aid can he, a belabored sinner, get through the ordeal before him. Gathered around him are both brethren and friends of the gospel, and preachers who are bitter enemies of numerous literal Scriptural controversies. Time and again the "onlarned"

disciples have matched their ministerial wits up and down the creek valleys, and each of them is familiar with the "tender spots" of the others.

The Hard-Shell minister requires a tremendous amount of "scotching" to push over a sermon. In his hard scrabble to make a living, the preacher has learned that a team can pull a loaded wagon over a steep rutted hill road only with the aid of adroit scotching at every stop for breath, and the same thing is true in preaching. A loud Amen tells him that he is rising "higher and higher." A friendly handshake is assurance that the trail is warm, and a loud handclap is an invitation to let go with all his might.

Before the primitive Baptist preachers can go far in ascending their spirals of emotionalism it is necessary to warm up the congregation with a song, a song which perhaps comes from somewhere deep in the ancestral background of the primitive church. There is the famous song ballad which pours forth a sobbing farewell:

> Farewell, mother, I am dying
>> But you must not weep for me—
> I am happy, cease your sighing,
>> Soon with Jesus I will be.
>
> Darling mother, stoop down and kiss me,
>> How I love you none can know;
> When I am gone you'll surely miss me
>> And your tears for me will flow.

Each respectable memorial requires the services of five or six preachers, and each succeeding minister achieves the paradoxical results of sinking his hearers deeper into a state of deathlike melancholy and of working their emotions up to the breaking point. Mem-

Facing (Bottom): Grave Houses to protect the deceased from the weather were thought to be the ultimate in burial sites by many in the Kentucky mountains.

bers of the deceased's family are bowed in grief, and audible sobs add deathlike gloom to the service by the time the third preacher has reached the peak of emotional intoxication in his sermon. The last preacher to occupy the pulpit is the man of power. It is he who is entrusted with the precious spiritual responsibility of pushing the services to a stormy finish in which the excitable members go on a rampage. He dawdles away no precious time offering awkward excuses for not being prepared. To do this would sweep away the high state of enthusiasm already at hand. Members of the family who remain without the pale of sanctity are made the victims of thunderous appeals. An accusing finger is waggled under their noses, and they are victimized with stinging personal remarks. Yet it is astounding how calmly some of them can sit through these spiritual lambastings. They have even been able to ignore personal charges and appeals with an indifference that does distinct credit to a rugged individualistic race of people. But where one determined member of a family has sat by without breaking down, scores have undergone emotional storms which left them physically and mentally unstrung for hours.

A powerful preacher, following his fellows who have labored successfully in preparing the ground, can always count on the "hair-trigger" sisters to help him. He appeals to them individually and as a group. Soon a tear trickles slowly down the face of the browned cheek of a sad-eyed, emaciated woman who bears the marks of many trying mountain winters upon her face. Her sunbonnet begins to bob back and forth, she swings her long bony arms, and her calloused hands come together in loud claps. She rises to her feet and in hysterical screams of holy terror proclaims her faith in the church. One wailing convert brings up another and

another until the crude platform is crowded with agonized women crying out in terrifying screams—screams
which ring with the pains and sufferings of countless
lost generations. This is the grand climax when a waver-
ing sinner gives in and comes marching up in a panic
to repent and be accepted into the church. At this
point the minister lines out another funeral dirge, and
the chanting prolongs the emotional outburst. A favorite closing song bears the astounding title "The Great
Speckled Bird." Through six halting verses it recites
the frightening story of death, and of the recording of
the names of the faithful who reach the great beyond.
The soul of the departed has long since taken the tangible form of a huge bird, and the mourners, in eerie
chant, recite line by line:

> What a beautiful thought I am thinking
>   Concerning that great speckled bird,
> Remember her name is recorded
>   On the pages of God's holy word.
>
> All the other birds are flocked around her
>   They watch every move that she makes
> But I am sure they can watch until evening
>   And really they will find no mistake.

The dying notes of the final line end the formal
ceremony in the stand, and amidst the wild hysterical
wails of stampeding female shouters the preacher announces "That the people are to take notice" that other
funerals will be held in the weeks to come in the neighboring graveyards up and down the creek branches of
the Kentucky River, or that another service will be held
for the same person a year hence.

From the stand the congregation moves to the
memorial grave, and there once again the song leader

steps forward and lines out a mournful recitation of death. Two favorite songs are "The Village Churchyard" and "Farewell, Mother, I Am Dying."

In all American music there is no more downright melancholy than is to be found in the wailing chant of "The Village Churchyard." The ballad recites a long grief-stricken tale of a lone orphan child wringing its pale hands beside a mother's grave. The child moans:

> In that dear old village churchyard
>   I can see a mossy mound;
> That is where my mother's sleeping,
>   In the cold and silent ground.

And then the lone orphan, bowed low with grief, finishes its sad account in complete defeat and despair:

> Looking at the stars above me,
>   Waiting for the early dawn,
> There mother I'll be buried
>   And no more be left alone.

One final act and the belated funeral is finished. A preacher kneels low over the head of the bare clay mound. With his head bobbing up and down on the dirt, and the congregation kneeling about him, he lifts his voice in loud and tremulous supplication. His appeal may sometimes be peppered with requests that Hebraic vengeance be visited upon stiff-necked loved ones who have refused to come through with a conversion.

With remarkable suddenness and informality, the morbid Hard-Shell funeralizing comes to a close. In a moment what was an emotionally upset Baptist congregation becomes a neighborly folk gathering. The storm has passed, and the dead have been served. Everyday life takes up again where it left off on Saturday morning. Even the mournful echoes of the primitive chants have died away, and laughter and banter ring out with a happier note. Hospitable mountaineers pass through the crowd insisting that people go home with them for dinner. Rural isolated America is enjoying the thing for which it hungers—company and a crowd. For the family involved, the memorial ceremony is their one grand social occasion in which they enjoy the spotlight of neighborly attention and sympathy. Grief for the departed one is genuine, but so is the interest in the company and friendly communion of the neighbors.

This is primitive America, and these Hard-Shell Baptists, who cling to foot washing and belated funerals, are our "contemporary ancestors." They have been caught up for more than a century and a half in the unrelenting clutches of geographical and social isolation. Both the people and their Primitive church have been forced back into the fastness of the Appalachian highlands in order to avoid the competition of an educated and snobbish outside world. In basic humanity, the Primitive Regular Baptist faith has served the spiritual needs of some of the most virile stock in America. It was the one religious faith which could accept realistically the primeval limitations of the country at the head of the Kentucky River and succeed in living with a degree of happiness.

13

A Kentucky Symbol

BETWEEN Brooklyn Bridge and Tyrone, the Kentucky River stretches out into a long gentle sweep of emerald-green water. On either side the steep, heavily wooded bluffs of Woodford and Anderson counties roll down close to each other. Near the middle of this long reach of the river is a sharp break in the steep Woodford County palisades. Grier Creek cuts a bold and sinuous swath through the blue-limestone bluff. It is a boisterous little Bluegrass stream which rises only a short distance back of the great Woodford hill. Where it flows into the Kentucky it has cut a deep bed, and there underneath a beautiful stand of slender gray sycamores it pours into the river a crystal contribution of fresh spring water. Here was a place where Kentucky's pioneer people could cross the river, and, likewise, here was located Sublett's Ferry about which a rich chapter in Kentucky's cultural history was to center.

It has always been natural in the history of the lower Kentucky River that where a satisfactory crossing could be effected a bit of romance has clung to the spot. The mouth of Grier Creek and its deep ravine stand out as extraordinary places in a rich countryside. Grier Creek valley was just the sort of place created by nature to please the aesthetic taste of homesick Frenchmen, whether from Virginia or the homeland. Like much of Bluegrass Kentucky, land around Sublett's Ferry and at Mortonsville, an old river village near by, was claimed by Virginia soldiers who had received pay in land warrants for their services in the Virginia Line. In the vanguard of these claimants was the tough old Indian-fighting General Charles Scott, who later became governor of Kentucky. There were also John Morton and his five sons: James, Jeremiah, John, Benjamin, and William. Their neighbors were Jeremiah Wilson, James and John Rucker, and James and Thomas Coleman. These sons of the American struggle with England were victims of economic displacement in their homes in Virginia. They came west to build new fortunes and to enjoy the fruits of a frontier democracy. Their sympathies in later years were on the side of the people who struggled to gain their individual liberties. It was with a keen sense of fellow feeling that they watched developments in revolutionary France. Among the settlers at Mortonsville and along Grier Creek were Huguenots.

A ship was built on the banks of the Kentucky and loaded with supplies for France. The ship, however, was sunk almost in sight of its goal. This community became a haven for refugees who found themselves so far west. Boatmen going to New Orleans aboard their Kentucky River broad-horns from Scott's Landing and Sublett's Ferry carried hearty invitations to the French immigrants in that city. Among the Huguenots and later French immigrants who settled here were the Ruckers, Subletts, Trabues, Muldrows, Dupuys, Mortons, and Mountjoys. Of these, four names became inseparable parts of the Kentucky River story. Lewis Sublett ran the ferry back and forth across the river while Joel Dupuy, Edward Trabue and Andrew Muldrow became landlords of considerable means.

Grier Creek ran down from the Bluegrass fields in Woodford County with a good head of water. Its current was strong enough to turn the wheels of flour mills and ropewalks. Its rich limewater was likewise fine for making a high quality bourbon whisky. One of the first pioneer enterprisers to realize this fact was Colonel Andrew Muldrow. He harnessed the current of the little creek and forced it through his millrace under the huge wheel of his mill and through the flake barrels of his distillery. His mill ground the rich grain from the acres of the Bluegrass which rolled out behind the big river hill. Farm wagons creaked downhill over the narrow Sublett's Ferry road to deposit their valuable burdens of grain and hemp fiber in Colonel Muldrow's storage houses. A half mile away sturdy flatboats tugged at the end of Kentucky hempen lines looped around the boles of stanch sycamores. In the spring boatmen dropped their lines and drifted away with their heavily loaded boats to the southern markets down the Mississippi.

In a short time Colonel Muldrow's vigorous commercial activity was to earn him a fortune. The colonel was one of the Kentucky pioneers who brought a sense of beauty with him over the mountains. He dreamed of the day when his fortune would grow and he could desert his log house and live the life of a gentleman atop the long point of land which stood above his mills and Grier Creek. This point was just the place for an affluent landowner and millmaster to build his graceful home. Around his place on three sides the creek is visible from the front porch, and the roadway to the ferry parallels the creek. The natural surroundings within the bow of the creek, with the outline sketched more boldly by the limestone road, place the Muldrow house in a perfect setting. Brick for the side walls of the house were burnt on the grounds from dirt taken out of the basement pit. Skilled brick masons laid these in British bond. Broad oval-topped colonial windows, flanked by side sashes, and a large door with side sashes, topped by a delicately designed and leaded oval overhead light, balance the front of the house. A porch supported by four slender columns, with a Palladian window in the gable end, gives a dignified finish to the front of the structure. At either end are large brick chimneys, and on either side of these large Georgian windows which give a sense of perfect balance.

Colonel Muldrow's aesthetic taste reached beyond exterior lines. He had a keen sense of appreciation for interior detail, and Matthew Lowery's imaginative wood carvings are distinctly works of art. Every cornice in the rooms is a delicately carved masterpiece. Carved mantels framing the fireplaces are the products of a master craftsman. To break the monotonous lines, Lowery carved every series of wood trimmings on a different pattern. The cluster of columns dividing the hall into two sections are different in design yet they show an astounding sense of harmony. Here on the banks of the Kentucky, Colonel Muldrow built one of America's architectural gems. Down at Frankfort John Brown had built Liberty Hall in 1796; and at Lexington, Henry Clay built Ashland in 1811; and Benjamin Gratz built his home in 1806; but none of these famous houses surpassed Colonel Muldrow's in beauty and sensitiveness of detail.

For twelve years more, after the colonel moved his family from his frontier log house to his miniature Georgian castle, his mills and distillery were to yield him a rich return. In 1829 Colonel Muldrow died, and in his will he requested that his distillery not be operated after his death, and that his slaves be liberated when the males were twenty-eight and the females twenty-four years of age. They were to be sent to Liberia if they wished to go. Among numerous other items listed in his will are the books from his library. Colonel Muldrow owned a fine collection of books, and he gave evidence during his life of having read them. On two different occasions he had served his county in the state general assembly. But of more importance, here on the bank of a Kentucky River creek Colonel Muldrow, an overland pioneer, had fought back the woods and the frontier environment. He had captured the wild current of Grier Creek and turned it into a sturdy foundation stone of western American culture. It perhaps would have given Andrew Muldrow's pride a considerable boost if he could have known that architects and lovers of graceful building lines would still be driving down the Sublett's Ferry road to admire his beautiful house more than a hundred years after his death.

Upstream a mile or so, a second Huguenot gentleman, Joel Dupuy, built a sturdy stone house on a sprawling ledge high above Grier Creek. Unlike Colonel Muldrow, Joel Dupuy used gray Kentucky limestone instead of brick. He went downstream a short distance on the Kentucky and quarried large blocks of Tyrone limestone. The Dupuy house is of a provincial American dogtrot design. Yet it combines the grace of its neighboring Georgian structures with the forthright ruggedness and honesty of line of the pioneer American log house.

Joel Dupuy was one of the early Huguenot Baptists who helped to plant that church beyond the Kentucky in the Bluegrass. John Taylor mentions frequently the work of the Dupuys in his *History of the Ten Baptist Churches*. Grier Creek formed a ravine which delighted the heart of the romantic Huguenot, but he, like Colonel Muldrow, delayed its current, in the shute of his millrace, long enough to turn his mill-wheel to a rich profit. His mill produced hundreds of barrels of flour and meal for the lower southern market. Likewise, both Muldrow and Dupuy were interested in Kentucky's other cash crop, hemp. Southern cotton farmers needed Kentucky hempen bagging, and later rope with which to wrap their cotton bales. Their rope-walks were busy places. Here yard after yard of strong coarse hempen bagging was wound by their slaves into rolls in preparation for the long river journey to the cotton belt.

Making money was a matter of primary interest with Joel Dupuy, but secluded as he was on the banks of the bubbling little Kentucky creek, he had time to satisfy a Frenchman's love of beauty. Above the grace-ful Kentucky stone house was Lucy Craig Dupuy's for-mal garden. This became one of Kentucky's most beautiful spots, and for years it attracted the atten-tion of travelers along the river.

The time came, however, when Joel Dupuy was to tire of his life at Reynaud Hall in the secluded glade under the great Woodford hill. It was a long journey to the county seat at Versailles, and like the gentlemen of means and dignity of his period of the nineteenth century, Colonel Dupuy enjoyed his frequent visits to his county's seat of justice. There he hobnobbed with other Woodford gentlemen and kept pace with both the times and state politics. When he journeyed to Ver-sailles, so it is said, he traveled east over the rough road with the sun shining straight into his face. In the after-noon he traveled west going home and suffered from the sun shining directly upon him. To remedy this situation he deserted his home on Grier Creek and built nearer the county seat so that he could put the sun behind him in his journeyings back and forth to town.

A third pioneer enterpriser along the bank of the Kentucky was Edward Trabue who had fought in the battle of Guilford Courthouse. He came west with military land warrants in his pocket in search of a fortune. Many of his friends and Virginia neighbors came to Woodford County. The fertile rolling plains of the Bluegrass region north and east of the river appealed to the land-hungry immigrants. Edward Trabue selected a thousand acres of rich land northeast of the river, and settled down to become a landed Kentucky gentleman. At a point three hundred feet above the stream he constructed a handsome Virginia house, and before its front door sprawled the long graceful stretch of the Kentucky. From Colonel Trabue's front door the view was almost too picturesque to be real. It had much the appearance of being the handiwork of some dreamy painter who had created an imaginative scene far too idyllic for reality. Colonel Trabue was proud of his house and its fine location. As a mark of pride in his ownership he scratched his record in the cellar: "Edward Trabue, October 11, 1794."

Here beside the Kentucky, western America was to experience an architectural beginning that was to do credit to the discriminating tastes of three pioneer sons. These houses still overlook Grier's Creek and the Kentucky River. They stand as proud and dignified monuments to another day when the violin in the hands of a slave rang out the Virginia and French reels, when their occupants tripped gaily over their thick but carefully matched Virgin ash floors. Frequently today a modern automobile climbs slowly up the hill and de-

posits its burden of architects before "Mount Miller."
Back at the foot of the hill where the driveway fords
the creek, tops of the foundations of the mill and distillery are visible above the ground. The mills and the
millraces, however, are gone. Even Lucy Craig Dupuy's formal garden is grown up in saplings. But
enough of the tangible documents remain intact to assist the historian in reconstructing the picture of this
other age.

A short distance away from Grier's Creek is the
village of Mortonsville. Today it is one of those sleepy
little roadside villages characteristic of Bluegrass farming communities. Perhaps not a single person lounging
lazily in one of the country stores, or leaning dreamily
against posts around the filling station, ever heard of
the rich river run to New Orleans from Scott's Landing. Their fortunes are now tied up with the tobacco
towns of Lexington, Winston-Salem, and Durham or
with the packing houses in Chicago and Louisville.
Overhead, on the old houses, however, is evidence of
the flourishing river trade. Boatmen, drifting away
from Scott's Landing, five miles from the village,
brought back ideas of fancy decoration from the iron
grillwork which they saw in the southern towns where
French influence was a factor. Today several old Mortonsville houses bear a fringe of this iron lace, reminiscent of the village's early trading days.

Nicholas Roosevelt came south in 1811 with his
self-propelled steamboat, and some other ingenious soul
had already brought the stationary steam engine into
Kentucky. No longer was Grier Creek a necessary
source of power. Mortonsville failed in its ambition to
become the capital of Kentucky, and the steamboat
destroyed the economic importance of Scott's Landing.
Versailles became the county seat, and this corner of

the Kentucky River country was almost forgotten. Sublett's Ferry, after fifty years of operation under that name, passed into the possession of John Shryock in 1830. He took up the business of ferrying travelers across the river where Lewis Sublett had left off.

The story of the early Shryocks in Kentucky is closely interwoven with the state in at least two important aspects. First, the name of Shryock is closely associated with the pillared mansion, a glorified symbol of Kentucky well-being. John Shryock, owner of the ferry, however, had ill-luck, or so it was considered to be by most Kentuckians of his day—he had eleven daughters and no sons. But at Lexington his Uncle Mathias was luckier. Mathias became the father of ten children, and three of them were boys. In the future the paths of the Shryock families of Lexington and Grier Creek were to cross, and the country around Shryock's Ferry was to become an important factor in their lives.

Mathias Shryock's second child was a boy whom he named Gideon. As the child grew, he showed a definite love for his father's trade of builder. Even as a student at Mr. Aldridge's "Celebrated Lancastrian Academy" in Lexington, young Gideon's mind ran to architecture. He read his father's books on structural design, and paid close attention to the development of American architecture. Benjamin Latrobe was the Kentucky architectural pacemaker until his death, and then William Strickland succeeded him as a pioneer in American design.

At Philadelphia, Strickland was busily engaged in completing the Bank of the United States started by Latrobe when the young Kentuckian, Gideon Shryock, presented himself as a prospective student. Gideon wrote his parents on October 21, 1823: "I have seen

Mr. Strickland and he says he will do anything in his power to instruct me. I am to go with him tomorrow to look at some of the public buildings of the city, and then he will let me know what I had better do. I have not tried to get work at any place yet, but I have no doubt that I can get enough to pay all expenses. . . ." His other letters tell in detail of his work with Strickland, and after a year in Philadelphia, Gideon Shryock came home, riding overland from Philadelphia to Kentucky. In his saddlebags he brought with him both new designs and many original ideas of architectural beauty.

From the very beginning of his practice Gideon Shryock was a successful architect. He introduced to Kentucky the architectural style, the Greek revival houses and classical public buildings, which was to symbolize the state of the future. It was Shryock's Greek revival architecture which put the Virginia-Georgian influence definitely in the background in the West. Before the end of his second year of practice, Kentucky was in need of a new statehouse. Such an important assignment as planning a statehouse was a task for an experienced architect, and young Gideon was too timid to seek the job until he was urged to do so by his friends. The plans which he submitted to the committee in charge of the erection of the new structure were selected, and in 1829 the building was ready for occupancy by officers of the state government. Its architect, just turned twenty-seven, had built a handsome monument to himself, and a symbol of the grand order of early nineteenth century Kentucky. He had caught the spirit of classicism on an upswing. Kentucky had been very much wrought up over the Greek Revolution, and both newspapers and public speakers had done much to stimulate an appreciation of Grecian lines of architecture and culture. The Old Capitol is an Ionic temple of Minerva with a front elevation of hexastyle, or six Ionic columns. Inside is its builder's pride and joy: the circular stairway which is a thing of beauty and captivating symmetry. So graceful is this winding double stairway that even the army of indiscriminating sightseers who blunder through the fine old building each year to stare at the gun and relic displays of the State Historical Society is impressed with Shryock's masterpiece of internal planning.

No artist, however, could have suffered a more unfortunate turn of fate with his matserful achievement than did the young Lexington architect. Some heartless romanticist started the unkind story that a convict at the state penitentiary designed and built the stairway. The story is absurd, as a sensible examination of the famous stairway and its keystone will prove, yet it is difficult in Kentucky to destroy a legend once it gets under way. Soon it becomes a sort of religion in which the righteous must believe.

Designing and building the Kentucky capitol was a dignified task for a young man, and Gideon Shryock approached the job with a sensitiveness that was to make his work outstanding. He brought to Kentucky a dignity of architecture that was to influence the taste of all future designers in the state. Next to his appealing design, his structural material was attractive. He used native stone quarried from near the Shryock's Ferry at Tyrone. This grayish Kentucky limestone, or "marble," was taken from the steep ledge which towers above the Kentucky River and drifted down to Frankfort on barges. In the walls of a building this stone presents a clear creamy-white face, and yearly it sloughs off just enough of its surface to free it of soot and smoke grime. Through more than a century, Gideon Shryock's honest building has stood as a gracious symbol of governmental authority in Kentucky. Its young successor of federal-classic design over across the river has not displayed such a degree of rugged integrity and of competent workmanship.

Five years after Shryock had completed his work in Frankfort, he was asked to design the statehouse of Arkansas. In 1833 his representative built for that new southern state a temple "of Minerva Polies at Priene, in Ionia." At the same time he designed and built the Doric temple, Morrison Chapel, on the Transylvania University campus. Later at Frankfort he was architect in charge of building a county courthouse and the Orlando Brown house.

Above Frankfort the river makes a wide sweeping bend and, after it passes the heart of the town, swings back gently to assume its general course. At this point there is a broad alluvium shelf, and here in 1796 John Brown built his Georgian house, Liberty Hall. As time passed and his son Orlando was married, the old Virginian, following the custom of men of affluence in his mother state, built a beautiful Greek Revival house for his home. And it is Greek Revival architecture at its best in a private home. Shryock was able to give it the proper small scale balance and to add a graceful touch so necessary to make of it a building of noble distinction. This house, built on a beautiful lot where the garden slopes down to the river, rivals its Georgian colonial neighbor, Liberty Hall, as an object of admiration.

Cincinnatus Shryock, young brother of Gideon, likewise turned to the study and practice of architecture. His first building experience was in the structural work on Morrison Chapel. He rounded out his apprenticeship at Frankfort, where he assisted in constructing the courthouse and the Orlando Brown house. Gideon moved on to Louisville when these buildings were completed, but Cincinnatus returned to his home in Lexington, and he worked here as an employee of John McMurtry. Where Gideon had emphasized the classic Greek Revival, John McMurtry's taste ran to the ornate Tudor Gothic. During the forties and fifties he catered to influential Bluegrass landlords who had considerable money and even more imagination. They wished to become the exciting romantic figures of Sir Walter Scott's Waverley novels. They wished to play at being knights fighting such dragons as they could conjure up locally. John McMurtry was sent off to England by Joseph Bruen to learn how to build ornate American castles.

Shryock's experience of working as an employee of John McMurtry was to leave its impression upon the young architect. He was able in his later years of practice to adapt the best features of the Greek Revival and those of the Tudor Gothic and to use them in many of the buildings he designed. His taste for the classic form was the influence of his brother, and it tended to soften the lines of his post-bellum houses.

Just prior to the Civil War, the architectural business in Lexington dwindled to nothing. McMurtry and Shryock broke off their business relationship, and the latter moved down to the Kentucky River to teach school and to operate Shryock's Ferry during the war years. When the war ended, Cincinnatus Shryock moved his family back to Lexington and began once again the practice of architecture. During the next twenty years he was actively engaged in building in the town the newer type of houses which were lining the streets in all the American cities. Many of his houses with mansard roofs, eaves trimmed with gingerbread scrollwork, and bay windows indicative of a certain pomposity of the age are to be seen up and down the streets of the town. Yet in all these houses of the latter half of the century there is a quiet dignity which distinguishes them from their gaudy neighbors which were planned by men who knew nothing of the earlier age of classicism.

Along the Kentucky River, in that long gently curving stretch which separates Woodford and Anderson counties, was developed the foundation for a brilliant chapter in the cultural history of Kentucky. The prosperous river trade, the rich return from the waving fields of grain, the shaded savanna pasture lands, and the mills along Grier Creek, stimulated the building of skillfully designed houses in which much high living took place. This taste for the popular and classic designs in homes and public buildings along the river spread to the rest of the state, and immediately it characterized the advance of a Kentucky civilization.

14

Graham's Springs

ALONE battered grave marker, stained by the ravages of time, stands on the grounds of the Graham's Springs Sanatorium in Harrodsburg. For nearly a hundred years this stone has been an object of the most imaginative speculation. It perhaps is more of a marker to the "good old days" of Graham's Springs than to the human ashes beneath it. Anyway, the story behind this mysterious stone is that of a headstrong southern belle who died on Dr. Graham's dance floor. It is said that a well-dressed southern couple drove up to the famous Kentucky River resort and registered. There was nothing mysterious about a beautiful southern girl and a handsome southern gentleman coming to the springs, because that was the everyday business of the hotel. But the couple did not clear up their identity in their entries on the guest book. When the clerk later investigated this record, he found them incomplete.

In the evening the famous slave band opened the grand ball and the dashing couple appeared on the floor. The young woman wore a striking gown, and her escort was likewise handsomely dressed. The woman was an excellent dancer, and before long she had attracted general attention by her graceful steps as she went through the sets with unusual vigor. The strange lady was beautiful; she possessed an odd beauty, set off by sad eyes, fair skin, and luxuriant curls. Her beauty had to be unusual to attract the attention she did in a company where beautiful women were almost commonplace. It was evident that the gay dancer came of good family and that she was used to wealth. Her speech was that of a daughter of the Old South who had been educated to the grand manner. The man gave evidence of polish, even if he did lean a bit to the temperamental, gambler-actor type of that day. He made his presence felt in the ballroom somewhat as a dark shadow from the background. This was a strange and exciting couple. Who were they? Where did they come from? All this is the fine material of the legend maker's fascination web.

Dr. Graham's musicians made the big dance hall ring with the gayest music of the season. Waltzes, reels, and promenades followed in gay procession. The strangers mixed with the crowd of gallant southern belles and beaux who had gathered at the springs for their health. As the dances progressed, the slave musicians, Reuben, Henry, and George, increased the tempo of their music until the ballroom was awhirl with quick-step dances. None was so excited or active as the beauty with the doelike eyes. She danced until she fell in a deathlike faint, and before the solicitous young bloods could lift her limp body from the floor she was dead. Her handsome "husband" had vanished. Someone recalled seeing him drive away in mad haste. It all remained a mystery. No one knew who the fair corpse was nor from whence she had come. Her body was buried in front of the hotel on the velvety green lawn underneath the spreading oaks of the resort grounds. Her tomb has been a mark of both mystery and romance since that fatal night.

What a shame it is that the telltale historian has to blast so pretty a tale which the people along the Kentucky River like to believe. But the beautiful girl who danced herself to death in Dr. Graham's ballroom was no mystery after all. She was the little spitfire Mollie Black of Tazewell, Tennessee. Mollie had become the second and unhappy wife of the wandering actor Joe Sewell. Her shiftless husband spent most of his time away from home satisfying his wanderlust. The life of a stay-at-home was not for Mollie Black. She loved a lively time, and she ran away from her young son and a bickering mother-in-law to enjoy a fling at the rollicking Kentucky watering place in Harrodsburg. Here she danced madly, forgetting her troubles back in Tennessee. Mollie rushed through one fast set after another until she fell dead on the floor. Her body was buried before the hotel, where a stone was erected bearing the exciting word "Unknown." Before this humble marker countless visitors have stood and indulged themselves in the sweet human pastime of wondering who the mysterious lady could have been.

Like a tattered piece of dress goods found in a sentimental girls' scrapbook, Mollie Black's headstone tells a tale of lavender and lace of the ante-bellum South. Once the Kentucky springs were retreats of safety to which Southerners fled to escape the low-country miasma which they believed bred malaria and yellow fever. The Harrodsburg resort was a place where no infectious atmosphere sapped the human system of its virility.

There were many other springs along the Kentucky River to which high-living Southerners could bring their sons, daughters, and malaria-ridden corpuscles to recuperate in pleasant surroundings. Among these were Drennon, Franklin, Crab Orchard, and

Estill. All these chalybeate watering places attracted swarms of low-country visitors each year. Every summer Kentucky River boats unloaded crowds of decrepit strangers who came to seek pleasure and physical restitution by the side of the sulphur-laden waters.

Most famous of all was that of Dr. Christopher Columbus Graham. This genial Kentucky gentleman completely mastered that delicate Kentucky art of making people feel at home. The little doctor had grown up with the rich country along the Kentucky River. He was born in 1787, the year that suave James Wilkinson was away in New Orleans persuading Governor Don Esteban Miro to open the Mississippi River to the roistering Kentucky flatboatmen and their rich trade. His boyhood was spent climbing through the deep ravines and up the rugged cliffsides of the steep river palisades. Young Columbus was truly a boy of the Kentucky frontier. In time to come he was the best rifle shot in the West. To his superior accomplishments with the rifle he added that of being an able flatboatman. More than twenty times the future host of the fashionable southern springs went to New Orleans aboard a flatboat loaded with fine Kentucky products for sale to foreign buyers. In 1812, like all red-blooded boys, he became a volunteer and saw service in the Detroit campaign.

Back home after the riotous frontiersmen's victory at the Thames, Columbus Graham went to Transylvania University Medical School and was its first graduate. He was an understudy of that stern, sharptalking, pioneer surgeon Ben Dudley.

In 1819 the young medical school graduate arrived in the pioneer town of Harrodsburg with twenty dollars and a medical education as his stock in trade. By a judicious marriage and shrewd foresight he was to make a national reputation for himself and his community, not in medicine but in amusement. He was quick to see that the chalybeate springs of that place could be made into an attractive resort to draw the attention of the people of the rapidly expanding West, and from those islands of cotton planting along the Mississippi River in the lower South. Purchasing the land on which the springs were located, and taking slaves with him to the Three Forks country up the Kentucky River, he dug fine mountain shrubbery with which to plant the grounds. The plants were drifted down on a flatboat to the Shaker ferry and then hauled overland to Harrodsburg. Likewise the diligent promoter of the springs scoured the countryside around Harrodsburg hunting beautiful plants for his grounds. He wished to create the most beautiful park in America. How well the aesthetic doctor succeeded is to be seen in the extravagant praise of that perennial seeker after health, N. Parker Willis. This pompous New England literary man found the grounds "laid out and shaded in exquisite taste," and "the grounds surrounding the hotel was a nobleman's park." N. M. Ludlow, the actor, was at the springs for an extended visit and he found that "the grounds of Harrodsburg Springs was then covered by the main building on one side of the front lawn, with a line of cottages on the opposite side and at one end, leaving the other open for an approach from the road. Between these tenements was a grass lawn, pleasantly shaded with lofty trees." Along the broad mile-long promenade many a romantic couple strolled while holding hands and looking at the star-laden sky which beamed through the gaps in the branches of the huge Bluegrass meadow oaks of the lawn.

Graham's Spring was an ideal place to fall in love.

Who could fail to respond to the soft gentle enchantment of a beautiful expansive bluegrass lawn sending up a sensation of earthly freshness in the moonlight, a freshness which caused human souls to transcend all worldly realities. One of Judge John Rowan's daughters was at the springs in 1829. She left her famous home in Bardstown to enjoy the pleasures of Harrodsburg. In a burst of wild and romantic enthusiasm she wrote one of the Bibb girls in Frankfort: "I should have written you sooner, but I have not had a moment, and it is now 1 o'clock and I have just left the ballroom. If I could only describe to you this lovely place, the many comforts and luxuries we have, together with the interesting gentlemen." Of great importance to the infatuated Rowan girl was the fact that "there are two gentlemen worth more than a million apiece." As if being courted by two millionaires was not thrilling enough, the fair daughter of Federal Hill continued: "The table is the best I ever sat down to at any place: *Ice Cream in profusion*. The cottages are furnished beautifully. All of them with large closets." A fairyland indeed, handsome gentlemen, ice cream in profusion, and cottages with large closets. What more could a woman ask?

That little Miss Rowan was not bubbling over as a tender love-struck girl is borne out by the observation of a more critical and mature visitor. N. Parker Willis on his famous *Health Trip to the Tropics* went by Harrodsburg "to take the waters." He was fascinated by the continuous procession of expensive equipages, the property of wealthy southern families, which rolled between the regal bronze lions at the gate. To Willis, as he observed this exciting resort crowd moving about him, Dr. Graham appeared such a hospitable host that the English language lacked the facility to adequately describe him.

The convivial master of the springs was on hand at all times. He had an uncanny way of appearing at just the right moment to hand an invigorating drink to a thirsty cotton planter, or to placate an "ailing" lady's desires for another bowl of ice cream. A young couple quarreled, and Dr. Graham was the first to learn of it and to draw upon his ripe experience for a happy solution which would send them down the mile-long promenade arm in arm.

Those decrepit old mortals who sat about the springs covered with heavy wraps, or on warm days leisurely fanned away annoying flies, were often entertained by their host's thrilling stories of flatboat days, of Boone, Clark, Kenton, and Harrod, or of the War of 1812. It was said that he could give such a vivid description of the Battle of New Orleans that his auditors actually felt themselves to be active participants in the combat. Many a spavined old pioneer who had dragged himself to the springs in the hope that he could drink profitably from this Kentucky fountain of youth fought the frontier wars over day after day. Graham's was a meeting point for reminiscent old age and the bubbling anticipation of youth.

Again N. Parker Willis bears testimony of the good doctor's complete hospitality. The poet was given the special privilege of riding over the countryside astride his host's personal saddle horse. Whenever Willis approached a carriage which had halted on the road, the horse dashed forward and halted before it, and not until the New Englander had conversed with its occupants could he get the animal to move on. Life's little affairs throughout the countryside were matters of deepest personal concern to Dr. Graham.

Occasionally difficulties arose which the adept master of the springs could not overcome. On a warm summer afternoon when the resort's activities were suspended in that hour between the digestion of a rich heavy meal and the lengthening of the afternoon shadows, a group began playing with a trained dog. They sat in a circle and each person in turn gave the animal an article and asked him to take it to his husband or wife. One smart aleck who had no wife gave a glove to the enthusiastic dog and asked him to deliver it to his wife, thinking the dog would be nonplused. The dog, however, hustled out of the room and found one of the colored maids and handed her the glove. That evening there was a vacancy at Dr. Graham's table.

In the evenings when there were no grand balls, gay parties gathered in knots under the sheltering oaks and one glorious anecdote followed another. Lemonade glasses, filled with a delicious concoction of citrus fruit juice and a dash of rare old bourbon, kept tongues wagging, and happy laughter ringing throughout the grove. Among these parties which gathered under the trees on the big lawn was N. M. Ludlow, a convivial soul who had been on the American stage for several years. He and his companions drank freely of the heavily spiked beverage and matched yarn for yarn with their host until late at night. On one evening they drank frequently from the silver pitchers of Dr. Graham, and between puffs on long cigars they were led gaily along in their merrymaking. Among those present was the enthusiastic German musician Koumar. The lemonade, cigars, yarns, sweet young girls in crinoline, a seductive south wind, and gentle moonlight falling in big splotches through the sheltering oak branches had infected the romantic German with a spell that called for musical expression. When less romantic souls proposed that the party break up and they go to bed, he exploded in a bitter storm of Saxon wrath. "Vas is das?" shouted the aroused Koumar. "Go to ped? Who would go to ped and schleep, like a dem fool, such a night as dees? No, let us have some moozick." He went off to get his famous guitar, and soon the resort grounds rang with the lilting strains of a German love song. Next Koumar and Ludlow sang "The Minute Gun at Sea." This duet brought the girls to their windows. Romance tore fiercely at the warm heart of Professor Koumar. This was his glorious moment, and he sang for them the popular "Woodpecker Song." In broken German-English he exclaimed, "I'll tell you vat, boys, I'll stonish dem vemmins. Dey dinks cause I sinks in German, I can't sink in English, vel, dey shall zee." He launched into a comic serenade:

I knowt py der schmoke dat zo greasefully kirlt
    Aroundt der kreen helms, dat a cottidge vas near
Undt I zed to mi zelf, if durs peas in dis vurldt,
    Der hardt vas hoompel mite hop for it hare.
Aver leaf vas at raste, undt I heerdt note a zound
    Put der voodpaker dabbing der holla peach dree.

The German's song was indeed astonishing, and it brought loud cheers from the men and numerous giggles from females clad in nightgowns who listened from their windows. Koumar was most pleased of all. He turned to his companions and crowed, "Dare, you zee, I tolt you I would stonish dem."

Gay little Miss Rowan wrote in glowing youthful terms of the daily arrival of gentlemen from Tennessee, South Carolina, and the interior states. Another belle, reminiscing years later, wrote:

I remember the long parties at Harrodsburg, with its great white columns up to the roof where beaux and belles walked up and down in what seemed to me a fairy procession. The ladies with their beautiful elaborately dressed hair in the New Orleans fashion, as from there we got our styles, and their organdy and muslins, which were not then to be bought outside of New Orleans. In the morning the walk to the spring with tan bark and shaded by locust trees, their branches meeting and arching overhead the whole distance. The ballroom at night was a scene of enchantment! Old Dr. Graham, the proprietor, the master of ceremonies and life of the party.

Arrivals and departures of the stages at Harrodsburg were exciting occasions. Visitors at the springs rushed out to see what prominent people were arriving or leaving. Girls hurried down to see if a prospective handsome and wealthy beau had arrived, and the young men to see if a new fair-haired charmer was on hand. Among the many prominent belles who came to the springs to enjoy the gracious hospitalities of Master Graham were Sally Ward and Fanny Smith of Louisville, Alice Carneal of Cincinnati, the Widow Shelby, the Preston girls of Lexington, and the Poignard daughters from St. Louis. Judge Rowan and Judge Bibb's daughters were on hand to make life pass along pleasantly. The Berger, Walsh, and Buchanan women came from St. Louis to stroll up and down the long promenade with interesting companions. There were scores of other beautiful southern women who came north with their families to avoid malaria, and to look for romance. Creole beauties from New Orleans added charm and love interest to the great patches of moonlight which sifted down onto the spacious grounds. These exotic and dark-eyed beauties, in their

Graham's Springs—the Saratoga of the West—with the completion of this four story brick hotel in 1842 was "the finest edifice in the West" as it was billed to vacationers from the South and North who made annual trips to the Kentucky resort.

"Unknown" reads the epitaph of the beautiful lady who "danced herself to death" at Graham's Springs at the height of its fame as Kentucky's most fashionable spa.

crisp New Orleans muslins and organdies made the "moonlight and roses" South a happy reality.

Among the male contingent which flocked to Harrodsburg were the Kentucky political celebrities, Henry Clay, Robert Letcher, Colonel John Rowan, Governor John Jordan Crittenden, George D. Prentice, William Graves, Robert J. Breckinridge, John S. Williams, William Preston, and John Hunt Morgan. Numerous notable visitors came from outside Kentucky. One of these was the flashy merchant prince, Glendy Burke, who followed sweet Alice Carneal there. Glendy was quite a blade in his day. Stephen Collins Foster wrote a famous black-faced minstrel song entitled "Glendy Burke" in honor of the steamboat which bore the rich merchant's name. Frederick Peel, son of Sir Robert, was there for a visit, and he caused considerable twittering among the ambitious mammas and their flirtatious daughters.

Grief-stricken Colonel Vick from Vicksburg arrived at Graham's Springs to recuperate and to forget the death of his fourth wife. The colonel had quite a personal history, and his grief, doubtless, was heavy. It took four beautiful girls crowded into his "splendid coach" to enable him to make the journey and to alleviate his sorrow. One female observer wrote that the poor man had had four wives and that, "He is such a good man, a devout Methodist, he surely deserves a fifth," and as another personal attribute, "he is so very rich." Too, there were Poignard, Rowan, Buchanan, and Berger men who added genuine interest to the long strolls along the tanbark promenade or to the grand marches in the dazzling ballroom.

Under the dark shade of the trees, men turned their conversations to subjects nearest their hearts. There were the inevitable male subjects of horses, races, and stables. There was a track at Harrodsburg, and meets were held during the height of the springs' resort season. Kentuckians pitted their horses against those of the rest of the South. When the subject of racing lagged, cards proved an effective change of interest. Many master cardplayers were on hand and not least of them was Henry Clay. Cockfighting was a lively pastime. Richly frocked southern colonels fetched their cages of spindle-legged game warriors along with their entourages of sons, daughters, and horses. N. Parker Willis jostled along the road from Lexington to Harrodsburg with four companions who had a fine game fighter. The scarred warrior lay hobbled and panting on the floor of the stagecoach. He had just killed three bold antagonists in the night stands at the Lexington track and was on his way to Harrodsburg to claim more victories. As they bobbed along, one of the sportsmen gave the garrulous Easterner a lesson in training a champion gamecock. "For three weeks afore the fight," said the cocksman, "feed the feller on egg, corn meal, rock candy and barley water." This, of course, was invaluable information to the effete New England man of letters.

Kentuckians took advantage of the social season at Dr. Graham's springs to facilitate trade between the regions. Southerners who had fled the hot weather and infectious miasma of the lower South came to the Kentucky River resort to enjoy the gay social life. Under the shade of the giant oaks they bought livestock from Kentucky breeders, arranged for supplies of pork to feed their slaves, and hemp bagging with which to wrap their cotton bales. Kentuckians anxiously conversed with delta cotton planters about land prices, and the uncertain business of cotton planting. Many of them wished to go South to make their fortunes in the new country down the river. Of a tenderer nature was the exchange of sons and daughters between the families of Kentucky with those of the South. The springs resort was a great mixing ground. Even today, Greenville, Vicksburg, Natchez, and New Orleans have connections in Kentucky. Many a Kentucky belle went south to become mistress of a cotton plantation or a fair Mississippian came back to Kentucky to live in a large brick farmhouse.

Among the hundreds of visitors who were guests at the mineral springs at Harrodsburg were many companies of actors. That humorous old manager-actor, Sol Smith, was there in 1827. He records in his autobiography: "From Lexington, we proceeded to Harrodsburg Springs, where our business again failed. We made a precipitate retreat leaving Crampton (whom we considered a sort of theatrical jonah)." N. M. Ludlow's company played at the springs with more success than the veteran master, Sol Smith. The company was made up of Samuel, Douglas, James, Martha, Julia and Alexander Drake, John and Harry Vaught, Mr. Blisset, Mrs. Lewis, Miss Denny, and N. M. Ludlow. They played to large audiences in the grand ballroom, and when they had finished their first performance a great shout went up for Mr. Koumar to repeat his serenade, the "Woodpecker Song." This company remained at the springs for a month, during which time they played *A Dissertation on Faults, Alexander's Feasts, The Hunters of Kentucky, Alonzo and Imogene,* and *The Day after the Fair.*

Competing with the professional actors for the entertainment spotlight were Dr. Graham's three grinning slave boys who composed the house orchestra. Reuben, Henry, and George's musical abilities were well known throughout the South. For years they had played for the gay dances in the large ballroom at the resort. When the summer season was ended their generous master allowed them to go to Lexington and Louisville and to play for hire at fashionable balls. Not only could they play musical instruments with real talent, but likewise they were excellent waiters, and from long experience at the springs they were able to make a party a booming success. Their services were in demand in the wealthy homes and on the Kentucky and Ohio steamboats.

In 1841, "Old Tippecanoe" (William Henry) Harrison visited Lexington to confer with one of his Whiggish political advisers, Henry Clay. The Log Cabin and Hard Cider Campaign had aroused Kentuckians, and the citizens of Lexington were anxious to give him a rousing welcome. Dr. Graham's musical waiters were sent over from Harrodsburg to assist in receiving the aged Whig warrior. The boys were placed under the supervision of a freeman of color named Williams, and after the reception at Lexington they packed up their waiters' coats, music, and instruments and went to Louisville, where they boarded the steamer *Zebulon M. Pike* and headed for Canada.

Dr. Graham followed his runaway slaves to their Canadian destination, and near Malden he was mobbed by a band of fugitive slaves. They pinched him, spit upon him, called him vile names and rubbed their calloused fists in his face. Perhaps he would have lost his life in the struggle had it not been for the gallant rescue by General Ironsides, half-brother of the famous Indian chief Tecumseh. The master of Harrodsburg springs came home without his sleeves, lucky, so he said, that he had escaped from "the fiery fiends of perdition."

Graham's Springs resort was in its heyday in the forties. In 1841 more than ten thousand persons met there to celebrate the founding of Harrodsburg. Militia companies flocked in from all the neighboring towns and paraded up and down the famous tanbark walk. Dashing militia captains strutted their companies back and forth on the parade ground. Among the units present were the Lexington Rifles, Greys, Grenadiers and Infantry, the Versallies Artillery, Frankfort Light Infantry, Georgetown Artillery, Danville Artillery, Harrodsburg Central Guards, Cloverbottom Riflemen, Athens Greys, and Jessamine Cavalry. Governor Charles Morehead was there to inspect the troops and to shake hands with the citizens of the state. Hundreds of Southerners were on hand to intermingle with the jovial Kentuckians in their proud moment of celebrating the foundation of the first settlement of their state. Eloquent old "Kitchen Knife Ben" Hardin delivered the oration. Ben was a leading Kentucky orator and wit. In a vein of true Kentucky philosophy he observed that "three things are mighty uncertain, who a woman will marry, what horse will win the race, and which way a jury will decide."

In 1845 the editor of the *Frankfort Commonwealth* visited the Harrodsburg resort and came home to write about it. "To those," he wrote, "who have ever been there a single word would be superfluous, but to those who have not, we are justified in saying they will find mineral water whose medical properties are highly beneficial; trees, and shades and lawns and shrubberies, and walks, that Shenstone might have envied; architecture of the English rural cottage order and noble Grecian; music as sweet as the voice of birds, or the laugh of fresh-lipped girls; society, men and women, the elite of this great and intelligent continental accommodations, the most agreeable and sumptuous that skill, taste, and liberality can provide, enjoyment to the highest bent, whether you prefer fashionable bustle or rural seclusion; host highbred, attentive amicable and liberal; in short everything that the heart may wish at such a place. Such is a *just* tribute as we know by experience." This was the enthusiastic opinion of a stern editor.

Kentucky mineral springs were the scenes of the gayest social life of that day when Scott's romantic novels helped to shape the South's philosophy. The springs were the exciting places where hundreds of visitors came to seek health, entertainment, and to associate with southern high society. In 1853, however, Graham's Springs as a resort center came to a close. The property was bought by the United States for a soldiers' home. But its history lingers as a bright chapter in the social history of the Old South.

15

Born to Be a Princess

THE NIGHT of July 8, 1896, was extremely warm. Kid Ed Rucker, the Louisville boy wonder, fought Kid Ed Levigne at Boss John Whallen's famous Buckingham vaudeville house. He made a date with Emma Carus the singing lady of the show. Kid Ed was a tender lad and did not know much about women and liquor, but this was the night of his initiation. In the whirl of the bout and the excitement which followed he forgot all about Emma and went off with the swaggering Levigne and his hilarious chorus girls. This was the day when the Galt House was the heart of Louisville's social life, and the boys had a room there. When Levigne suggested that they go to the bar and have a drink, Ed Rucker was certain that he meant of milk or soda pop, but it turned out to be hard liquor.

It was a boisterous party in the old Galt House that night. Nadine, a shapely chorine, hit upon the ingenious idea of kicking her heels at the chandelier to show her knees, and her companions were loud in mirthful encouragement after each kick. Just as the party was moving on in fine style, and someone had begun singing "After the Ball," a frantic hotel clerk knocked at the door and begged them to be quiet. "There's an old lady

dying across the hall. Her nurse telephoned begging us
to stop the noise. . . ."

Next morning the old lady died, and what a
famous old Kentucky lady she was. Sally Ward was
dead, and her death brought up many memories of an
old Kentucky way of life which had practically passed
from the scene. She was born, in 1827, on the Elkhorn
branch of the Kentucky River. The Elkhorn hitches on
to the Kentucky just below Frankfort, and in its upper
reaches drains some of the finest farming land in the
United States. Along its banks grows the famous Kentucky bluegrass in its most luscious state, and the beautiful rolling pasture lands have been grazed for a hundred and sixty years by the choicest livestock in Kentucky. Elkhorn Creek is the aristocrat of the Kentucky's
branches.

It was on the North Elkhorn that Sally Ward's
father and mother settled when their families pushed
through the mountains from the Huguenot settlements
in low-country South Carolina and from Virginia.
Robert Ward became an influential planter, then he
moved away to Louisville to become a lawyer, capitalist,
and politician.

Colonel Ward was a successful man. He grew
wealthy and tremendously influential. It seems that he
was entirely too influential never to have been more
outstanding in the state's services than he was. Perhaps he could have wielded almost as much power in
Kentucky as Clay, Breckinridge, or Crittenden. He was
far wealthier than any one of these men. His wealth was
a matter of table talk in the state. When his famous
cook placed an order for culinary supplies, it was no
measly package affair. Two stout Negro slaves shoved
wheelbarrows before them to the markets each morning
and returned panting under heavy loads of choice vege-

tables, fruits, and meats. The Ward table was always loaded with the rarest food to be had in Kentucky, a state where good food has ever been a religion. Colonel Robert had to dig up $50,000 a year to keep his famous family living on a "respectable" plane; a sum which to most Louisville people was a tidy fortune.

This is the environment in which young Sally grew to womanhood. An admiring neighbor commented defensively upon this famous southern belle by philosophizing that "genius comprehends all the loveliness of woman, and to be a famous belle one must be a genius." I would like to know—and our obliging "neighbor" does not exactly answer the question—was Sally Ward so overpowering in her beauty? Again, the good "neighbor" observes that her "beauty was not as great as that of many other women of her time." Then he begins to ask the rambling rhetorical question: "Her wit was often overmatched. What was it then that brought her homage of all men she met, and most of the women?"

One, of course, can never hope to stare at a rigid steel engraving and be much charmed by the lady whose impression is before one. But even in all its stereotyped rigidity, a steel engraving can impart some reasonable conception of feminine proportions. An oil painting is an even better source of information. There hangs in the Speed Museum in Louisville an excellent oil painting, and I hope an accurate likeness, of this famous woman who received "homage from all men." Yet it is difficult to reconcile her feminine attractions in life with her chubbiness in print and on canvas. Her face, if her portrayers were capable and truthful men, was that of a well-nourished cherub, and her figure was like those used to illustrate chastity in the romantic magazines of the fifties. The great painter, Healy, so it is said, thought that "she was the most exquisite woman that he had ever painted." Sally had what the simpering Mrs. Ellet called "aristocratically" small hands and feet. Her hair was auburn, and her blue eyes were shaded by delicately penciled brows. Her features were set in an exceedingly fair face.

Sally Ward seems to have been a contradiction in feminine history. Since time immemorial those women who have had men standing around them in humble supplication were willowy maidens. Earlier in female history Delilah and Cleopatra were sinuous charmers, and so it goes through the ages. Perhaps it was in the plushy forties and fifties, when family albums with heavily stuffed lids were popular, that plump women came into their own. Of Sally Ward's charm there can be no doubt. Chubby or not, perhaps no other southern belle attracted as much attention as she did.

At Graham's Springs Sally was the high light of the gay assemblies. At the huge dining table it was a three-cornered race among the famous belle, her witty neighbor, George D. Prentice of the Louisville *Journal,* and gracious old Dr. Christopher Columbus Graham. No one else dared interrupt when Sally and George were exchanging thrusts with their flashing wits. On the dance floor, Sally Ward was the leading belle. The idolizing Mrs. Elizabeth Fries Ellet, who put very sweet little stories of the famous American belles in a book, goes much into detail about the manner in which she dressed. Sally was never content with a single gown for a ball, with her it was a continuous rushing out to change a gown and rushing in to show the new one off. It was she who set the trend which the fancy balls were to take.

A fine example of the extravagance in dress indulged in by Robert Ward's oldest daughter was the fancy ball given by her relative, Lillie Ward, in Cincinnati for Alice Carneal, the famous Ohio belle. It was a matter of keen rivalry between Sally and Alice to see which could outdo the other in dazzling dress. The auburn-haired Kentucky belle appeared in light-blue antique moire set off with diamonds of "wonderful size and brilliancy." She had about her shapely neck a necklace of thirty-two costly solitaires, and over her shoulders was draped a delicately woven point-lace shawl. When she walked into the room she glittered like a drunken conquistador's dream of El Dorado.

Not to be outdone by the Bluegrass beauty, Alice Carneal appeared as a Polish princess at the Russian court. She wore a "heavy dress of white silk, the shirt trimmed with ermine, and four rows of wide scarlet bands embroidered with gold. The corsage was high, and striped across the front with scarlet satin bands and gold lace. A hussar jacket of scarlet lace, embroidered with gold and trimmed with ermine, hung from her left shoulder, fastened with a gold cord and tassel. A jaunty cap of scarlet satin, with a band of ermine and the emblematic Polish feather, fastened with opals and diamonds, completed the costume." Never had the Queen City of the Ohio valley seen such a gaudy display of femininity and feminine wearing apparel. Rivalry between the two famous belles grew fierce, and there is a tradition that a dispute broke out between them, when it was said that the blue antique moiré dress which Sally Ward wore was copied from that of another, and a lesser belle. This was indeed a mean thrust at so sensitive a woman, and only by adept counseling was a hair pulling averted in high society.

Young Miss Ward was a highheaded girl. She was so full of spirit and daring that it was hard to tell what she would do next. In personality she was both a wily practical joker, and a good psychologist. Kentuckians have not yet ceased telling the story of her wild and mischievous gallop through the Louisville market house. She was out riding with one of her army of beaux who, it seems, was willing to follow every move the impetuous girl made. Perhaps it was the devil in her or an impulse to test the mettle of her escort which caused her to rein her spirited horse into the market house doorway and dare her patronizing riding companion to gallop through with her. It was with a great deal of hesitancy that the gallant swain followed, but the pair loped down the long rows of vegetables, sending baskets of earthy cabbages, onions, beans, cucumbers, and potatoes sprawling. Scurrying market attendants fell back in fright, afraid, no doubt, that General Santa Anna's bloodthirsty Mexican raiders were bearing down upon them. Of course, when it was discovered that it was the high-spirited belle who was breaking the tedium of an afternoon's riding with a boring companion, all was forgiven.

When war broke out with Mexico, Kentuckians rallied quickly to the colors. Here was an opportunity for militiamen to show off in grand style. The brave men were anxious to be off to Chapultepec, Camargo, and Buena Vista to try their mettle. But gallant Kentuckians could not go rushing headlong into battle without the blessings of their fair women. Individually the volunteers rushed to war fresh from the arms of their sweethearts, but collectively as a regiment they were sent to war with a final blessing from the great Kentucky sweetheart. They say it was a great sight there in Louisville the morning the Louisville Legion made ready to leave. Before the proud troops were assembled at the point of embarkation, they were marched to the commodious home of Colonel Ward to receive their colors. Sally stood before the troops, looking her very sweetest, while a gentle breeze blew the flag around her beautiful body. She stood smiling upon the troops with the contours of her body showing clearly through the drapes of the silken flag, she was a living, embodiment of the goddess of liberty. It was a tender moment, and manly soldiers drawn up at rigid attention looked upon the beautiful girl with tears streaming down their cheeks. The crowd of patriotic onlookers sobbed aloud. This was a glorious personal triumph for the young girl. The girl, of whom an idolator had said "was intended for a princess, but by accident, lived under the flag of a republic," was sending brave men into battle with the indelible memory of a beautiful woman standing before them draped in their flag.

Sally followed the brave Legion to Portland to see it on board the steamer *Scott*. As the troops passed her carriage each man turned and smiled. She said later that, "as those brave fellows marched by the open carriage in which I sat, each one lifting his hat to me, it was the proudest moment of my life. I esteemed the honor of being selected to present the flag to these noble sons of Kentucky far greater than all the homage of a ball-room." Gentlemen were going to a gentleman's war, and their going was marked by all the tender graces of a gallant genteel age.

A year later Sally's darling troops were to come marching home "covered" in glory. Victory was sweet, and the Kentuckians had seen active service. When they reached Louisville, the Legion marched to the Ward home, where they found Miss Sally mounted on her horse. Brave men had come to tell their sweetheart of a nation's success in battle. The colors were unfurled. Again it was a tender affair in which the famous belle was recipient of the collective admiration of the Legion. The greeting, she said, was "such as only brave men can give a woman. And, in my whole soul, I bade them welcome. I gazed with pride upon those flags, borne with honor and success through so many battles by the brave men before me."

Two years were to pass in which the Ward daughters were sent to Europe and to eastern finishing schools. During the summer months they visited the fashionable springs of Kentucky and those in the East. The girls were taking both life and youth in a single bouyant stride. Their parents were indulgent to the point of being oversolicitous for the pleasure of their four beautiful daughters. Perhaps Father Robert was a bit vain in the fact that his family carriage hauled four women who were beautiful enough to turn the head of every man they passed.

It was at Saratoga Springs that the Wards of Kentucky met the Lawrences of Boston. Sally and young Bigelow saw a great deal of each other in the gay round of parties, and soon they were in love. Abbott Lawrence, the boy's father, was an influential New England businessman. He was an important member of the famous Lawrence mercantile firm in Boston engaged in selling cotton on the foreign market. He had dabbled in the China trade and in American politics. He had served in Congress, and was a member of the boundary commission which executed the terms of the Webster-Ashburton treaty concerning the Canadian-United States boundary. He was once a candidate for the vice-presidency, refused a seat in Zachary Taylor's Cabinet as secretary of the navy, and had given $50,000 to Harvard. All this, in the good Kentucky idiom, made Abbott and his family "some punkins." This was endorsement enough for the Wards, and they were satisfied on that cardinal question of whether Bigelow could keep Sally in the style to which she was accustomed.

Bigelow Lawrence, a New England Yankee, was to win the fair southern prize; a prize over which many a gallant southern man had made a fool of himself. The belle of the South was to get married! Gossips from Cincinnati to New Orleans could hardly believe the news. They had always regarded Sally Ward somewhat after the fashion of a prize watermelon in a county fair exhibit; a thing of beauty and joy, but really never to be enjoyed otherwise. For eighteen months her approaching wedding was the talk of society in the state.

Louisville had never seen anything like the wedding ceremony. The Boston *Post* sent a special correspondent to cover the affair. At this late date it is difficult to tell whether the man from the *Post* was a facetiously patronizing jackass, or pitifully naïve. I am of the opinion that he was the former. At any rate, his account was so fetching that the famous sportsman's magazine, the *Spirit of the Times*, ran it along with other sporting events from Kentucky. How the New Englander did pour forth the words:

The lady in question is acknowledged "belle" of the "ton" in every state, city, village, and hamlet between Pittsburgh and New Orleans. Books have been written about her, odes dedicated to her, she has been the heroine of operas, farces, and theatre events,—yachts, race horses, doll babies, and steamboats named after her, in fine, my dear fellow, she has been the chief subject of conversation, "the observed of all observers," for the last two years, ruling the city exquisites and belles with all the privileges and immunities of a queen. Every girl in this city is said to imitate her. All strive to dress like, all wish to speak, talk, sneeze, smile and flirt like her—so far has this feeling been carried, sir, that she has introduced an entirely new, original, and I must say rather *outre* manner, costume and style of conversation.

It is true that there were several steamers named *Sally Ward*, and likewise three race horses. She was the darling of those three famous Ohio River poets, George D. Prentice, James G. Drake, and F. Crosly. They say, too, that many an ambitious mother named her female offspring for her.

The wedding itself was the grandest show in Louisville history. No expense was spared, and the Ward home was an interior decorator's dream. Three drawing rooms were furnished in the most expensive style. Even the skeptical Yankee newspaper reporter had to admit that the house was furnished in such a style "that would do credit to a New York upholsterer. On the left was a magnificant dining room with a huge table loaded down with rare liquors and tidbits at which the big men of Kentuck paid frequent and dutiful homage."

During the ceremony the bride appeared chaste and pink. The groom was a bit pale, but, in the eyes of his fellow Bostonian, he appeared impressive, and his sensible and solemn New England countenance showed off to a good advantage. Eight beautiful girls from Kentucky and Mississippi escorted the lovely bride to the altar, and an equal number of handsome young men performed a like service to the groom. As purely a matter of mundane cash accounting the bride's gown cost $5,000, but it was said that "the dress was in good taste, and at the same time expensive."

In the dining room a huge pyramid supported by twenty cherubim, on top of which was mounted a huge vase which poured forth clouds of sweetly exotic incense. Someone facetiously remarked that the twenty cherubim symbolized the bride's age, as if twenty years was getting a bit on the shady side of life for matrimony. As a matter of fact, it had been twenty-two years since little Sally was born near the banks of the Elkhorn.

It was an illustrious crowd that thronged the Ward house on December 5, 1849, the wedding night. Among the top-line dignitaries was Ex-Governor Robert Letcher, who later was to tell a Taylor henchman that he would take anything "from a Minnesota Territory judgeship to a foreign ministerial appointment"; Governor John Jordan Crittenden, Lazarus W. Powell, Messrs. Fish, Dana, and Bigelow Lawrence, Sr., of Boston; and George D. Prentice, James G. Drake and F. Crosly, Sally's poetic friends. About four hundred other dignitaries of slightly lesser rank milled about the huge reception rooms and trampled on one another's feet. This was Kentucky's big wedding and it was being enjoyed.

There was no place where the young couple could go on a honeymoon and enjoy the same elegance which Robert Ward's home afforded them. A room had been fitted out for a bridal chamber, and the couple remained there several weeks in sweet postnuptial seclusion. Never before in the romantic Old South had so much been spent on a bridal bower. Lace hung in profusion about the room, the pitcher, bowl, and all other metal fittings in the room were of sterling silver. Truly the room was a dreamland. It was stacked high with expensive presents which had poured in from all over the world. The Ward-Lawrence alliance was to be a high point in extravagance for the rest of American society.

In all sweet things in life there must always, so it seems, be at least one flaw. At the wedding of Sally Ward to Bigelow Lawrence, Father and Mother Ward were shocked, as one observer said, in such a manner as they were "never to experience again." The lavish philosophy of the ante-bellum South clashed harshly with the strait-laced frugality of New England. Colonel Ward had not spared the purse in preparing for his beautiful daughter's marriage. Why should he? She was marrying a mercantile fortune, and his family was becoming allied with the upper crust of Boston society. Mrs. Ward, the bride's mother, appeared in the dress of a handsome dowager. Colonel Ward himself was diked out in the very best formal style of the gentleman of his period. In fact, the whole Ward part of the show outdid even the collective and vivid imaginations of those arbiters of style, Messrs. Godey, Graham and Peterson, in its erotic display of clothes and female surroundings. In contrast were Father and Mother Lawrence. They appeared at the wedding in the plainest and most unimaginative kind of clothes. Mrs. Lawrence was dressed in a modest cotton dress trimmed in, of all things, cotton lace, and about her neck dangled a string of the cheapest mock pearls. How out of place they were in the whole show; really the groom's father and mother innocently became a sort of inanimate pair of jesters before an audience of lavish Southerners. One can easily imagine the trend of conversation when Colonel Ward and his wife went to their bedchamber that night. How that cotton dress and those mock pearls must have haunted their sleep!

That plain little cotton dress should have been an ominous warning to the proud Sally. But when a famous belle is getting married she has no time to be staring at sleazy black-cotton omens. There were too many old suitors to be kissed, and too much flurrying around with squealing but ambitious maids to take up time with affairs of the future. It was a weakness of the ante-bellum Southerners that they displayed their wealth and influence with all the pomp and circumstance which the trade would bear. New England philosophy was in direct contradiction; the more wealth one had, the less he displayed it.

Boston society in the forties and fifties was unbending, even when a haughty southern girl surged against it. How shocking it was when the Lawrence daughter-in-law appeared in the city after her trip from the South in a pink beige dress, a flower-trimmed hat, and slippers. The girl flaunted herself in the face of staid, cruel convention wearing ankle-exposing slippers. Her ankles had been exposed in public, and she a Lawrence!

From the moment Sally crossed over the threshold of the Lawrence household it was a point between the two women to see which could do the most meticulous job of annoying the other. Madame Lawrence was determined to make over the flippant Kentuckian into a staid strait-laced Boston matron. She went about this task in a somewhat foot-patting "do as I say" schoolmarm manner. She demanded that her son command his wife to observe the Boston rules, one of which forbade the use of cosmetics. Industrious Bostonians, too, were up with the sun and about their business. The women did much of their own housework, and there was little or no place for the drowsy woman who whiled away her time in bed until noon. Mrs. Lawrence felt that her daughter-in-law should get up at a "decent hour," and this was further cause of friction.

When old friends of the Lawrence family came partly out of politeness, but largely out of curiosity to see the bride, she made them fidget restlessly in the parlor while she leisurely primped in her bedroom. One evening very special friends called to see the haughty southern girl whom Bigelow had married. They, too, were cooling their heels in the parlor when Mrs. Lawrence intervened and commanded Sally to come down.

This was her chance to strike a deft blow at her termagant mother-in-law, and the demure Kentucky girl stepped calmly into the parlor clad in her dressing gown, explaining sweetly that she just did not have time to dress properly.

One final lick back and Sally Ward's stay in Boston was at an end. She became a convert of the crusading Dr. Amelia Bloomer, who wished, if not exactly to put pants on women, to split the skirts and to gather the sections tightly about the ankles. The Lawrences gave a grand ball in honor of their Kentucky daughter-in-law, solely, one is led to believe, for the purpose of keeping up appearances. Sally was to disgrace them; she appeared on the ballroom floor dressed in beautiful satin bloomers with jeweled Persian slippers on her feet. The Bostonians were horrified, and so frigid did the company become that the impetuous Southern girl lost her temper, yanked off her bloomers in their presence and left the room. This was the end. She pretended that the weather was too vigorous for her health, packed her baggage and came home.

There followed Sally's departure from Boston a nasty bit of smearing in the papers. Robert Ward sued, through his friend William Preston, on behalf of his daughter, for a divorce before the Kentucky legislature. Back in Boston the Lawrences exposed private letters, some of which were published in Boston and New York papers. Bigelow advertised that his wife Sally had "abandoned his bed and board and that he would not be responsible for any debts she might contract." Charges and countercharges came thick and fast. The Lawrences with stern and vigorous Yankee determination spoke their minds freely. The son published a defensive pamphlet in which he presented his side of the case. But with it all Sally was once again a free woman, and she had come back to Kentucky just in time to catch a gay social season on an upswing.

Down on the Kentucky River near its mouth was a famous group of mineral springs which had a long and interesting past in Indian legend. It was to these springs that Jacob Drennon, the greedy surveyor who had bribed a Delaware Indian to tell him of the place, rushed ahead of his party in 1773, to lay the first claim. Finally the lands came into possession of George Rogers Clark, hero of the famous northwestern campaigns. In 1849 a popular Kentucky springs resort was built there by A. O. Smith, and hundreds of folks from all over the South flocked there. Dozens of proud belles were on hand to flirt until their hearts were content with the gallant beaux who had followed them up the Kentucky River.

It did not take young "Widow" Lawrence long to get back into the social whirl. She made her first public appearance at the famous ball given in honor of Madame Octavia Walton Le Vert, daughter of the governor of Florida. No one could tell from her frolicsome manner that she had undergone "that horrible experience at Boston." It seemed that divorce had only increased her attractiveness. She now drew men to her because they, perhaps, found her as a divorcee more exciting than before. Outwardly she was the same lively girl who had dashed through the Louisville market house on her pony, or the one who had presented the colors to the Louisville Legion.

Her indulgent parents gave a grand coming-out party in her honor. Again Sally was the center of attraction. At ten o'clock the Ward house was fully lighted, and Cunningham's band struck up the grand march. The gay dance kept up until one o'clock, and then dinner was served. After the dinner the band played again, and the ball continued in a lively vein.

Never before in all her experience of dazzling hilarious Kentucky parties had Sally reached the grand heights which she attained that night. When the evening began she appeared as Nourmahal from "The Light of the Harem." She wore "a pink satin shirt, covered with silver lama, the bodice embroidered with silver and studded with diamonds; the oriental white sleeves adorned with silver and gold; the satin trousers spangled with gold. Her hair was braided with pearls and covered with a Greek cap; her pink slippers were embroidered with silver," and splendid jewels formed extravagant decoration for the whole costume.

When the ball began once again after supper, Sally appeared in a second dress, this time as Nourmahal "at the Feast of the Roses." The dress was "white illusion dotted with silver, with a veil of silvery sheen and wreath of white roses, and white silk boots with silver ankles. She bore the charmed lute."

Sally was the gayest of the revelers. She was again a fair and eligible prize for some gallant who could forgive her the fact that she was a divorcee, and, as always before, there were swains aplenty. One, however, stood out in her affections. He was a quiet, dignified, and retiring young man. Robert W. Hunt, a member of an old Kentucky family, who had recently graduated from medical school, was to fall madly in love with her. It was love at first sight, for Sally captured him from the outset, and immediate plans were made for their marriage. There was one difficulty, Dr. Hunt's people were conscientiously opposed to his marrying a divorcee, which was a direct violation of Biblical injunction against such acts. Truly young Hunt was torn between loyalties, marrying the most beautiful woman in Kentucky or obeying the Hebrew Scriptures. Since Hebrew Scriptures had little of personal attraction to offer, his decision favored marriage. His decision was clearly set forth in a note to his family on the morning of the wedding. He wrote that he was very sorry they could not be present at the wedding, but understanding their opposition he could not ask them to come. Dr. Hunt said that he was conscious, that in his family's eyes he was committing an act which would eventually land him in hell, but at this point he became philosophical and rationalized his rash act by concluding that "he would far rather go to hell with Sally Ward than to heaven without her."

Dr. Hunt took his bride to New Orleans, where they lived in grand style. Their famous residence was furnished after the style of the Duchesse d'Orléans's apartment in Paris. There was much white chenille, satin, and rosewood. Gold frames and brackets held huge mirrors, and the halls and corners were filled with marble works of art. The dining room was an interior decorator's golden triumph, and this room opened onto a beautiful marble court. The fairest ornament of all, however, was the mistress of the house. Her table was a jousting ground for all the wits of New Orleans. Mrs. Hunt appeared occasionally with luscious natural roses pinned in her hair with large diamonds fastened in their centers to represent dewdrops.

Difference of sectional viewpoints was to separate Sally from her second husband. Dr. Hunt favored the cause of the Confederacy, and Sally, like her old friend George Prentice, favored the Union cause. This time it was a conscientious difference in political views that sent Sally Ward back to her family. Dr. Hunt went away as a medical officer to die in the Confederate Army.

Twice more Sally was to go to the altar. The third time she married Vene P. Armstrong, a wealthy merchant, and for a few years the couple lived at the Galt

House. This marriage was broken by death. Mrs. Sally Ward Lawrence Hunt Armstrong was once again single. Her fourth marriage was really a liaison of friendship. She married the wealthy Major George F. Downs and lived with him until his death.

Sally Ward outlived the Old South which had been such an important factor in her life. The mineral springs along the Kentucky River were gone, and the gay steamboats were either worn out or engaged in the vulgar business of making money hauling freight in the highly materialistic age following the war. George Prentice grew old and shabby, and then died almost deserted, the poets Drake and Crosly were gone. The Ward fortune was dissipated, and worst of all, Sally's beauty was disappearing. In desperation she went to Paris to have her face remodeled, but age showed through in spite of the "French enamel."

There was little else left in life for the famous belle but seclusion in the Galt House and plans for her funeral. Two years before her death she wrote out detailed funeral plans. The coffin was not to be opened, and only a small, carefully selected group of friends was to be invited to the burial at Cave Hill Cemetery.

She lies today near two of her husbands, Vene P. Armstrong and Major George F. Downs. The proud Bostonian's ashes and those of Dr. Hunt are elsewhere. Sally Ward was a definite part of the gay Kentucky social life which went on in the Bluegrass. Much of her life was spent near the Kentucky River, and much of her story was also its story.

16

Dr. Warfield's Colt Lexington

OFTEN the dignified halls of the Smithsonian Institution ring out with the echoes of the voice of a small boy asking his father what kind of skeleton that is in the big glass case. The placard tells the visitor that it is the exhumed framework of the great thoroughbred racer Lexington, but a small placard could never tell much of this astonishing horse's history. Lexington was foaled on Dr. Elisha Warfield's sunny Bluegrass farm, the Meadows, at Lexington, on a branch of the south fork of Elkhorn Creek. His birthplace was one of the choicest of the fine Bluegrass farms in the famous central Kentucky grazing country. Dr. Warfield was a prosperous planter and breeder. Many fast horses had come from his stable, and when the old master placed his stamp of approval upon a foal it usually turned out to be a winner.

As became a man of Dr. Warfield's distinction in the breeding industry of Kentucky, he built himself a fine estate just on the outskirts of the city of Lexington. A long avenue of trees led from the road to the front door of the large rambling pseudo Italian Rennaissance house. Downstairs were large parlors, and a huge dining room with an enormous plantation kitchen adjoining. The ceilings were high, and the walls were finished with beautiful native woods. It was an appropriate home for so famous a breeder and sportsman, and the fertile land which sprawled out for a mile behind it was as noble a place for a thoroughbred to find his legs as there was in America. Wide rolling meadowlands spread out under oak, walnut, ash, and hackberry trees, while underfoot was a matted carpet of fine bluegrass.

It was here in this breeder's dreamland that Lexington, first named Darley, was foaled on March 17, 1850. He was sired by the distinguished blazed-faced Boston, and damed by the shy but capable Alice Carneal, who was named for the famous Cincinnati beauty. Few horses could lay claim to such aristocracy of ancestery as Darley. His sire, Boston, was one of the best known in the country in the thirties and forties. It was he who had lost in the glorious race with Fashion at the Union Course on Long Island in May, 1842. But in losing Boston had forced his filly opponent to set a new world time record of seven minutes and thirty-two and a half seconds. Boston entered forty-five races, thirty of which were four-mile heats, and he won a majority of them. He was owned by John Wickham, a Virginia sportsman, who evidently was fond of cards. It is said that the colt was won in a game of boston, and thus the name was given him.

Back of the blaze-face Virginia colt were many distinguished ancestors—ancestors who had written their names large in the annals of horse racing. There were Timoleon, Sir Archy, Diomed, who won the first English Derby, Florizel, Herod, and others back to the very beginning with "The Byrley Turk." This was indeed a fine background for a Virginia horse and, later, Kentucky sire. It connected Darley by a direct bloodline with almost the entire American and English racing history.

There is a romantic story connected with the origin of the colt's Arabian ancestry. Three Arabian horses were captured by the English in their Eastern campaigns in 1684, and Captain Byrley of the English Army is said to have ridden his famous captive stud in the Battle of the Boyne in 1690. From these three Arabians the foundation for the English thoroughbred line was laid. The English soldier was going to battle with less cumbersome equipment than he had carried in earlier campaigns. Before this it was the carrying power of a horse that counted and the English breeds were rugged and slow. With the change in military tactics emphasis was placed upon speed, and the early type of heavy, clumsy horse was outmoded. At this juncture the light Arabian horse was brought in to build up a new English cavalry type charger and to introduce a faster type racer. This was the capstone of the thoroughbred industry which centuries later was to distinguish the horses of breeders in the Kentucky valley.

Darley ran his first race on May 22, 1853, at the famous Lexington Association track. He competed against a heavy field of twelve fast two- and three-year-old entries. Old horsemen, race-track followers, and others were busily sizing up the field. They soon discovered that there were many choices, but one especially was top favorite: Garrett Davis, named for Senator Davis, by imported Glencoe out of Too Soon. There was Darley's half brother, Big Boston, John Harper's Wild Irishman, R. P. Fields's Grey Eagle colt, Jim Barton, and John Clay's Madonna. Taylor and Earle were certain that their colors would ride on top with the fast Garrett Davis. A false start was made, and Dr. Warfield's Darley and John Clay's Madonna ran two and a half miles on a track knee-deep in mud before they could be stopped. The favorite drew up with an injury and was scratched from the race. On the second start Darley was off ahead, and came by the judge's stand first in both heats, to prove himself a powerful contestant on a soggy track. Five days later Darley started again, this time in the fast Citizens Post Stakes of two-mile heats, and again the gawky colt came in ahead of a fast field which included the favorite, Garrett Davis. Before the horses had gone to the barrier the aged Dr. Warfield, with keen insight into racing possibilities of thoroughbred horses, prophesied that after the race was run American breeders for many decades to come would trace their bloodlines back to his entry.

Primarily Dr. Warfield, then in his seventy-second year, was a breeder, and once he developed a promising horse he sold it and turned his attention back to his famous Meadows stud. After the Citizens Post Stakes race, Darley was sold to the itinerant sportsman, Richard Ten Broeck, who immediately changed his name to Lexington in honor of the Bluegrass city. Under the adroit management of his new owner Lexington was to have an illustrious racing career. The colt was sold for $5,000, $2,500 in cash and the remainder if he won the great States Post Stakes to be run at Metaire Track in New Orleans that December. Lexington, in this race, was to begin a long rivalry in the racing world. He was to pit Boston blood against all comers but more especially the get of Glencoe. His opposition in the States Post Stakes was a single entry, Sallie Waters, a Glencoe three-year-old, and the pride and joy of the rich Black Belt of Alabama. The horses were to run straight heats of three miles each with a purse of $5,000 to Sallie Waters, if she came home first, or $3,500 to Lexington if he came in on top. On the heavy track the son of Boston and Alice Carneal showed his four white heels to Glencoe's heavily backed daughter and won the two heats in the good time of 6:23½ and 6:24½. This was the beginning of a heated racing rivalry in the lower South which was not to end until the outbreak of the war. Because of the audacity of the sporting Richard Ten Broeck, Boston blood was pitted against the whole field of American and European breeding, and breeders were quick to take up the challenge. Ten Broeck offered to run four Boston entries against a like number of horses of other bloodlines at any time or on almost any recognized track. His challenge was a broad one, and, later, General J. T. Welles claimed, an indefinite one; at any rate, it was turned down, and he had to await a second running of the States Post Stakes in April, 1854, to enter his famous horses.

In his first show of strength in the States Post Stakes Lexington had defeated Sallie Waters, and had sorely injured the pride of the proud Alabamians. Previous to her race against Lexington in New Orleans, the Glencoe filly had outstripped everything in her state, and her backers had become exceedingly imprudent in their boasting of her prowess. They published her record in the *Spirit of the Times,* and in Alabama, New Orleans, and Kentucky newspapers. On at least one occasion they had flaunted themselves in the face of Kentucky breeders, daring them to produce a better horse. Challenges had been sent out, and her supporters went to New Orleans in 1854 with an overdose of confidence and large sums of money with which they hoped to bankrupt the Kentuckians. The race opened with the filly enjoying a 2-to-1 advantage in the betting over the Kentucky entry, but at the end of the first heat the long end of the betting had shifted to 100 to 10 in favor of Lexington. In the second heat the big rawboned Kentuckian galloped home in good time, and was easily the winner.

A New Orleans *Picayune* reporter became much excited over the race. He had gone to the track a Sallie Waters partisan, but he came away to sing the praises of the big Ten Broeck horse. When Sallie was stripped for display in the paddock she presented a graceful appearance, even though she was a bit tall and top-heavy. Lexington presented a radically different picture, and the reporter said, "As he walked past the stands he was by no means attractive, and he violated all the rules laid down in the purchase of a horse 'four white legs, deny him'; is the old maxim—and in addition to that eye sore, he has glassy or 'wall' eyes, and is a 'blazed young rip'; but when stripped his form did certainly command admiration. His style of going is the poetry of motion, and the horse that outruns him in a sticky, heavy track like that of yesterday must be a sort of steam engine in disguise." This outburst of unbridled admiration for his racing capacity came just at a time when Lexington was recovering from a spell of sickness, and while he was in the process of acclimatization to the muggy climate of the lower South.

Lexington's easy victory over the formerly invincible Sallie Waters stirred the southern breeders to action. The Old South's racing supremacy was being dangerously threatened by Kentucky horses. This was the period when cotton planting was in its heyday, Southerners had money or their credit was easy, and they were branching out seriously into racing. Along with their dreams of pillared mansions, Tudor Gothic public buildings, and knightly living stirred up by the reading of English novels, the southern bloods wished most of all to become swaggering sportsmen. There was a surging period of prosperity in which puffing river boats hauled down from West Tennessee, the Mississippi Delta, and Alabama's Black Belt thousands of bales of cotton which found ready sale at good prices. It was under these conditions that Southerners, who hitherto had satisfied their sports yearning with meaner horses at local tracks, or had followed the less expensive interest of fox hunting, turned to fantastic racing. Bloods at Natchez, Vicksburg, and around New Orleans began to take great pride in the accomplishments of their horses at the fashionable Metaire track. Quickly the States Post Stakes became the leading sporting event of the southern planter aristocracy. It was an ideal race at which thousands turned out to engage in that age-old vain human sport of "seeing and being seen." Spectators came garbed in flashy new spring clothes, with pockets full of money to bet themselves broke and to yell themselves hoarse for their state's entry. Never in all the long history of the Southerner's notorious provincial love for his state was he so vociferous in proclaiming that fact than at the running of the famous State Stake in New Orleans.

April, 1854, came in wet, but even with the heavy rainfall, foliage was out in waxy profusion. Fortunately the first day of April was fair, and work went nicely at the Metaire track, where four horses were entered in the raging all-states duel. Alabama, the state which had bet so heavily on its entry the year before, was sending Highlander, a Glencoe colt owned by Judge Hunter, to regain a place of honor for the state. Louisiana nominated Arrow, a Boston foal owned by Richard Ten Broeck, Mississippians named LeComte, a second Boston offspring and owned by General J. T. Welles of Rapides, Louisiana, and the Kentuckians, of course, stood by the white-footed, wall-eyed Warfield colt Lexington. The race was to be in four-mile heats, with the best two out of three, or two straight, to be declared the winner. Excitement ran high, and the owners had their eyes on the highly coveted stake trophy, and the rich $20,000 purse.

Before midmorning of the great match, crowds swarmed out of the city toward the Metaire course, and men and women thronged the grounds of the track. Fair Mobilians were loud in their declaration for Highlander, and they were answered by Kentucky belles who wondered how any remotely sane person could bet against Lexington. Restive Mississippians and Louisianians smugly supported LeComte and Arrow with their bets. The *Picayune's* "man-on-the-grounds" took in the scene with wide and incisive reportorial oversight. With something approaching poetic intoxication he babbled:

The day was fair, bright clear and mild; the sky was all blue, the air all balm, the earth all beautiful. A lovelier day was never born of spring—fitter to be the first of spring's fairest months. The warmest expectations that could have been formed of what the coming "day would bring forth," must have been more than doubled by the first glimpse at the morn that broke upon their waking vision. It was a day formed by the hands of nature expressly for pleasure, and there seemed no room for so much as the possibility of disappointment. From an early hour all the roads, avenues and means of approach, by every possible kind of conveyance were put in requisition. The city was practically deserted. Business seemed (we, who were among the couldn't get aways were told) to be suspended; everybody who was anybody or wanted to be anybody had gone to the race. Dinner hours were postponed, engagements were forgotten, and we should not at all wonder if bank notifications, in some instances slipped some memories. The race for everybody, and everybody for the race.

Never before had a horse race created such a stir in the great city where stirs were fairly commonplace. The

Old South was supremely happy, and its fashionable, and even its not so fashionable, citizens were out to preen their feathers in rollicking good company. Had a stranger suddenly come upon the excited throng leaving the city he would have thought that a deadly yellow fever epidemic had occurred. Again our happy newsman was on hand to picture for us the colorful hegira from the city:

The variety of the modes adopted by which to reach the course, was a source of no little amusement to the curious lookers-on. The luxurious private carriage, taking its leisure and rolling on with confident security of being in time without hurrying, and as it turned out for a dashing pair of bloods, regarding its rivals with a bland, *festina lente* kind of compassion; the coach, the cab, the cart, the carriage of every sort, with one horse or four, and some even with the humble animal that the Prophet Balaam was not ashamed to ride, made up a variety that was, in its way, far from unexciting, and then, the plodders on foot, or *en cheval* (whose name is legion) and the many passengers on cars (whose names were many legion) all helped to swell the great stream of life, whose ocean was the race course. Such a moving panorama has never before been exhibited in these parts.

Inside the Metaire gates there was great excitement. State partisans were bantering each other—plug-hatted gentlemen were naming bets to other plug-hatted gentlemen. Ladies, dressed in huge hoopskirts, and shaded by delicately petite umbrellas twittered with other ladies who bore like burdens of crinoline. Kentucky's daughters were a sight to behold. We are told that it was truly inspiring "to see the bright eyes of her daughters sparkling with joy, and to hear their ringing laughs and exultant shouts, as the champion of their state was going on 'conquering and to conquer,' and adding another to·the already many noble trophies that have been gallantly won by Old Kentuck."

In the judges' stand were five distinguished southern gentlemen. Representing Alabama as its field judge was Colonel Wade Hampton of South Carolina. Colonel Robert Evans was on hand to see that Kentucky got a fair deal, Colonel J. J. Hughes was selected by Louisiana, Judge Pinckney Smith was Mississippi's choice, and Judge J. G. Cocks of the Metaire Club presided. Betting was heavy, Highlander was favorite with Lexington trailing in second position, and Arrow and LeComte were fighting nip and tuck for third and fourth place. Some reckless sportsmen were wagering $100 to $50 that Highlander would sweep the first heat, and they were giving long odds that he would take the race in straight heats. The course was heavy from March rains, and the gumbo clung to a horse's hoofs with dogged tenacity; the race was definitely to be a test of strength and staying power.

At the tap of the drum the start was a clean break, and Lexington went ahead of Arrow at the first turn, LeComte was third, and the favorite, Highlander, fourth. In the second mile LeComte went ahead for a moment, but the powerful Lexington stepped back into the lead and the field quickly shuffled into its original position. The third mile was a repetition of the second, and in the fourth the Louisiana entry slackened, and Highlander climbed into third position and then made a brush with LeComte. LeComte, however, had more power, and he surged forward to push Lexington home three lengths ahead.

Before the second heat began, the betting shifted to Lexington against the field, with LeComte first choice to place. In the second start Highlander dashed ahead with Lexington at his heels. LeComte made a brush in the second mile and forced the field to run in quick time. At the opening of the third mile Highlander was again in the lead for a moment, and LeComte went out eight lengths ahead when they entered the fourth, but when they rounded into the final mile Alabama's darling weakened and left the field to LeComte and Lexington. It was now Kentucky against Mississippi, and the powerful Lexington pushed up to close the gap, and in the third quarter of the final mile the two colts were plunging ahead in a deadlock. They entered the stretch with their noses together, Boston blood was under fire on both sides, and it was standing up nobly, and for a moment the hushed crowd thought the contestants would come by the post in a dead heat. Lexington, however, had enough reserve left for the call, and he rushed by the judges' stand ahead.

Twice in the all States Post Stakes the big Warfield colt had come home ahead in a heavily supported field. Kentucky was proud of her famous horse; indeed, the sparkling eyes of her daughters were filled with joy. The famous Kentucky River grazing country had triumphed in the big southern racing contest, but its moment of victory in the States Post Stakes was of short duration. Backers of LeComte were certain that if the two horses could run a return race their favorite would win. Throughout the week crowds which thronged to Metaire track, the streets of New Orleans, and the hotel lobbies begged for a second race. On Friday night of April 7th, the owners agreed that they would on the next day run their horses in a race of the best two out of three four-mile heats for a Jockey Club prize of $2,000. For the first time Lexington was to meet an opponent on a dry track, and with only two entries against him. Judge J. S. Hunter entered his horse Reube, playing for any breaks which might develop against the Boston horses. Again the crowd swarmed out to Metaire to see the reopening of the racing duel between Mississippi and Kentucky. The belles were once more on hand in the ladies' box shouting and squealing for their favorites. Many of the pretty and shy creatures, with an eye for business, bet their bags, dainty handkerchiefs, and trifling little parasols against the hard cash of any young gallant who would stop long enough to come to terms. Betting among the serious followers of each horse was fast and furious, with Lexington enjoying a 100-to-60 advantage. Some money was placed against time with a specified minimun of 7:32, a half second slower than that of Fashion in her race with Boston. Clearly the crowd was aware that it perhaps had come to see a world-famous race, and some individuals believed it to the point of betting a substantial sum of money that the world's best time record would be broken.

At the tap of the drum, LeComte broke into the lead, with Lexington second and Reube trailing. For three miles Lexington trailed closely on the heels of General Welles's fast entry, once he moved up for a brush, but LeComte quickly covered his lead. They entered the fourth and important mile with LeComte holding a good lead and running at a brisk rate of speed, but, at that, he gave indication of abundant reserve strength and speed. Lexington's jockey pulled him up for a brush, realizing that the moment to win was at hand, but LeComte held out, and came home in 7:26, the fastest time for a four-mile heat in racing history. The crowd was stunned into silence; persons who had privately timed the race thought their watches had suddenly gone wrong.

Never was there such milling about among the gamblers. Those who had bet on time were collecting their money, and were turning it back on the race itself.

Lexington lost his edge of favoritism and the odds shifted quickly to LeComte at the rate of 100 to 40. Again the horses appeared at the post, and the tap of the drum sent Lexington away in the lead, a position which he held for two miles, but at the entry of the third mile LeComte moved and went ahead to come home by three lengths, and to set a world's record of 7:38¾ for a second heat. Richard Ten Broeck's great Kentucky colt was defeated, and by a horse he had distanced by a great show of reserve strength only a week before.

It was hard for Ten Broeck to accept defeat for his gangling colt. Impulsively he challenged General Welles to a renewal of the rivalry on the following Wednesday, but the latter wisely refused the invitation. Ten Broeck believed in his horse, and through the *Spirit of the Times* he offered to run four miles between April 1 and 15, 1855, against the fastest time on record for a purse of $10,000, or to challenge any horse in the country for a purse of $25,000. A hot dispute broke out in public print among thoroughbred owners, one of whom was General Welles. He claimed that Ten Broeck had given such a short time in which to accept his challenge that no one could take him up. Nevertheless, Colonel Calvin Green and Captain John Belcher, of Virginia, accepted the time challenge and guaranteed a purse of $10,000 against LeComte's record of 7:26. Never had an owner displayed so much audacity, and because of the hot dispute carried on in the papers, the race attracted nation-wide attention.

New Orleans was crowded with visitors, and on April 2, 1855, the road to Metaire swarmed with sporting bloods on their way to see the Kentucky horse compete against heavy odds in time. When he lost to LeComte, it was said by many people that because of a misunderstanding on the part of the jockey, Lexington was pulled up momentarily and was thrown off his stride at a critical moment. This time, however, shrewd Dick Ten Broeck had the seasoned jockey Gilpatrick astride his horse, and if Lexington failed it was not going to be the result of a faulty ride. For the fourth time at Metaire the drum tapped to send Boston's proud son away to a long and grueling drive. He ran the first mile in 1:47¼, and the fourth in 7:19¾ to come home 6¼ seconds under LeComte's world record of 7:26. This was a proud day for the people in the Kentucky River valley, and especially in the fertile Bluegrass. An Elkhorn Creek horse had galloped past the judges' stand to set an almost unbelievable world's record.

Once again Lexington was to take up the gauntlet to prove his superiority to southern antagonists. This last time he was to demonstrate his speed and endurance so thoroughly that even Colonel Ten Broeck's bitterest opponents had to admit that he owned America's superior horse. General Welles challenged Ten Broeck to a matched race between Lexington and LeComte twelve days after the thrilling time race. Immediately the challenge was accepted, and the two horses were brought to the post on April 14th, to determine once and for all which was the better horse. Lexington met the challenge with a record of one victory over LeComte, one defeat, and a victory over his rival's time. So much publicity was given the big race against time, and close on its heels came the announcement of the matched race, that a large crowd of racing people gathered in New Orleans to see the final act in the long rivalry. Betting was $100 even. At the break Lexington went ahead, and at the second mile LeComte moved up strong to make his brush, but Lexington staved him off and maintained his lead. Ten Broeck had Gilpatrick ride his mount under a tight rein, while LeComte's jocky rode with a whip. When the horses came into the stretch General Welles's rider was applying the whip so furiously that LeComte dropped his tail and slackened his gait. Lexington never gave any doubt as to where he would finish, he came past the post in good form to set a new world's record of 7:23¾ for the first heat of a matched race. So decisive was Lexington's victory that General Welles withdrew his entry, and the second heat went by default. This was a glorious victory, and sweet vindication of Lexington's failure in 1854 to stave off the stubborn lead of LeComte. There was no further doubt that Lexington was the greatest horse in America. He had brought honor to Dr. Warfield, the Meadows, and to the Kentucky thoroughbred industry. Lexington had made seven starts and had won six of them. His total earnings of $56,000 sounds like pin money when compared with those of Twenty Grand.

Betting men watched Lexington enter his last mile against LeComte and begged frantically for takers at odds of 100 to 10, but no one was interested. Nothing short of sudden death could have stopped Boston's charging son. When his rider brought the winner back past the post, an observer thought that the horse was conscious of his fine showing. He said, "I will add, that no one who saw Lexington walk quietly through the cheering crowd that flocked round him at the close, as if his triumph were a matter fully understood, doubts that he has sense, memory and powers of reflection—horse sense at least."

His racing days were over, and Lexington came back to the Bluegrass country aboard a Kentucky River steamer to spend the remainder of his long life in darkness. First he went to Colonel W. F. Harper's farm at Midway, and later Colonel R. R. Alexander bought him from Richard Ten Broeck and transferred him to his near-by Woodburn Farm. For sixteen years Lexington led the American sires' list, and before 1880 his get earned almost a million and a quarter dollars. He died in 1875, having lived to a ripe old age for such an active racer and stud. It was a matter of great pride with Lexington admirers that in 1864 he had three sons, Norfolk, Kentucky, and Asteroid, who were unbeaten except when two of them ran in the same race.

17

Lion of White Hall

I⸗ was July, 1903. The sun bore down upon
the roof of the tall house at White Hall. Long streamers
of heat waves danced crazily over the wide meadowlands which spread out before the commodious Bluegrass house. In the yards the chickens were clucking im-
patiently to one another, and about the windows of the
house flies droned lazily. Within the house in the large
oval library was a bed, and on it was stretched the huge
frame of an aged man. General Cassius Marcellus Clay,
"Lion of White Hall," was both tired and sick. His
kidneys had ceased their normal function, and the
weight of old age bore heavily upon him. The heavy
shock of glossy black hair, which had hung so nobly
over his wide brow in early years, had now become
scraggly and white. His once handsome clean-shaven
face was now covered with a grayish unkempt beard.
The black eyes, which on so many famous occasions in
his life had flashed fire, were now buried deeply in dis-
colored and wrinkled sockets, hidden away under
shaggy, overhanging eyebrows. Those huge masterful
hands, which had once wielded a bowie knife with fatal
results for his antagonists, now were bony and shook
with palsy; and the one in which the muscles had been
cut by his own knife in his fight at Foxtown was practi-

cally useless. The old Lion lay in his bed and stared aimlessly at the high ceiling of his room.

One of the giant flies which buzzed about the windows worked its way into the room, and whipped itself from corner to corner. Its noisy flurries in the corners of the molding bothered the old man. He commanded the young tenant boy, Henry Perkins, to bring him his rifle, and he drew a bead on the fly and killed it. For one brief moment those fiery old eyes and massive hands performed as of old. The fly was spattered over the ceiling, and the Lion of White Hall had won his last major physical encounter with an opponent.

Until the very day of his death, Major General Cassius M. Clay displayed an indomitable will power. He had boasted that he did not intend to die until Pope Leo had passed away. As a matter of fact, General Clay's life-and-death race with the aged pope became somewhat of a sporting affair in Kentucky. The general was successful in outliving the pontiff, and it was with something of a spirit of triumph that he came to the end of his weary old age. General Clay died at 9:30 on the evening of July 22, 1903, at the age of ninety-three years. During the night a storm raged over the Bluegrass, and in the early morning of July 23rd, by weird coincidence, a bolt of lightning demolished the head of the Henry Clay monument in the Lexington Cemetery. Cassius M. Clay was dead. At last the bold trumpeter of freedom was silenced.

Not far from White Hall the Kentucky River stretched itself into a long gentle sweep below Boonesborough. It had cut its bed deeply into the blue limestone, but at one place a roadway drifted down the sides of the palisades, and the river crossing was called Clay's Ferry. This crossing was named for Cassius' father, Green Clay, a big landholder and a prominent Virginia soldier and legislator, who had come west to the Kentucky country. For more than a hundred years the ferry had been a landmark. Once it was a point of departure for flatboatmen on their way to New Orleans. All the logmen from up the stream knew the ferry, and they looked upon it as a happy landmark on their difficult journeys downstream.

Close by Clay's Ferry was a second point of interest. Where the gray-limestone banks pushed up to a high point was a spot called "Bull's Hell." The origin of this name is somewhat legendary, but the story pertains to the quick temper of Cassius Clay. It was said that he had a pure-bred bull which was difficult to handle. On one occasion he tried to catch the animal; and when he was unable to do so, he ran it over the steep bank and smashed it against the rock shoulder two hundred feet below. When inquisitive neighbors inquired about the bull, the high-strung Cassius replied that he "had gone to hell," or at least he had gone to "Bull's Hell" on the Kentucky River.

Every aspect of General Clay's life seems to have been stormy. In 1833 he married Dr. Elisha Warfield's daughter, Mary Jane. His courtship with her was an instantaneous affair. He was just back from Yale and full of the ardor of youth. Unfortunately he went hickory nut hunting with a party of friends, one of whom was Mary Jane. According to Cassius she had her cap set for him, and she played her part well. In a colorful paragraph he described years later how she had dropped down in his lap and coyly smiled and whispered that she would be his. The hot blood of the young squire had surged in his veins, and he was swept off his feet.

So enamored did Cassius become of Mary Jane that a kinsman immediately detected it and warned, "Cousin Cassius, I see that you are much taken with

Mary Jane. Don't you marry her; *don't* you marry a Warfield!"

His cousin's warning was in vain. Years later Cassius recalled with great delight the moment when the young Warfield girl had brushed her hair against his face and had given herself to him. Cassius Clay was the most eligible bachelor in Kentucky in 1833. He was a Yale graduate and a large landholder. No one doubted but that he would settle down at White Hall and become an important Kentucky planter.

The Warfields, however, objected to Clay. When Dr. Warfield was pushed for a reason why he did not approve of young Clay, the best he could offer was that "Green Clay was not what he ought to be." Socially in Kentucky this feeble excuse covered a multitude of sins and was specific about none of them. Like so many headstrong men, Cassius Clay forgot to ask his prospective mother-in-law for her daughter's hand. Dr. Warfield, master of the Meadows, was considered a bold and courageous man, but around his wife his actions were decidedly dilatory. The doctor failed to make a prompt reply to Clay's request for his daughter's hand, and Cassius put the pressure on the daughter by telling her that he would not call any more. This forced Mrs. Warfield to make a decision. In the family council it was thought best to send an affirmative note, but Mrs. Warfield was not to forget the pressure under which she was made to assent.

Mrs. Warfield held what she hoped was a trump card in this highhanded game of bluff. There was another suitor for the hand of Mary Jane. He was Dr. John P. DeClarey of Louisville; and when he learned that his fair prize was lost, he wrote a somewhat derogatory note about Clay to Mrs. Warfield. The old lady saw in it a chance to involve her future son-in-law, and she showed him the note. The contents of the letter were not too damning, but Clay believed it placed him in an unhappy light before his future mother-in-law. This was the beginning of the career of Kentucky's most sensational duelist. Enlisting the services of James S. Robbins, who was to be his best man at the wedding, Clay went to Louisville for the purpose of giving Dr. DeClarey a whipping. He bought a small black hickory stick; and when he met his rival on the steps of the Louisville Hotel, he gave him a "threshing" in public. Within a short time DeClarey challenged Clay to a duel beyond the Ohio River.

The duel never occurred between the rivals for Mary Jane's hand. When the antagonists reached the field there were so many people present that it was called off. Dr. DeClarey wished to fight it out in Louisville that night, but Clay refused to do so. He had to rush back to Lexington for his wedding. DeClarey published him as a coward and theatened to "cowhide" him if Clay ever visited Louisville. This was too much for the proud Cassius, and he went to Louisville to meet the braggart soon afterwards.

It was with some difficulty that Clay found DeClarey. When he did meet him, the Louisville man showed a marked fear of Clay. A day later the doctor committed suicide, and Cassius and Mary Jane were left free to live their stormy lives.

As a normal and ambitious young Kentuckian just out of Yale University, Cassius left off delivering tirades against his mother-in-law and fighting with his rivals long enough to become a member of the Kentucky legislature. His first trip down the river was made in order to respresent Madison County in the assembly, but after his first term the voters refused to reelect him. Cassius said that the reason he was not returned to the legislature was because one tobacco-raising old cynic said the time had come when he should be stopped and allowed to spread. In a rollicking campaign in Fayette in 1840, Dr. Warfield's son-in-law swept the field before him, and once again he returned to Frankfort to continue his good work in behalf of internal improvements. His failure in his home county of Madison perhaps was because he had favored improvement of the rivers for transportation purposes. The "plant had spread" by 1840 as the political sage of Madison had said it should. "Cash" Clay was already showing the lionish tendencies which were to make him the most rip-roaring character in all Kentucky A diminutive bully named Sprigg took Clay to task in the house of representatives, and the gentleman from Fayette was, as Cassius' mother said, "not mild in his mode of statement." This tiff led to one of Cassius' famous encounters. Sprigg, once under the influence of bourbon, had revealed to Clay his mode of fighting. He approached his opponent in a gesture of reconciliation, he said, and then knocked him down. When Clay reached his hotel in the evening, Sprigg rushed toward him with outstretched hand, but Clay landed him with a blow between the eyes, and several times more he knocked Sprigg down. When the two were pulled apart, the conciliatory bully had both eyes blacked, his nose was bleeding, and his coattails had been jerked off. This led to a comic duel in which neither man was harmed.

In the early part of 1840 the national presidential campaign was already under way. Cassius Clay was a delegate from both Fayette and Madison to the Whig convention. After Harrison was nominated, the young Kentuckian returned home to work the Ashland District in behalf of the famous Ohio nominee. It was in this campaign that he first became an ardent and outspoken opponent of slavery in Kentucky. According to Cassius, he had gone to Yale University in 1830 "with my soul full of hatred to slavery." In the campaign for Harrison, he matched wits with the Wickliffes and other large slaveholders of the Bluegrass.

For the next four years, the eloquent Cassius M. Clay was to attack from the Bluegrass with tongue and pen the sacred institution of slavery. From every convenient public stump he shouted opposition to the "peculiar institution." He was bearding the lion in its den. A son of a big slaveholder and a slaveholder in his own right, he gave active voice to the destruction of the enforced system of labor. Clay's speeches were not those of an enraged abolitionist. It was true that he had heard William Lloyd Garrison at New Haven and had met other opponents of slavery, but he claimed that his opposition was that of a gradual emancipationist. He wished to see slavery gradually, peaceably, and constitutionally driven from the borders of the state. In his fiery speeches he shouted to his embittered audiences, "Kentucky will be richer in dollars and cents by emancipation, and *slaveholders will be the wealthier by the change.* . . . Until Kentucky is prepared to go all lengths for slavery, she is powerless; not pro-slavery enough for the 'chivalry,' nor free enough for the *free,* between two stools she flounders on the ground. Christians, moralists, politicians, and merely let-live laborers feel these bitter truths. Kentucky never will unite herself to the slave empire, born of southern disunion: then let her at once lead on the van of freedom."

Oregon and Texas were major political and territorial issues. Meeting the militant Thomas F. Marshall in debate, Cassius Clay had contended that if Texas was annexed it would only expand the influence of the slaveholder and involve the United States in a needless

war. In his speeches he echoed the contentions of his
distant cousin Henry who sought the Whig nomina-
tion in 1844. Oregon, Clay believed, should be annexed.
He thought that if it belonged to the United States,
then the United States should have it, and he was willing to make a sacrifice to bring about annexation.

By 1845 Clay's opposition to slavery was well
formed, and his sphere of influence reached far beyond
the borders of Kentucky. He had visited the East in a
speaking campaign against both the institution of slavery and the abolitionists. The ground was prepared for
a major attack upon slavery in his native state. His plans
were complete, and by June, 1845, Cassius M. Clay
began the publication of the *True American,* an emancipation paper published in the heart of Kentucky slavery. On June 3rd, the first issue of this paper came
from the press carrying a clear statement of its policies.
"The paper," said the vigorous editor, "is devoted to
universal liberty, gradual emancipation in Kentucky;
literature; agriculture; elevation of labor, morally and
politically; commercial intelligence, etc."

In the editorial columns of the *True American,*
the bold Cassius thundered at the slaveholders, declar-
ing always that he "desired to bring about the abolition
of slavery in a constitutional way." His promises of
moderation were sometimes violated. He despised the
slave trader, and in an eloquent flourish he denounced
the practice. "In the name of advancing civilization,"
Clay wrote, "which, for more than a century has, with
steady pace, moved on, leaving *Cimmerian regions of
slavery* and the slave *trade* far in the *irrevocable* and
melancholy past, I denounce it. In the name of the first
great law, which at creation's birth was infused into
man, self-defense, unchangeable and immortal in the
image in which he was fashioned and in His Name,

whose likeness man was deemed not unworthy to wear, I denounce slavery and the slave trade forever."

With even more vengeance Cassius M. Clay dug his pen deeply into the paper and spread the gospel of fear among the Kentucky slaveholders. In his tirade against the "peculiar institution," they read the spirit of bloodshed and revolution. Cassius warned: "But remember you who dwell in marble palaces—that there are strong arms and fiery hearts, and iron pikes in the streets, and panes of glass only between them and the silver plate on the board and the smooth skin woman on the ottoman. Where you have mocked at virtue and denied the affairs of men and made rapine your horrid faith; tremble for the day of retribution is at hand— and the masses will be avenged." This was the fire of a determined man shouting a stern warning to a frightened people. The citizens of Lexington were afraid of the editor of the *True American*. They wished to maintain freedom of the press and the sanctity of slavery. Neither, they believed, would be safe from harm with Clay's paper enjoying free publication.

An irate reader replied to Clay's thunderous denunciations of slavery in a letter written in either blood or red turnip juice.

C. M. Clay: You are meaner than the autocrats of hell. You may think you can awe and curse the people of Kentucky to your infamous course. You will find when it is too late for life, the people are no cowards. Eternal hatred is locked up in the bosom of meaner men, your letters, for you. The hemp is ready for your neck. Your life cannot be spared. Plenty thirst for your blood—are determined to have it. It is unknown to you or your friends, if you have any, and in a way you little dream. [Signed] Revengers.

Cassius knew in June, 1845, that such avengers would thirst for his blood. Never was he without his bowie knife, and the *True American* office on Mill Street in Lexington was a veritable arsenal. The building was made of brick, and the doors were lined with sheet iron. Two brass four-pounder cannon were purchased in Cincinnati, and they were loaded with shot and nails and placed on a table breast-high so they could be touched off in an instant. The doors were so secured with a chain that they could be opened and the intruding mob could be fired upon with the cannons. There were Mexican lances and guns enough to arm the six or eight persons who Clay believed would help defend him. A trap door was prepared in the roof so that in case of defeat the defenders could make their escape. Clay placed a keg of powder in such a position that upon his retreat from the office he could touch it off and blow the building to pieces. It was behind this militant spirit and equipment that Cassius M. Clay made an attack upon slavery from the Bluegrass.

By August of 1845 the situation had grown tense in Lexington. The powerful proslavery forces were up in arms, and they were determined to stop publication of the *True American*. A Committee of Sixty was called together on the fourteenth, and resolutions were adopted requesting Clay to discontinue publication of his incendiary paper. They said that it endangered the peace of the commonwealth and the safety of their families. At the time the committee met, Cassius M. Clay was sick with typhoid fever at Thorn Hill, or the old Morton house. A special committee which contained two of the determined editor's bitterest enemies called upon him to present the resolution. In a patronizing manner they explained to the emancipationist that they did not offer a threat, but they were concerned about his personal safety. The rugged Lion poised on one elbow in his sickbed and listened to the insincere solicitations of his callers. Then he denounced them in fine Clay style. He charged them: "Traitors to the laws and the constitution cannot be deemed respectable by any but assassins, pirates and highway robbers. . . . I treat them with burning contempt of a brave heart and a loyal citizen. I deny their power and defy their action!" This was a positive, unflinching answer to men who were about to deny the constitutional rights of one of their fellow Kentuckians. It was with a guilty conscience that the committee walked down North Limestone Street to their fellows to report Clay's reaction.

During the next three days in Lexington, when the town was upset over the possible removal of the *True American*, charges and countercharges came fast. The town was in a state of civil insurrection. From the sickroom of Cassius Clay poured vitriolic denunciations of those citizens who were taking advantage of his weakened condition. He accused them of base cowardice and informed them, "Your advice with regard to my personal safety is worthy of the source whence it emanated, and meets with the same contempt from me which the purposes of your mission excite." Then with the stinging eloquence of the courageous crusader, Clay commanded, "Go tell your secret conclave of cowardly assassins that C. M. Clay knows his rights and how to defend them." It must have been with considerable shame that the committee listened to the sick man's condemnation. They knew that for a month he had been in bed, and they knew the reputation of the men of their state for gentlemanly action. But in this moment they were torn between their sense of chivalry and constitutional scruples and their determination to remove the dangerous paper of Clay forever from their midst.

The press, type, and other equipment of the *True American* were packed in boxes and shipped to Cincinnati. In a letter to Messrs. January and Taylor, James B. Clay, a son of Henry, writing for the Committee of Sixty, informed them that the equipment of the *True American* had been sent there. They were instructed to take the boxes into their possession and to keep them until they were called for by their owner. In Louisville George D. Prentice, ever a defender of the freedom of the press, was critical of the actions of the Committee of Sixty. He believed that it was the work of a small headstrong group of men who were determined to retain the power of dominating the policies of Kentucky. Prentice was quick to say that Clay had acted with moderation. True to his promises to live within the Constitution, Cassius Clay had, upon the court order of Judge Trotter, delivered the keys to a county official, who in turn gave them to the Committee of Sixty. Publication of the *True American* with a Lexington imprint was continued for a time in Cincinnati, but it never reached the high point of attainment which it had when it was published on North Mill Street.

Not to be outdone by the highhanded action of his neighbors, Cassius Clay entered suit to recover damages from the Committee of Sixty. In April, 1848, the court decided that he was entitled to damages and the committee paid him $2,500 for damages done to his press. At least he had recovered the intrinsic value of his property if not the constitutional loss which he had suffered.

Always the reformer, Cassius Clay spent his time delivering long lectures on public education, internal improvements, divorce, southern women, and any other subject that came to mind. Usually he was able to warp his discussions of these numerous subjects into an attack upon slavery. Using the convincing device of comparison, he anticipated later attackers of slavery by holding up Ohio and Kentucky for comparative purposes. It was with a spirit of embarrassing ridicule that he pointed to the greater economic success of Ohio.

It was with the eye of an experienced judge in such matters that he turned his attention to the subject of women. The female figure had great fascination for the fire-eating Kentuckian. He leaned against a column in front of Jones's in Chestnut Street in Philadelphia, and indulged himself freely in the sidewalk pastime of staring at the passing throng. Before him passed faces "with noses to them" and faces "with no noses." There were "necks with no heads" and "heads with no necks." There were "old gals" lean, dry, and sallow. They had "thin and wind-blown hair, wiry, like a cataract of cork screws—some platted, some crisped"; and then there was the lassie with a "yellow mane." Waddling along in squads of threes and fours were the fat German women of the city, and the staring Cassius snorted, "fat—not plump; yes, by Jove, fat —a fat woman has no soul." Three fat women who passed in a row brought to Cassius' mind an agricultural simile: "They were the same size, had the same step, all loaded with cotton bales; and they beckoned east, and then to the west." Their strides were those of three cradlers swinging in unison in a heavy field of wheat.

Dresses were shocking. They were one- and two-story affairs. Cassius said that there were some of brick, of stone, and of mud. Skins of all sorts were to be seen: old leather, chalky, brick dust, and indigo. Dropping into the lingo of the frontier, the Kentuckian shouted, "Wolf in camp!" Philadelphia's stream of female cari-

catures provoked him to swear by the "Mammoth
Cave, the wild Crab Orchard, the raccoon dog, the best
rifle, the snapping turtle, and the half horse and half
alligator, and the small touch of an earthquake that
there was not a pretty woman out of old Kaintuck."
There was one of the passing throng, however, who
caught his eye. In rapturous prose he described a delectable angel who glided past him wearing a dress
which closed at the waist and widened at the shoulders. It widened in the skirt and closed sympathetically about the feet and ankles with the undulations
of the lady's walk. In the exact descriptive language of
a Kentucky horseman, Cassius wrote of her features
"not classic, but passionate, and full of poetry and soul;
the large expressive mouth; eyes large, wide apart, and
wide awake, under seeming sleepy lids; rich auburn
hair, so judiciously braided as to fill out to perfection
of outline, a most beautiful head." This was the female
ideal of a man who spent much of his energy lambasting
the bustle.

Cassius tied up his fight against slavery with his
feminist reform movement. The fair southern woman
was not to escape a scathing from his tongue. He was
free with advice in his famous "forked radish" speech
in which he commanded the southern belle to give up
her slaves. "If you want a drink," he wrote, "go to the
pump or the spring and get it; if to bathe, prepare
your own bath, or plunge into the running stream;
make your own clothes, throw away your corsets, and
nature herself will form your bustles. Then you will
have full chests, glossy hair, rosy complexions, smooth
velvety skins, muscular, rounded limbs, graceful tour-
nures, elasticity of person, eyes of alternate fire and
most melting languor; generous hearts, sweet tempers,
good husbands, long lives of honeymoons, and—*no*

divorces." The woman who was waited upon hand and foot by her slave servant was compared by Clay as being an owl, "when stripped of its feathers its skin is flaccid," and its form that of a "forked radish."

Within two years after the removal of the *True American* in 1845, the antislavery crusader volunteered his services in the Kentucky militia. Captain James S. Jackson resigned his command of the Old (Lexington) Infantry, a mounted company, and Clay was unanimously selected as its captain. It was a long step from the vitriolic denunciations which Cassius Clay had heaped upon the large slaveholders of central Kentucky to a command of a militia company on its way to fight in the Mexican War. This move on the part of the great social crusader came as a hard blow to his antislavery associates. They were at a loss to know why the editor of the *True American* had turned about-face on them. But as usual Cassius was ready with what he believed to be a complete answer. Texas, he said, had become a part of the Union, and he as a good citizen was willing to help fight his country's battle. It was curious logic that he used. The annexation of Texas he had declared was a "disgraceful and degrading act," and he had preached in the *True American* that it meant a useless war with Mexico. Clay's excuses for going to the slaveholders' war left much to be desired from his antislavery friends. Silas M. Holmes wrote James G. Birney: "How strange and inconsistent was his conduct, after taking the position that he did upon the subject of slavery, to abandon his post as editor of the *True American,* when he was beginning to exert in his own state a powerful influence, for that of the field of battle, to engage in a war for the extension of human slavery."

Silas Holmes could never have understood Clay's

motives. Neither could James G. Birney, a fellow Kentuckian, nor William Lloyd Garrison, editor of the *Liberator,* understand why Clay shifted his position. They did not know that there was no such thing in Clay's whole temperamental make-up as consistency. Likewise, Clay was, first and last, interested in local politics, and the Mexican War was popular in Kentucky. It was with an astounding bit of naïveté that Clay always confided to his readers that what he was doing was largely for purposes of gaining a political advantage. He said in his defense that he believed when he returned from the war he could take the stump and get a more effective hearing on the subject of emancipation.

Captain Clay's military history in the Mexican War was of doubtful glory. Near Salado, on January 23, 1846, his command was captured by three thousand Mexican calvarymen, under the command of Colonel Mendoza. The rest of the short war he spent in a prison camp, but his popularity in Kentucky grew and that was the thing which counted. His neighbors in Madison County gave a public dinner for him when he returned, and he was given a jeweled sword as a token of appreciation for his heroism. True to his predictions in his numerous explanations to his critics, he came home from Mexico a more popular man than he was when he left Kentucky.

He was to give this popularity an acid test within a short time. Again he took up the editorial cudgel against slavery. Soon he was speaking against the institution in various central Kentucky counties. Beyond the Kentucky River at Lawrenceburg was a proslavery community. From this region had come the famous Salt River Tigers who had fought so gallantly under Zachary Taylor's command. They were the soldiers who, while fighting under William R. McKee and young

Henry Clay, had frightened "Old Zach" by their apparent failure under fire. When the pressure of battle developed and it appeared that the Kentuckians were retreating, General Taylor turned to Colonel J. J. Crittenden and shouted, "By God, Mr. Crittenden, this will not do. This is not the way for Kentuckians to behave themselves when called upon to make a good battle. It will not answer Sir." General Taylor was too hasty. The Tigers were crouching for their mighty lunge against the enemy. Within a moment the Kentuckians had marched victoriously against the Mexicans, and the old general rose up in his stirrup straps and shouted with pride, "Hurrah for Old Kentucky! That's the way to do it; give them hell damn them."

These victorious Kentucky Tigers were Cassius Clay's friends. They knew of the captain's misfortunes at Salado, and they honored him for his courageous efforts. But Captain Clay's stand on slavery was to them embarrassing. On April 14, 1849, he invaded Anderson to denounce slavery. He rode alone from Lexington through Versailles, across Shryock's Ferry, into Lawrenceburg. At the hotel he was the only guest. Even the streets of the town were deserted. It was necessary for Cassius to go out into the hotel yard to bathe his face; and while he was at the public washstand, a committee of citizens waited upon him with a petition begging him not to speak in the town. His answer was positive. "Gentlemen," he said, "I stand upon my constitutional rights to discuss any subject whatever that pleases me. Say to your people that I shall address them at the hour published at the courthouse." Again it was the crusading Clay of old. Again it was the old warrior, who had arisen from a sickbed to call the famous Committee of Sixty a band of cowards.

In the morning before Clay's speech, Lawrenceburg had somewhat the appearance of a town awaiting its moment of doom. The hotel was a forbidding ground and no one came near. As the hour for the speaking approached, the courthouse was crowded with anxious people awaiting the appearance of the famous speaker. At the hotel Cassius M. Clay made preparation for battle. He packed his bag carefully. In the top of it were two loaded revolvers, and in his belt he carried his famous bowie knife honed as keen as a razor. When he entered the courthouse, he found a path through the crowd from the door to the rostrum. A hush fell over the audience as he walked to the vacant seat on the platform. The self-appointed chairman who greeted him was a Mexican War soldier named Wash. As Clay seated himself, Wash stood up and addressed the crowd: "I understand that this is Cash Clay. You all know who I am. The boys who went to Mexico all say that Clay was a friend in and out of prison, standing by the soldiers, and dividing everything with them. I had no hand in the public meeting held here. But this I do say, that the man who fights for the country has a right to speak about the country. As I said, you all know who I am. I have lived on Salt River all my life. I have forty children and grandchildren, and they are all here. The 'Salt River Tigers' were out in Mexico; and they are here too. Now, we will stand by Clay, or die." For two hours Clay lambasted slavery without an interruption. Grandfather Wash's ominous warning had guaranteed him an attentive audience.

Not far from White Hall in Madison County is Foxtown. Here it was on June 15, 1849, that Cassius M. Clay had his first opportunity since the Mexican War to use his bowie knife on an opponent. A dispute arose among the candidates for the legislature as to the amount of time one of them had used in speaking.

When the dispute grew hot, Clay left the scene a moment for the purpose of strapping on his knife. He said that it was his policy never to go into a fight unarmed, and never as a useful citizen to suffer an indignity. Squire Turner's son, Cyrus, called Cassius a liar, and the fight was on. The Turners held the warrior of White Hall and caused him to drop his knife. He grabbed the blade in his left hand and held on, cutting the muscles in his fingers. He was hit over the head and for a moment was insensible, but he recovered his knife and fatally stabbed Cyrus Turner in the abdomen. For a time Cassius thought he, too, would die, but again, in his own mind, Divine Providence spared him to carry on his fight in behalf of the common people and against slavery. To Cassius M. Clay there was one happy memory of the Turner fight. His son, Warfield, had stood by him. It was he who had pushed through the angry crowd with a pistol for his father to use on the Turners.

Henry Clay died in 1852, and the Whig party in both Kentucky and the nation went through a long and painful process of dissolution. Its immediate successors in Kentucky were groups of intolerant political jackals who stirred up bitter racial and class hatreds. In 1856, to escape these unhappy political groups, Cassius M. Clay became a member of the Republican party. As the issue over slavery in that trying decade before the Civil War grew hot, he became more and more an ardent Republican. He was present at the Wigwam Convention in Chicago, and it has been said by one of the delegates from Kansas that it was he who turned the tide for Lincoln. Perhaps this is a figment of the Kansan's imagination, but Cassius Clay did work for the election of Lincoln in Kentucky, and his faithful services were not to go unrewarded. Lincoln made him minister to Russia. When the war got under way, Clay came home to become a major general. In Washington he organized the famous Clay Guard and stood brief watch over the White House. Perhaps this was one of his famous political gestures. When he sought a command along the Mexican frontier in order to turn back foreign invaders, he and General Halleck became involved in a personal conflict, and Clay resigned his commission and went back to Russia. The history of his years in Russia is hazy. Perhaps the unexploited records of the State Department contain more of the story than has yet been told. Clay and Seward were at dagger's points most of the time, and much of the published correspondence indicates that Seward did not always consult his minister at St. Petersburg. Apparently the secretary of state did not always inform the Kentuckian of the exact state of relations between the United States and Russia. In 1888, Cassius Clay made a speech in Berea in which he said that the one accomplishment he wanted recorded on his tombstone was the purchase of Alaska. However, if official correspondence tells the truth, Alaska was not his child.

Socially, General Clay cut a wide swath in St. Petersburg. It was said that his affairs with Russian women became the subject of gossip in high social circles. When he was challenged to a duel by a Russian gentleman and was accorded the privilege of selecting the weapons, he chose the bowie knife. This was an unknown instrument of honor in the Russian capital, and the experienced Clay had decidedly the upper hand. Shortly after he returned from his Russian appointment, a strange woman appeared at White Hall and presented him with an illegitimate son which he acknowledged as his own. This boy, Lonnie (or Launey), grew to mature manhood, but his presence at White

Hall caused a rift in the family that was never healed. Cassius' wife and children moved off to Lexington and left him with his Russian offspring, and on February 7, 1878, he and Mary Jane were divorced. The press was somewhat harsh with the general because of his domestic troubles. On March 29, 1879, the Cincinnati *Enquirer* carried the caustic note that "You see an early champion of freedom walking about boastfully with a bastard son, imported like an Arabian cross horse and swearing at his family."

General Clay, after the Civil War, was not a happy man. He, like all his fellow reformers of the antebellum period, was left without a substantial philosophical mooring. He switched from one political party to the other. He supported Tilden, Greeley, and Blaine. Cassius Clay was ever the reformer, and the numerous reforms of the postwar years interested him, but in none of these did he make any headway, except in the foundation and promotion of Berea College. He stood by John G. Fee in establishing in Kentucky a school which offered equal educational opportunities to the underprivileged of both races. He gave his land, which he called the "Glade," to the school, and this democratic institution has remained after him as a highly satisfactory monument to a man who professed and crusaded in behalf of beleaguered humanity.

The long days and nights at White Hall were lonesome ones. General Clay's friends were either dead or were busy with other affairs. His family had long since moved off to Lexington and left him, with his illegitimate son and his house, or, as he called it, his "thirty room armed castle." His daily associates were tobacco tenants from the Kentucky River cliff settlement. Among these was Dora Richardson, a fifteen-year-old orphan girl, who made a romantic appeal to General

Clay. In a short time he had proposed to the girl, and on November 9, 1894, they were married. General Clay had taken unto himself a wife on his eighty-fourth birthday. Newspapers all over the country carried the news. Central Kentucky became highly excited over the affair. The Lexington *Transcript* carried a splendid interview between one of its reporters and General Clay. He had shown the reporter through the house and had talked freely about his life, but he would not permit the reporter to see Dora. She was to remain away from the curious public's gaze until he could have her dressed up and prepared to meet people.

The *Transcript* reporter was certain the general was not crazy. He had reached a childish stage in which very simple favors appealed to him. He was flattered at having his picture taken, and was happy when the photographer took a picture of him standing before White Hall with his dog.

White Hall was built for a fortress. Its thick brick walls were made of carefully selected bricks held together with mortar containing a high percentage of lime. No wood was exposed except the window frames. General Clay prepared his huge house, at a cost of almost $100,000, to be a safe place of refuge. When the war was over, he armed it and was prepared to stand off a siege by the Ku-Klux Klan, which threatened him with violence. After his marriage to Dora Richardson, General Clay again fortified it as his "castle" against the attempts of the Madison County sheriff and his posse to take Dora away from him.

General Clay's marriage to the timid tobacco tenant girl, whom he told the *Transcript* reporter he "loved better than any woman he ever saw," stirred up the moralists of his community. An effort was made to separate the aged groom and his black-haired Kentucky

River cliff bride. The sheriff of the county was sent out to take the girl, but General Clay's answer was positive. He said that as a Kentucky gentleman he had never kept a woman against her will. If Dora wished to go, she was at complete liberty to do so. If she did not, then the fortress at White Hall was there to protect her. It was said that Dora shouted her refusal to leave White Hall from a second-story window, and General Clay drove the sheriff and his posse away by firing one of his famous brass cannons at them.

In time General Clay's second marriage, like the first, was to go on the rocks of misunderstanding. He was too old and Dora was too young for the coalition to succeed. It is a sordid tale which the papers of *C. M. Clay* v. *Dora Clay* tell. On August 17, 1898, a petition for divorce was filed. Dora had abandoned Cassius in July, 1897, and had gone back to her cliff folks at Valley View. The divorce was granted and she married the shiftless Riley Brock, but General Clay never forgot her. He wrote his friend, Dr. Perry, of Richmond, a frantic note in red pencil in January, 1900:

Dear Dr.: Brock and Company have driven Dora crazy & taken her off with the *sick* baby.

They will return in force & rob my house—*Help* me— & send Sant Oldham to *help* me. *Come* at *once*. C. M. Clay.

His fear of "Brock and Company," however, was soon allayed, and he continued giving Dora silverware, art objects, and money. Occasionally he visited her when she moved away to the little village of Pinkard in Woodford County.

When Dora went away and left General Clay alone, the old man became lonesome and sought female company wherever he might find it. He wished to marry a third time, he said, provided he could find a woman of the great middle class who would give him friendly companionship. Already he had married women from both the aristocracy and the peasantry. Clay's letter proposing matrimony publicly to American womanhood appeared in March, 1898, in the New York *Journal*. Once and for all, as far as the public was concerned, he closed the child-wife story. He wrote:

This is my second letter and last about Dora and myself, my poor orphan girl wife is now vindicated by events from all calumny. We have played our part on the sea of life and the curtain drops upon distinguished lights, leaving us alone with a just and benevolent Almighty God. My private griefs are sunk in the greater woes threatening my dear native land, and I follow in humiliation where duty and honor lead. Allow me to return recognition of the more than a thousand letters of sympathy and requests—mostly from women—which I have but glanced over and cannot possibly answer. These come from every class of society and are varied with every motive of human action. As I have laid down my idea of equal rights in the sexes in case of marriage, I shall select twenty of the proposals of marriage and answer in their turn if fate decrees, upon conditions: I must have a photograph and full statement by express company of all essential facts—character, age, fortune etc. I seek a companion, and prefer one over 40 years old, but all ages allowed. My real estate, entailed, is worth say $150,000, but unproductive, leaving, by unjust taxation, nothing to others. Whatever money or other property a companion and wife should bring—if $150,000 or $100,000 would be secured to her by legal contracts before marriage. I am sorry to bring my personal affairs before the public, but I have no other means of freeing myself from an impossible duty, and after all it may turn out to all our correspondence "loves" labor lost.

General Clay never found a third wife. He spent his declining years making wills. To Dora, he bequeathed $10,000; to Joe Chenault, whose mother, Florence Dillingham, had been a steadfast friend, he left his shotgun "which has done me many good services for 75 years." To his sister Pauline Clay Rodes he left an old painting of the Virgin Mary which hung on the wall of his "boudoir." There were many other gifts included in the will. It was a strange document. General Clay had become a pitiful old man whose mind was unstable.

Fortress Green Clay, as Cassius often called his house, was invaded in July, 1903. His family forced him to permit a physician to wait upon him, and they went so far as to hold a trial to investigate the state of his mind. Cassius was too weak to resist. He was afraid that someone would poison him, but he was unable to fight off the attack of his determined children.

Cassius Marcellus Clay died, perhaps, a disappointed man. He never had an opportunity to fire off his two famous cannons mounted on breast-high pedestals at an infuriated mob of his opponents. For a long lifetime he had fought the cause of the common man. He had fought for freedom of the press, and had opposed slavery until it was destroyed in Kentucky by the Thirteenth Amendment and then he had taken up the cudgel in behalf of any cause that came along.

The old Lion of White Hall left to the world a long written record of himself. In 1886 he published his memoirs to that date. The book was designed to have more than one volume, but Cassius became too engrossed in other things to bother with other volumes. His friend Horace Greeley collected in 1848 his writings against slavery and combined them with those in favor of reform in female clothing and published them in a thick volume. There were hundreds of newspaper articles, broadsides, and pamphlets. One manuscript especially was of interest. Cassius wrote on the fine art of fighting with a bowie knife. Speaking from broad experience, the old master advised his reader to stay away from the fatty portions of the human body, and to drive the knife home where every thrust would count. The first movement in the expert duelist's procedure was to lock an arm around an opponent's head and to make vigorous use of the knife with the free hand. This was a matter of technical detail only, as Cassius would have said, in the gentlemanly art of defending the dignity of the people. When not contemplating the fine point of knifing an opponent in a vital spot, the hoary old reformer turned his attention to the gentle and attractive subject of charming females. When newspaper reporters were interviewing him about his poor orphan, Dora, they found that he was far more interested in the publication of his proposed book of twenty-five sketches and photographs of the world's most beautiful women.

Not far away from White Hall is the Kentucky River. Cassius M. Clay loved the stream. As a young man he went swimming in it, and as a legislator he supported with diligence the laws to improve it for navigation. The river stood out in his life, as both a matter of sentimentality and a channel of practical commerce. He crossed and recrossed it hundreds of times in the days when he was fighting for the liberties of the underdog. The spirit of the Lion of White Hall still lives along the stream. Many an interested listener today hitches his chair up close so as to hear the fantastic yarns which are spun about the grizzly old bowie-knife fighter. His life story is richer than the hair-raising tales fetched downstream by the flatboatmen and raftsmen. Clay's life story, like his reforms, is a badly disjointed one. Many prospective biographers have backed away, shaking their heads and muttering, "He lived too long."

18

Shryock's Ferry

O<small>N THE</small> morning of September 18, 1861, two men drove leisurely through Versailles in a buggy. They were headed for Shryock's Ferry, but if anyone on the streets of the Woodford county seat noticed them, it was to observe that Captain John Hunt Morgan, commanding officer of the Lexington Rifles Company of the State Guard, was going to start his fall fishing a little early. Fishing poles stuck out of the back of the buggy, and Captain Morgan and his companion lolled comfortably on the seat as the horse jogged along at an easy gait. Many times before John Hunt Morgan had ridden through Versailles. On several occasions he had ridden through at the head of his proud militia company made up of veterans who had distinguished themselves in the Mexican War. In his command in the Lexington Rifles were some of the gayest young bloods in the Bluegrass. But this September morning things were different. People on the streets of Versailles were too vitally concerned with bitter issues involved in the War Between the States to speculate on John Morgan and his bobbing fishing poles.

Everywhere in Kentucky it was the same confused story. Some people were rampant in their southern partisanship, while others were equally ardent in their sup-

port of the Union. Kentucky's governing authorities
were torn between personal prejudices and the seriousness of committing the state actively to either side of
the question. Many of her influential sons, such as Robert J. Breckinridge, Governor Beriah Magoffin, and
George D. Prentice, were able to overcome strong personal prejudices and to convince the state's government
that it should remain neutral in the war being waged
between the sections. Throughout the Bluegrass, however, families were being torn asunder. Brother was
being set against brother, and father against son. Robert J. Breckinridge, who had pleaded for neutrality but
personally wished to see the Union maintained, saw his
four sons divide on the issue. Two of them went to the
southern army, and two enlisted in the northern army.
Courtlandt and Clarence Prentice went off to the Confederate Army to the embarrassment of their neutral
father. Already that September morning, General Leo-
nidas Polk was in Kentucky with a Confederate command. Up the Kentucky River at Camp Dick Rob-
inson, "Lincoln guns" were being distributed to
Kentuckians on the pretense that they could use them
to protect their homes.

Just before Captain Morgan left Lexington, a
regiment of Union troops had moved into the town and
were encamped on the county fairground. Morgan
knew the time had arrived for him to move, and move
quickly if he was to take the State Guard away to the
Confederacy. Behind him on the night of September
19th when he went to join the Confederacy, he had
left twelve or fifteen of his men to tramp heavily over
the armory floor to give the impression that the Lexington Rifles were at drill. His wagons were on the Versailles road headed for Shryock's Ferry and the South.
State Guardsmen were instructed to leave for the Con-

federate Army on such short notice that few of them had an opportunity either to say good-bye or to secure their personal belongings. John Morgan with his fishing poles sticking out the back of his buggy rode on ahead of his command to make arrangements for it to cross the Kentucky River.

Morgan went to the river two days before he was to leave the state, on the pretense of fishing, but actually he wished to secure the services of his old Lexington friend, the architect Cincinnatus Shryock. Times had become so hard back in Lexington just before the outbreak of the war that it became impossible for an architect to make a living. He had broken off his relationship with John McMurtry, and he could not make a new start in such troublous times. He had married his second cousin, Olive Shryock, one of John Shryock's eleven daughters. Since times were so hard, Cincinnatus moved down to the Kentucky River to operate the old Shryock's Ferry. Likewise he got the job of teaching the Grier Creek School. His pupils were much interested when the strangers from Lexington drove up in their buggy and stopped. They called the teacher out for a long conversation, but little did they know that as they played merrily at blindman's bluff or stealing dry goods that plans were being made to ferry the runaway Kentucky State Guardsmen and their equipment over the Kentucky River.

One night later at eleven o'clock Morgan's wagons rattled down the long hill to the ferry accompanied by a dozen men. The drivers were hot and thirsty, the trip from Lexington was a long one, and the road was dusty. Before they went aboard the ferry, Cincinnatus Shryock filled a jug with liquor from the supply in his grocery. Across the river was Anderson County, and truly southern soil. As yet no Union troops had crossed the Kentucky. Beneath the shade of a spreading sycamore tree over the river on that moonlight night, the State Guardsmen drank heavily from their jug and bade farewell to their friends the ferrymen. They were on their way over the steep river hill south to Tennessee and the big Confederate fight.

A few nights after Morgan's men had crossed over the river, and their escape from Kentucky had been discovered, a hackload of Union troops pulled up before Cincinnatus Shryock's door. They informed the ferrykeeper that they were on their way to Lawrenceburg to make several "military arrests," but before they went on they wanted supper. Independent and straight-talking Olive Shryock refused to prepare a meal for them, but she did allow the soldiers to use her kitchen to cook a meal if they wished. While they fried ham and boiled coffee on the Shryock stove, Cincinnatus sent his son John hurrying across the river to tell their neighbors, the Cobbs, to warn the people in Lawrenceburg that the Yankees were coming to raid the town. Mrs. Cobb hated the Union cause, and in a moment she had her slave Cale riding off to Lawrenceburg at breakneck speed to tell the Confederates to hide out. The Cobb family in a short time was to become the Confederate lookout on the south side of the Kentucky River. If a Yankee soldier crossed the river, they knew it, and before he could begin the climb of the river hill, Cale was on his mule scurrying away to Lawrenceburg to tell the Confederates to be on their guard.

While Ole Man Cobb's Cale whipped his foaming mount headlong into Lawrenceburg to carry the disturbing news that the Yankees were coming, Cincinnatus Shryock engaged the commanding officer in an argument. The river was running at flood stage, and a heavy drift of logs and other debris tumbled downstream to make a crossing in the ferryboat a ticklish job. Shryock was trying to get the officer to give up his idea of going on to Lawrenceburg that night and to wait until the next morning to go across the river, but the officer was stubborn and insisted that his orders be carried out. This was the beginning of a fine bit of comic bluff that was to wear the Yankees down before they could reach the other side of the river. The troops were traveling in horse-drawn omnibuses, and a third of the command went aboard the boat in one of the buses. Under the most favorable condition and with even the most sympathetic and diligent boatmen at the oars, the crossing would have been difficult. But with a bunch of boatmen sympathetic to the southern cause setting out with a boatload of Yankees, anything was liable to happen other than reaching the opposite bank at the right place. There was more than one way to win such an argument. The current piled up against the sides of the clumsy boat and forced it off its course. Nevertheless, the boat was pulled upstream and then turned toward the other bank. Cincinnatus Shryock was at the steering oar, but before he could ram the snub nose of his boat in the soft mud of the south landing, he ran afoul of a log, and the boat was completely out of hand. Debris drifted against them, and the boat started downstream at a hazardous rate. If Yankees could not be delayed on the bank, they could be drifted downstream and frightened out of their wits. It all had the earmarks of being purely accidental. Cincinnatus Shryock's boat had accidentally run afoul a drift of logs, and now it was going downstream out of control. A glance upward at the cliffs revealed the troops' predicament; the palisades were gliding by at a disastrous rate. In a short time the beleaguered boat was abreast of Tyrone, more than a mile and a half downstream.

Then it was brought under control, but it was impossible to land the bus and the troops on the sheer rock bank. It was necessary to maneuver the boat all the way upstream to the regular ferry landing before the company could be set ashore. As a part of his devilish scheme, the Confederate ferryman had loaded on a coil of rope just before he cast out into the stream.

Not only had the Confederate partisans planned craftily to delay the Yankees, but likewise to work them half to death doing so. The officer commanded his men to attach the rope to one corner of the prow of the boat and to get ashore and "cordelle" it back to the landing. It must have been with a great deal of self-satisfaction that Cincinnatus Shryock and his helpers listened to the frantic heaving and grunting of Yankee troops as they towed the boat upstream. The south bank of the Kentucky came down abruptly to the water's edge, and it was extremely difficult for a man to find stable footing. It was daylight when the tired, muddy, and bedraggled troops dragged the boat to a safe mooring back at the regular landing. A third of the company, including the commanding officer, was in no condition to go ahead with their raid on Anderson County when they drove up the hill from the ferry at nine o'clock that morning.

Old Lady Cobb, watchdog of the Confederacy on the south bank of the Kentucky, became a comic actor in the hot intersectional drama enacted in Kentucky. She was outspoken in her southern sympathies, and Union officers were soon to learn of her spying activities upon their troops as they crossed over the river. Several of their failures on the south side of the river were partly due to the old lady's southern leanings. All their raids upon the Confederate stronghold, Lawrenceburg, were failures owing to the warning of Mrs. Cobb and her mule-riding messenger Cale. At last this diligent Confederate partisan was fetched into Lexington and locked up in the federal prison.

In jail, as well as out, Old Lady Cobb maintained her determined attitude to help the South. As a youthful sentry, clad in the repulsive blue Yankee uniform, tramped up and down the corridor outside her cell and clicked his heels at the turns, Mrs. Cobb sat patiently by, knitting long gray woolen socks for the Confederacy. She was bringing the gentlest of domestic endeavors into sharp conflict with stern military discipline. Her persistent activities in the behalf of the Confederate Army while confined in a Yankee prison were disconcerting. The officials would release the old rebel only to imprison her again for some other outrageous act against the Union Army. She and her rabid Confederate daughter Kate were finally sent to a military prison in Louisville. There they kept up their knitting of long gray socks, and the clicking of their knitting needles added to the monotonous sounds of the tramping and heel clicking of the handsome sentry. He was a courtly sentry indeed, and even the two rampant southern women, his prisoners, could see that. Soon the rugged wall of bitter intersectional hatred was pierced. The prisoners were in love with their guard. Kate became confused in her own mind as to whether her love for the bonny starred and barred flag of the Confederacy or for the Yankee sentry was greater. Each clicking step of the sentry was a tormenting sound in her ear, and a glance at his face was a vigorous tug at her heartstrings. He was so handsome and fine. He was real, and the Confederacy began to seem so intangible. Kate married the guard, and by the end of the war she and her mother were idolizing Unionists.

There was one serious hitch in the Cobb-Yankee

romance. Back at Shryock's Ferry, Old Man Cobb, his son Joe, and their slave Cale, the dusky messenger of the Confederacy, had not fallen under the congenial and softening influence of the attractive Illinois volunteer. They remained loyal until the bitter end to the southern cause. When Ma and Kate went to live in Illinois, the Cobb family was torn apart. The steadfast Confederate menfolk swore they would be damned if they went to live among the Yankees, even if one of them had become a son-in-law. It took three years to iron out the social kinks and to persuade Father Cobb to sell his farm and move off to Illinois to live.

John Hunt Morgan was once again to call on his old friend Cincinnatus Shryock for aid. Early in July, 1862, Morgan and his hard-riding men galloped across the Kentucky border from Tennessee near Tompkinsville. They were headed toward the Bluegrass. As they advanced up the line, "Lightning George" Ellsworth, the clever telegraph operator, tapped the Louisville and Nashville line at Bear Wallow. Morgan informed the command at Louisville that Murfreesboro, Tennessee, had fallen into the hands of Nathan Bedford Forrest, a thing that actually happened. Then he threw the federal troops at Louisville into a state of confusion by reporting Morgan's menacing raid into Kentucky. Morgan's mounted command rushed northward to Harrodsburg, and then feinted toward Frankfort on the Kentucky River. On the morning of July 4, 1862, the main body of the command was on the Anderson County side of the river at Shryock's Ferry waiting to be passed over. For the second time John Hunt Morgan was seeking the assistance of his old Lexington neighbor.

When Morgan's men arrived at the ferry, however, they found things in a state of turmoil. The Bluegrass was alive with excitement. Ellsworth's telegraphic antics had every central Kentucky town in an uproar. People were afraid that Morgan would raid their communities in a surprise attack. A company of Union troops had rushed down to Shryock's Ferry where they forced Cincinnatus Shryock to knock planks out of the end of the boats and to sink them near the Woodford bank. This he did skillfully, however, for with his knowledge of construction he was able to knock off the planks in such a way as to do the least harm. Within a short time Confederate sympathizers gathered around the mouth of Grier's Creek, and with the aid of the soldiers the boats were put back into operation. The Confederate troops were ferried over the river for their famous raid upon Midway and Cynthiana.

Among the men who crossed over the Kentucky that morning were two characters who stood out above the rest in interest. One of these was solemn-faced George A. Ellsworth, a comic technician who possessed only one talent, that of sending messages on a telegraph instrument which could cause consternation among the receivers. He carried a portable instrument in his saddlebags which he used to keep up with the activities of the Union troops, and to mislead them as to the whereabouts of his commander. It was on this portable instrument that he had tapped out a jocular message to George Prentice that Morgan was on his way to Louisville with four hundred Indians to scalp him. Likewise he chided the Union officers in Louisville, especially the pontifical commander Jeremiah Boyle. He wired Boyle many frivolous messages, greeting him with "Good morning, Jerry," and sending his respects to Mrs. Boyle. When at last Morgan's men were leaving the state, Ellsworth greeted the officious Jerry with his "General Order No. 1":

When an operator is positively informed that the enemy is marching on his station, he will immediately proceed to destroy the telegraphic instruments and all material in his charge. Such instances of carelessness, as were exhibited on the part of the operators at Lebanon, Midway, and Georgetown, will be severely dealt with. By order of G. A. Ellsworth, *General Military Supt. C. S. Telegraphic Dept.*

Young John Shryock, walking among the men that morning at his father's ferry, spotted the second famous character in Morgan's command. He was the British soldier of fortune, St. Leger Greenfel. Greenfel had served with both the British and French armies in Africa, and had come to America in search of excitement and adventure He brought to Morgan's band of galloping Confederates a semblance of military order. It was he who supplied the knowledge of strategy used by the famous cavalry units to strike terror into the hearts of central Kentuckians. Colonel Greenfel impressed the young boy with his military bearing and his odd uniform. "He was about fifty years old," wrote young Shryock, "over six feet tall, as straight as a shingle. He had a large scar on one cheek. As a uniform he wore a grey-colored cape, a red cap without a brim with a red tassel on top. He was very strict with the men, sending them to the guard house, or making them carry a rail for the most trivial offense."

When the command had crossed over the river, Morgan galloped up the hill astride Black Bess at the head of his rowdy men. They were on their way through Midway to Georgetown and on to Cynthiana and the Central of Kentucky Railroad. Morgan wished to cut off Lexington's supply line from Cincinnati and to starve out the Union troops. At Midway, Morgan and Ellsworth perpetrated one of the most amusing hoaxes of the war on the officers at Lexington, Frank-

fort and Louisville. He and his men became so fascinated with their grand telegraphic comedy that they
almost forgot to move on. At Louisville, Jerry Boyle
aroused every mayor within a radius of a hundred and
fifty miles with his idiotic message of Morgan's advance. His report of the number of men in the Confederate command grew with the sending of each
dispatch. Jerry even invaded the sanctity of the White
House on Sunday morning with one of his frantic tele-
grams. He asked that Lincoln order General Don Carlos
Buell to his rescue. At last the president wired General
Halleck, then at Corinth, that "they are having a stam-
pede in Kentucky. Please look to it."

19

Nancy Hanks

THERE is a sort of provincial consciousness about a Bluegrass community which is fascinating. Its proud moments have made deep impressions upon the memories of the local sons, and because of this fact the man on the street can at times make some astounding blunders. A hundred stories of incongruous occurrences could be told about Lexington alone. Perhaps the most amusing of all of these is the persistent tale of that well-meaning group of women visiting in the town who wished to go to the grave of Nancy Hanks and to place some flowers on it out of admiration and respect. These visitors, however, were somewhat more ardent in their ambition to pay tribute to the famous pioneer woman than they had been in the reading of American history and in their search for geographical information. They reasoned, no doubt, that Abraham Lincoln was a Kentuckian. Since his mother died when he was quite young and since Lexington was in Kentucky, her grave must be in Lexington.

It might have been true that these women came to Lexington with the misinformation that the famous grave was near the town. Some ill-informed source might have given them the wrong directions before they started on their sentimental journey. At any rate, this group of patriotic women found themselves in Lexington searching for the grave of Nancy Hanks. They made the mistake of asking a bystander in one of the hotels if he knew where Nancy Hanks's grave was located. "Nancy Hanks's grave? Why, of course. It is," said the obliging local son, "four miles out on the Winchester Pike on Hamburg Place." They could not miss it. If they looked carefully to the right of the road going out, they would see it on the little knoll above the bridge. Thus it was that the party of good ladies gathered up their flowers, and got themselves in the proper frame of mind to stand for one brief moment over the grave of Lincoln's mother.

It was with feelings of deep patriotic emotion, so goes the story, that the Lincoln admirers placed their flowers upon the central grave in the cemetery. But underneath the air of solemnity there arose a tormenting question. Nancy Hanks, it was true, was a somewhat obscure pioneer character in American history. There has always been enough doubt of her origin that Lincoln biographers have seen fit to present a mass of documentary evidence in an effort to straighten out this historical snarl. But even the confusing issues of the legitimacy of Nancy Hanks's birth had never been quite so strange as was the monument over her grave and the weird surroundings. Why, for instance, was the gray stone fence built in the shape of a horseshoe? Why was Lincoln's mother's gravestone crowned by the figure of a horse? And who were the strange people buried about her? Then perhaps it passed through the minds of the visitors that the people of the Bluegrass were just a bit daffy on the subject of horses, and that was the way they paid tribute to their dead.

Back in Lexington, the visitors had their questions answered quickly. They had reverently placed their handsome flowers, not upon the grave of Nancy Hanks Lincoln, the humble pioneer mother, but upon that of the great trotting mare of the nineties. Even yet this fantastic story goes on its ridiculous rounds involving people in its meshes. Thomas R. Underwood, editor of the Lexington *Herald* and secretary of the Kentucky Racing Commission, has been swamped by Lincoln scholars and admirers with letters. At Hialeah Park, the Lexington editor was interviewed by Bryan Field of the New York *Times* sports staff. While they were waiting to begin the broadcast, Mr. Underwood repeated the story of the misplaced flowers and the grave of Nancy Hanks. A few moments later the New York sports writer introduced the Kentuckian to his radio audiences and said that he had just been told an interesting story about Nancy Hanks which could not be repeated over the radio. He meant, of course, that he did not have time to repeat it. But many of his listeners got the notion it was a defamatory yarn, and for the sake of decency it could not be repeated. Letters poured in from Lincoln scholars asking if it could be repeated in writing. They hoped he had uncovered some new evidence on the life of Nancy Hanks. Others lambasted him for defaming President Lincoln's mother. *Hoof Beats,* a trotting horse magazine, accused him of being prejudiced in favor of thoroughbred horses.

Perhaps few of these defenders of the Lincolnian maternal honor had ever heard of her namesake, the famous Kentucky trotter. Nancy Hanks was foaled on the Hart Boswell farm, on the banks of one of the branches of the pleasant Elkhorn. She was trained on William McCreary's adjoining old Kentucky Stock Farm, today called the "Old Kenney Farm." In the early nineties this was one of the most lavishly equipped breeding establishments in the Bluegrass. It had been developed by the impractical Philadelphia actor, Richard Penniston, who had won $400,000 in the Louisiana Lottery. The barns were well equipped; fine hardware adorned the doors and gates; and there was a mile trotting track enclosed behind a picket fence. This was an ideal place for training horses for competition on the regulation tracks of the country.

In 1887 Hart Boswell's favorite mare, Nancy Lee, foaled a filly by Happy Medium. Within a short time Boswell discovered to his disgust that Nancy Lee's bay filly was a pacer, and he disliked pacers. On May 14, 1888, he sent a Negro helper mounted on Nancy Lee over to the Kentucky Stock Farm to deliver the foal, Nancy Hanks, to the Kenney's where he hoped it could be taught to trot.

Ben Kenney took Nancy Hanks in charge, and after much patient work managed to change her gait from pacing to trotting. He put the filly through an elaborate series of tricks which involved shifting the weights of her shoes and placing fence rails across the track to break up the even shuffle of the pacer's feet. The next year at the Harrodsburg Fair, Nancy Hanks made her first start in track competition. Ben Kenney held her, or, in the horseman's vernacular, he "laid her up" for the first heat, and then let her out to win the race in succeeding heats. Immediately Hart Boswell's pacing filly became a promising trotter. As a three-year-old in 1890, she set a track record for the half mile on the Danville track. The next year at Lexington the bay entry trotted a mile in 2:14½. At Pittsburgh a short time later she lowered her record for the mile to 2:14, and on August 13th on the Grand Circuit track at Rochester she trimmed her time down to the fast clip of 2:12¼, and before the season was over was trotting the mile in 2:12.

Nancy Hanks finished the trotting season of 1891 a sporting enigma. She had showed real promise of lowering her track record with additional training. Ben Kenney had made such a reputation driving her that he was given a job training horses in 1890 for Marcus Daley's stock farm in the Bitter Root valley of Montana. His famous charge was sold for $35,000 to J. Malcolm Forbes of Boston. She now faced her mature racing career under the careful training and driving of the veteran Budd Doble. Nancy Hanks opened her record-breaking trotting season at Washington Park in Chicago on August 17, 1892. She was five years old, stood fifteen and a half hands high, and weighed 850 pounds. Her whole muscular system had become so completely coordinated that she trotted around the track in a perfect symphony of motion. Sports writers who watched her in action became highly rhetorical in describing her easy, graceful track form. Doble used the new type ball-bearing, low-wheel sulky which had just come on the market. It weighed sixty-two pounds, and added to the mare's burden was Doble's weight of 150 pounds.

At Washington Park, late in the afternoon of August 17th, Nancy Hanks was competing against her best time of 2:09, made on that track a week before, and the world record of Maud S of 2:08¾. She was out to snatch track-record honors away from the famous Alexander horse from Woodburn Farm on the South Elkhorn that had set the fast pace at Driving Park in Cleveland seventeen years before.

There were ten thousand cheering fans crowded behind the rail at Washington Park on the afternoon when Budd Doble proudly trotted his bay mare up the stretch in the first warming-up exercise. Again he came out in midafternoon to exercise the fast trotter before she was to make a serious effort. On her second journey down the stretch, the large crowd was expectant that perhaps before the sun had set behind the flat country the little bay mare would have set a new world record.

Promptly at five o'clock at the barn entrance the gate to the stables swung open, and Doble again paraded his fast trotter past the cheering stand. At her heels was the faithful Abe Lincoln, brought out to spur Nancy Lee's filly on to a new time record. The weather was fair, and a gentle, cool breeze blew down the stretch from off Lake Michigan. It was an ideal day for a fast-time race.

Twice Budd Doble brought his charge up to the wire before he nodded to starter Frank Walker to send him away to a fast start. When he went under the wire, Doble had Nancy Hanks trotting at a remarkably fast clip. She went past the first quarter post in .31 $\frac{1}{4}$; at the half mile the time was 1.03 $\frac{3}{4}$; she went past the third in 1:36 $\frac{1}{2}$; and came under the wire for a record-breaking mile of 2:07 $\frac{1}{4}$, a second and a half under Maud S's record, made at Driving Park in 1885.

Galloping up behind the fast-trotting Nancy in her furious circuit around the Washington Park oval was the gentle-natured ex-circus horse, Abe Lincoln. Abe was a strange and eccentric animal. He had broken a tradition of long standing among horses by being fond of elephants. Doble bought Abe from the elephant trainer Urban of Forepaugh's Shows. Urban told Doble to hit Abe Lincoln over the head if he failed to behave. The horse was a fine asset with which to urge on a promising trotter because he was a fast runner. He could run the mile in 2:00, and he took the whip without a flare-up of temper. It was to the easygoing Abe that the mare Nancy Hanks owed much of her success.

When Budd Doble sailed under the wire behind Nancy Hanks, there was a moment of breathless silence.

Then somewhere down in the crowd an excited spectator threw his parasol into the air. Then hundreds of coats, hats, canes, and parasols were flying over the heads of the howling mob. Doble's gray coat, cap and bay filly were soon obscured from view. People rushed out on to the track to rub their hands over the flanks of the game little mare. It was a happy day for the fans at Washington Park. That night the president of the park wired the president of Driving Park in Cleveland to pull down the charmed shoe of Maud S, which was nailed over the main entryway because they were nailing one of Nancy Hank's over the main entry of the Chicago track.

Three days after she broke the world's trotting record, Budd Doble drove Nancy Hanks once again over the Washington Park track against time. She was to shave her time of the 17th, but she failed. She trotted under the wire in the good time of 2:09¼, two seconds over her record.

News of Nancy Hanks's record-breaking trotting in Chicago stirred the Bluegrass people. Within two days her name was a household word in Lexington. By that time Overly and Bond, "bottlers of fine whiskey," were running a special box advertisement in the *Kentucky Leader*, listing their fine old "Nancy Hanks Whisky (record 2:07¼)."

On August 31st, Doble had moved Nancy Hanks and Abe Lincoln on to Independence, Iowa, to seek a new crown. At that popular northwestern track he trotted the mare once again against her best Chicago time. The Independence track was a kite, one with slightly diagonal turns. There was a contention among the trotting horse men that a horse could make better time on a kite than on an oval track. This contention, however, seemed not to disturb the successful Doble.

He went through his regular routine of exercising his famous trotter up and down the stretch at 2:30 and at 4:00 P.M. At five he rushed past the judge's stand, followed by Abe Lincoln and a newcomer, Ned Gordon. This was to be Nancy Hanks's supreme effort. On the first trip down the stretch toward the wire, Frank Walker sent the Kentucky mare away to a fast start. She rounded the first quarter post in .30; the half in 1:01; the three-quarters in 1:34; and she finished the mile in 2:05 ¼. Old-timers looked at their watches and shook their heads. Was it true that a trotter had gone past the first quarter in thirty seconds, and had lived to come under the wire in 2:05 ¼? Nancy Hanks had lowered the trotting record again, and had reduced her fast Chicago time by two seconds.

Eight days later in St. Paul the little Elkhorn trotter was again pitted against her best time record. A big crowd had flocked to this popular track from all over the country to see the sensational Kentucky mare go against her two world records in an effort to shave a fraction of a second from the lower of them. Fortunately the late summer weather in the Northwest was ideal for trotting, and late in the afternoon of September 7th, Budd Doble drove past the stand in a warming-up exercise. At the regular time of five o'clock he drove Nancy Hanks around the oval regulation track in the fast time of 2:07, to lower by one-fourth of a second the record for this type of track.

Nancy Hanks's supreme triumph was to come at Terre Haute, Indiana, near the end of the trotting season of 1892. Her fame had spread over the nation, and on the late afternoon of September 28th the rail around the oval track was crowded with trotting fans. A keen spirit of hopefulness ran through the crowd that this was the day on which the world trotting record would be shoved to a new low.

When the famous mare trotted past the stands in both of her warming-up periods, she was greeted by loud, nervous cheers. Later when Frank Walker signaled to Budd Doble that he had made a fair start, Nancy Hanks was going an eighth of a mile in .15½. A deathly hush fell over the crowded stands as Budd Doble's gray jacket was whipped past the first quarter in .31, and the silent emotion of the crowd built up when she went by the half-mile marker in 1.02½. A question was raised in many minds: Could the fast trotter hold her pace? At the three-quarters she had a mark of 1.32½. Down the stretch came the saucy Kentucy mare trotting at a furious pace, with the clumsy Abe Lincoln crowding up close behind. She went under the wire in 2:04. Clockers snapped their watch stops. At last a trotting horse had broken what was believed to be the minimum time of 2:05. This was an important day in trotting horse history.

When the officials announced that the little mare had stormed under the wire, trailed by the singing low-wheel, ball-bearing sulky in the startling time of 2:04 for the mile, there was panic. The air was filled with paraphernalia thrown by excited witnesses. Across the track the starter, Frank Walker, led the fans in three rousing cheers for the famous panting trotter and her calm driver. Men jumped up and down and embraced each other. Strangers grasped strangers by the hands and pumped up and down in hysterical congratulations. Down at the sulky, cheering trotting horse lovers gathered Budd Doble upon their shoulders and galloped up and down before the stands with him. This was a proud moment for the Bluegrass and the Old Kentucky Stock Farm back on the bank of the gentle Elkhorn. Another

Kentucky horse had lowered a world record. Nancy Hanks, like the famous runner, Lexington, had brought honor to the rolling pasture lands north of the Kentucky. It was this world record, "2:04," which the innocent women visitors to Lexington saw when they placed their flowers on the grave of Nancy Hanks.

Nancy Hanks was brought home to live out her life. In the rich pastures of John E. Madden's Hamburg Place, she led a lazy, easy life while several fast-trotting offspring nuzzled her side. Among these were: Admiral Dewey, 2:04½; Lord Roberts, 2:08¼; and Nancy McKerron, 2:10½. The name of Nancy Hanks was to go on in trotting history in the fast records of her colts.

When Nancy Hanks set her fast time record for the mile in Terre Haute, Budd Doble thought he would win the $5,000 Bonner Prize offered to the first horse that would break 2:05. Bonner, however, did much hedging on the question. He claimed that his offer was good only on regulation tracks of the Grand Circuit. He contended that the Terre Haute track was not a regulation one and that his offer was good only on tracks east of Cleveland. Likewise he objected to paying Doble the prize because Nancy Hanks had drawn a ball-bearing sulky instead of the old-style, high-wheeled, plain-spindle cart.

There followed a bitter newspaper controversy over Bonner's failure to pay the prize. By a misunderstanding on the part of a newspaper reporter, General B. F. Tracy, secretary of the navy, was drawn into the dispute. He was misquoted as having said that the time was near at hand when a horse would break two minutes. Many letters arguing this point were published, and General Tracy publicly denied the statement attributed to him. He published the statement that he doubted the time ever would come when a horse would trot a mile in less time than two minutes. There was some slight hint that the general believed it would be impossible for a horse to go at so fast a clip and live. He would have been amazed, I am certain, if he could have known that in the Kentucky Bluegrass in September, 1938, the big gray trotter, Greyhound, foaled at Almahurst Farm, a Kentucky River estate, would set a new world record on the regulation Lexington track of 1:55¼.

20

The Log Run

ADVENTUROUS pioneer huntsmen who visited
the upper Kentucky valley were impressed by the huge
trees thrusting their towering limbs upward. Here, at
last, was truly the land of happy hunting. Trees, magnificent ones, grew everywhere. This was an unspoiled
huntsman's Valhalla. Yarns as tall as the virgin Kentucky poplars were carried back over the mountains.
Yarns of deer as fat and sleek as canebrake hogs, of
bear, elk, fur-bearing animals, and of fish, so it was
said, that actually choked the streams.

There was that old Virginia colonel whose fancy
was overwhelmed by the size and number of Kentucky
trees. He said they grew so close together that a "spare-
built" man could scarcely crowd his way among them.
There was scarcely room for one of these veterans to
fall to the ground if it was cut. Elk? Why, man there
were the finest elk in all the land grazing along the
Kentucky River! Why, they had horns eight and ten
feet in length. Kentucky was the country of promise.
Virginia's scrawny red hills, in the expansive colonel's
eyes, were poverty-stricken by comparison. Jealous bystanders befuddled the colonel when they asked him to
explain the inconsistency between his tale of the tim-

331

ber, and of the prodigious long-horned elk which trod beneath the spreading branches.

The old colonel, in his comic bewilderment, might well have had in mind that rugged hill country which rises abruptly on either side of the Kentucky River. Not so long ago there stood along its banks millions of virgin trees leisurely ripened by time, and unscathed by the wasteful hands of profit-seeking men. Looking down upon the river from their lofty footings were tulip poplars straight and gray with many winters and summers of growth and with girths that were astounding when viewed in terms of a timberman's scaling rod.

Many of these forest patriarchs had boles containing enough lumber to build a half dozen mountain cabins, or several pretentious Bluegrass homes. Boards of beautiful golden heart could be cut wide enough to make a tabletop without a seam that would hold even the most bounteous Kentucky dinner.

Red and white elms, which had never been victimized by the insidious foreign Dutch beetle and blight, rivaled the massive poplars for a position at the head of the forest hierarchy. White sycamores thrust their hardy roots deep into the rocky ledges of the Kentucky and its fledgling tributaries. Their clean white stocky bodies held up long and sinuous arms which, on moonlight nights, gave them the appearance of leafy spirits. The sycamore loved the nourishing caresses of the hurried mountain streams. Perhaps, too, these stately gray trees stood as silent but wise guardians to see that no tributary went on a rampage and choked its bed with the frugal fertility of its neighboring hillsides. Their gnarled roots snatched at every runaway grain of mountain soil to see that none escaped, thereby impoverishing the hills.

Crowding in among the aristocratic sycamores,

leafy elms, and paunchy tulips trees, were oaks, which like mountain families were numerous in variety. Red oaks grew to dizzy heights in an effort to avoid suffocation by leafy neighbors. In growing toward life-giving sun, beautiful slim trunks supported spreading slender branches. When one was impervious to the lure of a virgin forest he reckoned the worth of these rough-barked grandees in terms of thousands of feet of clear flooring for Bluegrass and city mansions. White oaks, post oaks, black oaks, scarlet oaks, and oaks even unto the remote third and fourth botanical cousinhood stood as sturdy company to their proud maroon relation. They, too, were sought out in time by men who loved the forest because they made revenue-producing rafts to float on the Kentucky.

It was not a parsimonious nature which clothed the Kentucky valley. A discerning forester who looked upon the primeval Troublesome cove listed in his catalogue the following trees: black and blue ash, black walnut, chestnut, holly, blackgum, linden, beech, red haw, buckeye, pawpaw, pine, spicewood, sumac, swamp alder, cedar, dogwood, and umbrella, or wahoo.

Here was a land that was breath-taking in its rugged beauty. Steep knoll after knoll—or point after point, as the mountaineer would say—rolled back from the river. Around every bend lay billowing masses of virgin branches.

This was the upper Kentucky River country when the Civil War ended. Everything in the modern Kentucky has an uncanny way of going back to "The War." The history of its vast mountain timber industry is no exception. Down in the Bluegrass lumbermen and cabinetmakers had systematically cut back the huge black walnuts, wild cherry, river bottom tulip, maple, buckeye, linden, and sycamores. Hundreds of fine homes were furnished with native copies of European and English period furniture. Kentucky woods finished beautifully, and a native sideboard in time presented the same mellow effect as its foreign cousin. Level lands, too, were cleared by slave hands for tobacco and hemp or for pastures in which to grow blooded livestock. Timbermen now turned their attention to the rich woodland resources upstream.

In the thirties, millmasters at Frankfort bought a few rafts which were run down by mountainmen. This was the beginning of a business, which after 1865 was to grow into major proportions. Log booms were constructed in the river at Frankfort before the mills, and opposite the "Craw." Mountainmen, home from the war, heard of this market for their logs and built splash dams along their creeks all the way from Beattyville to Manchester. In the fall of 1870 the men along the Laurel Fork of Goose Creek cut and assembled 3,000 fine poplar logs. They were ready to make rafts of a hundred logs each and set out for Frankfort when the heavy "tide" of 1871 sprung the trigger in the dam and a winter's work rushed unbridled downstream to destruction.

From the calamity of 1871 the loggers learned to drift their wooden chattels into booms, or chains of logs, stretched across stream in such a way that they rose and fell with the tide.

Once rafts were formed and headed down Goose Creek they ran fast with the swift current. The rafts— or raaves, as they were called—were about 100 to 120 feet in length, and 10 to 16 feet in width. Mounted fore and aft were long poplar or basket-splint oak poles shaped at the water end into an oar. Running out of the country above and through Goose Creek narrows required five or six men to the raft. One ran as a steersman, and the others as pikers. The rapids, or narrows, were called "Clay County Narrows" between Upper and Lower "Teges," and it was said that this consti- tuted the most treacherous mile of navigable water in the western country. There was a fall of twelve and a half feet within a mile. When a raft sailed into them it took hard fighting on the part of the logmen to bring it through right side up and with its spine in good con- dition. Occasionally a raft ran lopsided into the ripples and turned over, unloading raftmen, tools, and equip- ment. When a raft turned over it sometimes took a luckless piker to a watery grave. The slightest mistake on the part of the steersman resulted in calamity. He had to ride his pole with the tenacity of a mountain- bear dog, and he had to place his craft in just the right spot to make the run. His front end would be riding ten or twelve feet in the air at one moment, and his stern was up the next.

Once through the narrows, the raft was combined with two other units, and a crew of three took these "drifts" to Frankfort. The first day saw the South Forkers through the rapids, the second they were in the main stream at Beattyville, and five days later they rounded the big bend at Frankfort and boomed their logs before the Craw.

Every logman knew that the necessary equipment for his run down with the big tide consisted of a peavy, a sixty-foot cable, a frying pan, an ax, a half dozen hickory linchpins, and two well-oiled forty-fours tied with strong buckskin thongs to his britches top. A log- ger couldn't afford to drop a valuable pistol overboard into the murky Kentucky, nor could he take chances of meeting a feuding enemy unarmed. Too, he had to run the damnable palisades down in the Bluegrass and their gauntlet of rock-throwing hoodlums.

Overleaf: Log rafts ready for delivery to the mills.

Running point by point—Island Creek, Whiteoak, Indian, Cow, Buck, Buffalo, Paw Paw, Ford, Boonesborough, Clay's Ferry, Ravens Bar, Fort Nelson, High Bridge, Clifton, Tyrone and Frankfort—raftsmen had to be alert. If a snag or stone jutted out of the water he had to be quick enough with his clumsy pole to swerve his raft away from danger. Steersmen were master craftsmen, and a good one was at a premium. They had to understand every point on the river, and to know at every moment just where they were. In their own individual way these rugged navigators became well-informed local geographers. They knew to a foot where the numerous county lines touched the river. Rocks, ripples, snags, eddies, bars, and rapids were given special names. Trees even bore names, and many of them stood out against their abrupt backgrounds as friendly sentinels of fair water or as frightening omens of trouble ahead.

In a night run, the steersman turned his oar over to a piker and took the head of the drift to search out the way. Squatting near the water's edge he listened to the wash of the stream against the rocky sides of its bed, and kept his eyes focused on the timber line. All the time he kept up a chatter of instructions to his substitute at the pole. When dark settled down upon the valley, the towering mountain slopes, in league with the goddess of darkness, appeared as walls which tried to crush the disturbers of the calm. So somber were the neighboring ridges that even a keen-eyed steersman was unable to pick out a friendly landmark.

It was always better policy to tie up for the night and to secure lodging at a neighboring farmhouse. Kentucky River farmhouses above Clay's Ferry have never been commodious structures. Characteristic of these modest buildings are the small double houses with rooms

on either end, a lean-to across the back, and an obliging trot for the dog through the middle. The family
occupied one end, the stove and table were in the shed,
and the other room was available to loggers.

Sometimes the rafting bullies beached their drifts
near a farmhouse where the landlord refused to provide them with floor space, hot biscuits, and coffee.
When this happened it was woe unto the landlord, for
the logmen pushed in and spent the night whether they
were wanted or not. They were determined men, and
they were also of the opinion to the point of backing
it up with a forty-four, that no man-beast should be
made to spend the night outside.

Wrestling with stubborn rafts during the day
worked up considerable appetite; in fact, it was said the
rivermen could eat a crowbar with a sauce of wire
staples and digest it. When a landlady undertook to
cook for thirty or forty voracious upriver tigers she
made an all-night affair of it. Hot flat biscuits, fried
meat, and white gravy disappeared in gulps. Steaming
mugs of black coffee, and frequently hefty swigs of
potent corn liquor of domestic manufacture, enlivened
the weary upriver rowdies. Many a capacious raftsman
wore a coat with huge pockets which he stuffed with
biscuits and meat for the next day's travel.

Eating was the main reason for a raftsman's living.
However, he presented a bit of comedy at times. At
High Bridge a landlady had an old-fashioned table with
a revolving center, and logmen would stop and eat with
her just to get to spin this table. The table was the butt
of many a ribald joke upstream. There were others who
took the business of eating even more seriously. A bystander recalls seeing a mountaineer swagger into a
riverside restaurant at Jackson, order a cup of coffee,

measure out a single handful of sugar, and then stir it with the barrel of his forty-four.

Piled on the floor, dressed in their heavy sweaty clothes and boots, thirty logmen created a veritable bedlam with their thunderous snoring. Few knew or cared, once they had stretched their stiffened limbs upon the floor, whether they slept on a mattress or not. It is a matter of amazement today to come on a shanty and have its owner reminisce that "many's the times I've had forty loggers piled up in them two rooms for the night."

The rafts came down during five of the twelve months. Most of the time one strong tide ran in November, and summer logs were drifted down on it. It was not until the spring tides, however, in February, March, April, and May, that the big runs were made. February was fair, but the weather was terribly cold. March was a little better, but April was the main month. Wise loggers knew, when the snowballs were in bloom and the blackberry briers had put up rabbit ears of green, that the tides were right. Overanxious timbermen usually left with their winter's cut on the February run. This was the trip which tried the mettle of the men. Footing aboard the rafts was at best uncertain, and when the logs were coated with ice it was practically impossible to stand up, except on the salted end logs at the stern and prow. Once logmen notched their timber to ensure safe footing, but this process lowered the value of the logs. "Blowey Jim" Bishop, a hardy old-timer, recalls that he ran to Frankfort on an early tide and was caught in a blue "dominecker" snow which chilled the crew of three drifts to the marrow. Jim became exhausted and lay down to take a nap under his oilskin slicker, but at three o'clock in the morning he awoke to find that he was sealed in by the ice.

Thousands of rafts were caught in the ice jams, and frantic owners and raftsmen stood by to see their precious timber crushed and ground to pulp by the demoniac fury of the river in its effort to shake off the icy paralysis which settled upon it. At no other time during the year did the Kentucky River impress more indelibly upon the natives the fact that it was powerful. It reared and pitched, drifted and flooded, groaned and tore to pieces unfortunate boats and rafts embroiled in its labors.

A cold night in February, such as that of February 13, 1905, and the downriver papers carried pitying accounts of destruction. Marse Henry Watterson's *Courier-Journal* newsmen sympathetically recorded this fact:

The heaviest loss by the ice gorge will fall upon the log men of the extreme mountain counties, whose timber has been lying for two years in the valleys waiting for a tide. These men have no other way to earn a living, and with their timber buried in the rivers, their entire labor of three years past has been swept away.

When the winters were mild and the coves were filled with fog, old-timers knew that the Kentucky would flood. So accurate were most of the weather prophets who lived close to the stream that they could foretell not only an approaching tide to within a few hours, but likewise its probable stage. This was a business, the exactness of which meant the difference between a livelihood and a meager living. If a tide caught a timberman napping, he was ruined.

Old Bill Peters, veteran Island Creek logger, spent a fall and winter "banking" three hundred fine poplar logs. When the spring tide came Bill would "drift" three rafts together and float away to Frankfort to find a purchaser. Bill missed a guess, however, on the change of the weather and was awakened one dreary February morning to find the South Fork of the Kentucky spread out like a highland biscuit. His log boom was gone! Four skinned poplar logs lingered on the water's edge to mock him. A winter's work had silently drifted away on the tide. If it was to be ruination, philosophized the stunned raftsman, then it should be complete. He rolled the four remaining logs into the current and watched sardonically until the last chocolate butt drifted out of sight.

Bill Peters was not alone in his heartbreaking loss. Timbermen up nearly every creek and along all three main forks lost thousands of precious logs in 1915. The river went on a rampage in March, and overnight there was a twenty-foot rise. Logs by the thousands rushed into the main stream. Booms at Jackson and Beatty-ville were spread to trap runaway timber. At Jackson preachers, lawyers, doctors, bankers, and businessmen mounted log booms with spike pole and helped to herd the runaway timber. As the tide rose, logs rushed by Jackson at the rate of 15,000 per hour—potentially enough lumber to build a town.

When a log went wild many things could happen to it. If it was an oak, beech, hemlock, or hickory its fate was liable to be a sad one. Once the rioting waters of the Kentucky had thoroughly penetrated its pores it sank to an ignominious grave in river-borne muck. Poplar, chestnut, walnut, buckeye, and basswood stood a reasonable chance of being captured by timber thieves who waited along the banks to pounce upon strays. These river hijackers snared and beached stray logs, and dehorned them of their end brands. It was an easy matter to dehorn a log when the brands were near the end. Each year dozens of rafts appeared in Frank-

afted logs moving down the river near Frankfort.

fort as the property of the river banditti. Log stealing became a real menace on the river, until "side brands" were deeply implanted and raftsmen with badly scarred logs became suspect.

Through blue dominecker snows, around snags, through ripples and around one angular bend after another, through freezes and floods, thousands of roistering log-running bullies arrived in Frankfort. Sweeping down beneath the towering palisades from Clay's Ferry to the Cemetery Hill in Frankfort, the rafters carried on a continuous warfare with the Bluegrass folk.

Just who started this eternal strife is, at best, a matter of conjecture. Riding the rafts were drunken rowdies who had patronized frequently the john-boat liquor salesman down from Beattyville. Their last four days had been lived close to hell and they were ready for a fight or a frolic. Like those rambunctious Kentuckians of an earlier day who made a shambles of Natchez-under-the-Hill, the hillmen were ready for any eventuality.

Many old loggers recall the hazardous passage underneath the steep palisades. Someone dropped a stone on Dan Parker's raft and it barely missed two oarsmen. Another raft floated silently under the covered bridge at Fort Nelson. The crew was cooking dinner, and just as the frying pan passed under the bridge someone dropped a rock squarely into it. This was too much. The mountainmen literally studded the sides of the bridge with bullets.

At High Bridge an innocent raftsman was hit in the shoulder and crippled by a malicious rock-hurling native. Partners of the crippled man beached their raft, and one of them went back and emptied his pistol into the culprit and escaped without detection or arrest. Fear of these rock throwers partly explained the gun toting of the logmen.

From High Bridge to Frankfort was a comparatively short distance. As the rafts cleared Horse Shoe Bend the capital city hove in sight. There was a large boom in which rafts could at last be deposited to await consumption by the sawmills. The long journey from the mountains was ended, but before the return trip there was much carousing to be done. Down in the Craw logmen could forget their trials and tribulations and give themselves over to at least one night of complete debauchery. Away from the mountains and their families they could enjoy complete freedom. A good place to start was either Salander's saloon or Jim Jenning's "Last Chance." Maybe a copper-lined moonshine lover could stand enough "factory-made" whisky to patronize both places. From Salander and Jenning's the logger wandered deeper into the Craw section, which clung to the famous river cliff like a half-drowned animal. Here, behind the staid and dignified Greek Revival capitol building, was all the wickedness of the Biblical twin cities in concentrated form.

Sometimes hundreds of mountain logmen tramped the streets of Lexington, and a majority of them would find their way to the famous dens of the town. Here was the one community in the Bluegrass where the welcome sign hung out in earnest to the upcountrymen. Only one place on the hill frowned upon such trade, and that was the three-story palace of assignation watched over by the snobbish Madame Belle Breazing. No hobnailed steersman or rough piker was welcomed within the famous octagonal hall with its fine novelty horn chairs and stately gilt-frame mirrors. Such privileges were reserved for a gentlemanly carriage clientele.

From Lexington the returning logmen divided into

two parties. Northern and Middle Forkers went home by way of Winchester. The South and Main Forkers went by Richmond. At Richmond most of the men bade farewell to the wicked delights of the "outside" by taking a final fling in the dives of Irvine Street.

Richmond was the jumping-off place for the return home. For years most of the men who unloaded in this place walked the rest of the way. From here it was a long and arduous journey overland.

Many South Forkers who came from near Manchester went to London on the Louisville and Nashville trains. Their travel manners were no more refined than those of the hoard which drifted eastward through Lexington, Winchester, and Richmond. They antagonized people all along the road by shooting at everything in sight. At Junction City the tension ran high between the citizens and the logmen. Especially was this true when there were colored men in the crowd. On one trip the white men had boarded the train when the citizens of the village started an attack on the Negro raftsmen. In a moment the train was unloaded and rivermen proceeded to shoot it out with the local citizens. But generally the raftsmen were peaceably inclined toward each other. There was some fairly good-natured rivalry between the men from the various creeks and forks, but remarkably few fights.

There were other famous characters along the river whose names have almost become legend. There was that unimaginative gentleman from Buckhorn Creek who struggled bravely through life under the name of William Nathan Decipitation Tyro Jefferson Heser Ceser Honeysucker Noble—later abbreviated to Honeysucker. On one occasion the sweetly named bumpkin was beset by a determined "hell-fire," Irish, Hard-Shell Baptist preacher. Brother Noble had been wicked in his ways, there was no denying the fact. Finally he broke down and came through with a "big red" case of religion. In his testimony to the congregation, however, he showed infinitely more knowledge and interest in the Kentucky River and the log trade than in heaven. When Brother O'Barn asked if he wished to live in the church he said, "No, sir, I live on Buckhorn and don't want to move." Honeysucker was then asked if he had traveled from "nature to grace," to which he replied he had been down the Kentucky River to High Bridge and Frankfort.

Dan Parker, a lanky mountaineer, who in a cowtown would pass for an old top hand, spent many days steering rafts. Dan was considered one of the best steersmen ever to spin a raft before the Craw. Today he sits under a bare hillside, and looks longingly at a river that is placid one moment and a raging torrent the next.

"Turkleneck" Eversole, Dan Parker's old buddy, is still on the river. He has a houseboat, and watches over an assortment of barges and worn-out steamboats. Turkleneck's rafting history was one of a superman, but when he rode the last raft down years ago, he settled in the Craw and he and his wife raised too many children for an old man to count. Old Turkleneck will never forget the glories of the river and its raftsmen. No longer can he relax in the Craw because the efficient Frankfort police force insist upon interfering with his memorial plans in honor of the old run. He has spent a lot of time just "setting and looking at Frankfort" from the vantage point of the city jail. Only once since the last rafts came down has the old long-necked raftsman been himself, and that was in the flood of 1937. When the Kentucky went wild and tried to drown Frankfort, he was a hero. The old riverman understood the stream. Something about its ungoverned surging about the city streets offered a challenge. With an oar and skiff, Turkle rescued an army of frantic dry-land citizens and delivered them to high ground.

At Beattyville, high on a rocky ledge overlooking the river, Blowey Jim Bishop dreams away much of the time. Jim was a sturdy raftsman with an uncommon amount of sense. Neighbors say he saved his money. At any rate, he has been to Florida to spend the winters. He loves to recall the old "run" to Frankfort, and none can remember as much of its human history as he.

But the log run is history. Scores of old raftsmen who spend most of their days thumping time to lonesome tunes on the lower rungs of their tilted chairs are more nearly historical documents than human beings. Kentucky hills are bare, the river is muddy, and a green-poplar log-scaling 300-foot board measure is a museum piece. Occasionally salvagers dig up huge logs from the river bed, but this is not a part of the lusty history of the rafts and their hard-driving crews.

The machine age of the New South came at last to the Kentucky River valley, and the sawmills moved upstream to meet the log run. The first mills were built at Valley View, then Ford, and finally, the big mills at Jackson halted the run at that place on the North Fork. Too, the government built locks and dams in the river, and these interfered with the drifts.

21

Moonshiners

A HISTORY of the Kentucky River without an account of moonshining would be like considering the river without the water flowing within its banks. Moonshining has been a major industry up and down the tiny branches which trickle along to pour their floodwaters into the big stream.

The upriver country is ideally adapted to the making of illegal whisky. A perfect maze of deep ravines, watered by flush spring branches, make it a simple matter to hide away from the prying eyes of revenue officials. Near-by mountain cornfields supply much of the basic grain needed for distilling purposes. Too, from the very beginning of highland settlement there have been rugged Scotch, German, and Irish settlers in the country whose taste for whisky was as robust as the terrain in which they lived. Fancy factory-made liquor never has been exciting to the primitive American taste. In the beginning the business of supplying this taste was as legitimate as making soap or maple sugar. Distilling was a community enterprise, in which experienced distillers converted the neighborhood grain into liquor on shares. But with the formation of the United States government the whole situation changed. One of Alexander Hamilton's earliest tax recommendations to Congress

349

was that an excise tax be levied on distilled spirits. News of this reached Kentucky, and soon revenue agents invaded the western country to see that the law was obeyed.

At Lexington in March, 1792, a dignified Virginia gentleman visited John Bradford's print shop. He was Thomas Marshall, father of the future chief justice of the United States Supreme Court. Colonel Marshall had come west to live in Kentucky, and he was given the job of state federal inspector of revenue. It was he who was entrusted with the ticklish responsibility of enforcing the new tax laws pertaining to the distillation and sale of bourbon whisky. He perhaps did not understand that his journey to John Bradford's little print shop that morning was to begin the century and a half fight which has raged between the unregistered and unlicensed distillers and the revenue officers. His notice which appeared in the *Kentucky Gazette* for March 17, 1792, told the distillers that the federal government was determined to collect the taxes on distilled liquors. A rumor had been afloat among the distillers that they would not have to pay the tax, but Colonel Marshall's notice distinctly contradicted this belief.

From 1775 to 1792 Kentucky corn and small-grain fields produced huge quantities of excellent grain, but there was no market for these raw products. Demands for bread were quickly supplied, but vast quantities of grain remained in the cribs or in shocks in the fields. To ship this unprocessed surplus grain overland to the Atlantic seaboard was out of the question. A horse could not carry enough corn to feed himself during the journey, let alone to make a profit. A bushel of corn was worth about fifty cents; a gallon of whisky was worth from one to two dollars; and a bushel of good plump mature grain yielded three to five gallons of prime whisky. Thus it was that the Kentucky whisky business began. There was little doubt but what good Kentucky whisky could be sold even if it was extremely difficult to sell corn, wheat, and fruit. This condition gave rise to the belief that only whisky and ginseng would pay their way to an overland market.

When the Mississippi River was at last opened to Kentucky traders, their boats were loaded with charred oak kegs filled with red bourbon whisky. Southerners and Easterners along the seaboard became fond of the creamy-smooth liquors which came from the small Kentucky stills. Limestone water (in the day before commercial distillers began using distilled water) was an important factor in the production of Kentucky whisky. The name of Kentucky was closely identified with the business of distilling, and within a short time "Kentucky" whisky became a prime article in trade. Even in New Orleans, where a large portion of the population was foreign, Kentucky farmers found ready buyers for production from their stills.

Kentuckians themselves liked the thin white fluid which trickled through their thumping kegs and worms. As they descended the upper Kentucky valley through the mountain passes or as they followed the river eastward upstream they took their stills with them. It was easy to conceal the small domestic manufacturing plant so that it would not be too conspicuous to curious visitors in the community. Federal agents, however, were impetuous souls, and they came searching into ravines and secluded spots. They had a special ability for ferreting out both illicit stills and their owners. Red bourbon whisky distillers, in contrast, paid their taxes to Colonel Marshall and his deputies, and they built many of their businesses to large proportions. Many of the small farm-owned and operated plants became foundation stones

for huge commercial distilleries. Those distillers who refused to pay their taxes resented interference from the
federal government. Making whisky was an easy means
of solving transportation problems, and at the same time
of boosting meager standards of living.

Wildcat stills appeared all along the river. Colonel Marshall and his deputies met with resistance
on every hand. He was burned in effigy by irate
moonshiners. The bootleggers were turning out thousands of gallons of whisky, and the problem of finding
them was a complicated one. No revenue man in all
the history of moonshining in Kentucky has ever believed the business could be destroyed. At best they have
hoped to curb the practice as much as possible, and to
give themselves a nuisance value.

As the moonshiners pushed their surreptitious business up the river valley, jokes began to be fabricated
round the making and drinking of raw corn liquor.
An old story has gone the rounds for more than a half
century of the neighborly Kentucky River mountaineer who shared moonshine with a poorer neighbor.
He gave his neighbor three gallons of "lightning," and
in a couple of days he was being asked for more. The
neighbor explained the rapid consumption of the liquor
by the fact that his family was a large one of growing
children and that he did not own a milk cow. A salty
philosopher has popularized drinking of illicit corn
liquor in his observation that the Kentucky mountaineer
"Shunneth water as a mad dog, and drinketh much bad
whisky," and that he "Goeth forth on a journey half-
shot and cometh back on a shutter full of shot. . . .
He goeth forth in joy and gladness and cometh back in
scraps and fragments." Kentuckians have long been embarrassed by the old story that all of them, especially
those from the mountains, drink from jugs thrown over

their left shoulders or, worse, the story told by so many imaginative after-dinner speakers that it has long ago become threadbare. It is said that a stranger went into the mountains to see one of the native sons, and when he arrived at the mountaineer's cabin he asked a little boy where he could find his father. With some hesitation the boy explained that he was up the ravine, and the stranger tempted the child with a petty bribe to lead him to the old man. The boy agreed, but asked that he be paid in advance; the stranger demurred, saying that he would pay when he came back. The boy, however, made known the awful truth that the visitor wasn't coming back. All these stories, coupled with many comic poems and "hillbilly" songs, have given the Appalachians of Kentucky a fantastic reputation.

As with the manufacture of "red," the making of good sugar-top liquor requires a deft hand, if not a modern mechanical setup. An experienced mountain moonshiner, with a keen sense of humor, has contributed this recipe. "Making Whiskey, Good Old Sugar Top" he calls it. Step by step he outlines the process of extracting "good old sugar top" from corn meal and sugar:

First thing to do is to get the things that you use which is the following: (a) the tank, cap, arm, staff, thumping keg, connector, flake stand, worm and barrels. (b) Things to use for the mash, meal, sugar and malt corn. These to be used in the proportions of one bushel of corn meal, one peck of corn sprouts, twelve pounds of sugar, water to cover. (c) How to mash the stuff. Cook the meal, then put it in the barrels, let the meal cool down. Put the sugar and malt corn in the meal, cover it over good and it will start to work. (d) How to put the things togeather [sic]. Build the tank in a furnice [sic], let the furnice come about half up the tank. Put the cap on top of the tank. The arm joins the cap, goes to the staff, the staff goes in the thumping keg. The connector goes from the thumping keg to the worm, the worm goes from the connector down the flake stand and part of the worm sticks out through a hole about six inches from the bottom. Water is used in the flake stand to chill the steam. (e) When the beer is ready to be boiled, exchange the beer from barrels into the tank then build a fire in the furnice. Heat the beer until it is nearly to a boiling point. (f) How the whiskey gets through these parts. When the beer starts up the cap through the arm down the staff into the thumping keg there is double boiled, then the steam starts on through the connector to the worm, when it hits the worm it is chilled down to a liquid by the water around the worm in the flake stand. The first is called alcohol as it boils it gets weaker when it gets too weak to bead [form air bubbles] you start catching what is called backings to weaken the alcohol down to good high whiskey. Then the whiskey is made. There you are ready for a big drunk and a good time ho ho.

The old fight between the revenue officers and the moonshiners, except they now make liquor in the day-time, has gone on for a long time. Federal revenue men have been diligent in their search for unlicensed stills, and moonshiners have tried to hide their activities from the inquisitive raiders. None has ever been more famous than Colonel J. W. Colyer, deputy collector of internal revenue from the Lexington office. Colonel Colyer was one of those shrewd woodsmen who could look at a ravine and tell if it sheltered a wildcat distillery. He kept the daily newspapers filled with accounts of his raiding activities. At times he reported as many as three large stills captured in a single day. Perhaps his most famous capture was that of bad "Red Bob" Baker on Laurel Fork of Buffalo Creek in Owsley County. For thirty years Red Bob had escaped capture, and he had become the most famous distiller in all eastern Kentucky. Red Bob's business was no fly-by-night affair which moved just one frantic step ahead of the raiders. It had a stone pen for the mash barrels, and a rough covered stillhouse. Colonel Colyer and his men called on the old red-bearded lawbreaker in May, 1897. They arrived at a time when the Laurel Fork was dressed out in its gayest spring foliage. It seemed that all the world, including Bob Baker, was happy. His mash was working perfectly without artificial stimulation in the fine weather. Bob was in his stillhouse stirring beer. The fire was burning slowly under the still, and the low gurgling thump, thump, of the thumping keg indicated that all was well. Perhaps Red Bob had lapsed into an idyllic daydream; at any rate, he neither saw nor heard the approach of Colonel Colyer, who now stood between him and his old Springfield rifle whose barrel was rammed half full of powder and iron slugs. Gently the courtly colonel from down in the Bluegrass said, "Hello, Bob, what are you doing here?" Never in all of old Red Bob's adventurous life had he been so taken by surprise. He whirled around and shouted in panic, "What are *you* doing here?" He knew the answer. Colonel Colyer's large-bore pistol appeared as a huge cavern of destruction before the old mountaineer's face. After thirty peaceful years in which the rusty Springfield had leaned against the doorjamb ready for immediate action, Red Bob Baker was vanquished at last.

In recent years, the Kentucky legislature has added woes to the moonshiners' lot. Not only are they now pursued by the federal "revenoors," but likewise by the state tax men. State revenue men, for the most part, are shrewd native sons who have graduated from college. They work methodically to curb the moonshine business in Kentucky. Unfortunately for the 'shiners, the state men are somewhat in rivalry with the federal agents, with unhappy results for the revenue blockaders. Their liability of capture has increased enormously. In nine days of 1941 active state agents chopped to pieces seventeen stills, broke up an impressive number of glass jugs, and poured several thousand gallons of ripe mash into muddy spring branches. The federal agents claimed 441 stills for the fiscal year 1940-1941.

A single day in the raider's life is interesting and exciting enough to be recorded here. On the day of a raid, the agents are up early and dressed in coarse clothes and heavy shoes, for their duties carry them into rugged hill country. Secretly they wonder if today might be the one on which a 30-30 rifle will dig a brutal channel across a shoulder, or maim an arm, or perhaps . . . After a drive by automobile through the Bluegrass across the Kentucky River and eastward up the south-side ridges, there appears a long chain of steep ridges, gray with the morning light. The road over which the car bumps is a crude, unimproved dirt road which dips its way several times across a winding creek. On either side log and frame cabins begin to show up at the foot of bare gutted hillside cornfields. People crowd their noses against windowpanes and stare at the strangers. Frightened children rush into their ramshackle cabin homes to report the presence of strangers. They know who the strangers are. From the cradle some highland youngsters have a seventh sense regarding the identity of revenue agents.

At the country store a homemade billboard lists its major commodities for sale as corn meal, rye, yeast and sugar. Here is the supplier who caters to the illicit still operators of the neighborhood. Revenue men know, of course, that this is a part of the moonshine business, but under the law they are powerless to stop the trade, except that the federal government requires the merchant to report abnormally large sales of sugar, meal and rye. Mountaineers do eat sugar and corn meal, but seldom do they buy rye and yeast.

Over the hill beyond a portable sawmill is a heavily wooded hollow; halfway down the opposite slope is a pond of stagnant water; and beyond, perhaps, is a still. The revenuers tramp over the ridge in Indian file. A dog barks at a cabin, and each agent can sense the stares boring into his back as he passes into the woods above the house. Across the ridge, the raiders begin looking for telltale trails; they sniff the air for mash odors. On the point opposite the ridge an agent holds up his hand, and the cautious move down the hill begins; but it is all in vain, the still has been "pulled." A pile of devitalized rye is all that remains. At the foot of the hill, however, is a maze of foot trails. One oily trace turns abruptly across the branch and leads up the ravine. The raiders are alert; the signs are right; they hurry quietly along the trail; and a hundred yards up the ravine there it is. A dirty greasy soot-stained still sits across the trail, and above it the branch is dammed to catch the flow of clear cold spring water.

Back down the trail at Copper Creek the main trunk path leads downstream. A hundred yards away a second lateral leads off to the left, and again the revenue officers prepare for action, but it is the same story over again. Another still blocks the path, and another pool of clear spring water is collected near by. Down at the point where the trail emerges from the woods and skirts a dormant cornfield, another lateral leads off, this time to the right, and two hundred yards away is a third still.

At each stillsite are six barrels of fermenting rye, capped rusty oil-drum cookers, thumping kegs, and oil-drum flake barrels. The worms are missing. These expensive bits of equipment are too precious to have chopped to pieces by revenue men. Good whisky is made on copper stills, but times are hard, whisky is cheap, and revenue men are too diligent to invest a meager supply of capital in copper boilers. Only the worms are of copper. Half-inch copper plumbing pipes are bought from plumbing supply stores or from mail-order houses who can supply sixty-foot coils for approximately $8. Where the pipe comes in straight rigid length, it is filled with sand and wound around a post to make a spiral worm.

Other equipment used in setting up a moonshine still is expensive in proportion to the moonshiners' ability to pay for it. At least six charred oak barrels discarded from legitimate whisky warehouses are needed, and these cost a dollar each. Two used oil drums, one for a cooker and the other for a flake barrel, are necessary. A two-gallon oak keg makes a thumper, and an assortment of tin pans, a short link of rubber hose for bottling purposes, a zinc washtub, a square-sawed length of tree trunk, and a collection of glass jugs and self-sealing fruit jars complete the equipment.

Mash barrels are placed, usually, in batteries of three or four. In the wintertime they are buried underground in beds of straw with dirt tamped tightly about them in order to keep them from getting chilled, which would stop fermentation. In the summer the barrels are placed in log cribs in batteries above the ground. In each barrel is poured a bushel of rye (if the whisky is to be a rye distillate), fifty pounds of sugar, and a small quantity of yeast. Approximately the same proportions of corn meal, corn sprouts, and sugar are necessary to make corn "sugar top." Some Kentucky moonshiners cheapen their brew by using laying mash,

A Kentucky River moonshine still and its proprietors and staff. At the peak of the distilling ade in the Kentucky mountains, illegal manufacture of whisky became a way of life.

flavored with concentrated lye, soap, or chewing tobacco. A part of a cake of soap will build up a bead in the whisky, and this is the only test that the purchaser has that the liquor is of high proof.

Three stills in one day is a nice piece of work from the standpoint of law enforcement, but it means physical drudgery for the leg-weary raiders. They have to dig the mash barrels out of the ground, dump their fermenting contents, and cut the steel hoops and smash the staves into a pile of kindling wood. An ax blade is thrust into the metal drums, the jars and jugs are smashed, and the thumping keg is pounded to pieces. The revenuer's work is complete, the moonshiner can salvage nothing. Sounds of raiders pounding away on a steel flake drum ring out down the valley as a sort of ominous warning. Cabin doors are closed tightly. A mountaineer comes by driving his cows home from the woods. On the hillside above him the revenue officers stand over his still, but he looks straight at the ground. For once the hillman curbs his rural curiosity to know who the strangers are. He knows already. In fact, his family has known who they were for several generations back.

At the foot of the hollow are a two-room clay-chinked log cabin and a T-shaped flimsy boxed house. These are the homes of the 'shiners. Above these cabins is a bare hillside where corn was grown the year before, and where a part of the ground is broken for another crop. Underneath a pile of sweetgum brush at the edge of this field is a cache of sixteen gallon jugs and across the fence under a pile of leaves are ten more. These are the containers for the liquor that was to come from the ripe mash which bubbled away when the raiders arrived at the stills up the creek. The sound of crashing glass brings an old lady to the door with a pan in her hands to feed her chickens. Twenty-six times she hears the crashing of glass against glass, and each time she knows it has cost her family another precious dime.

At last the valley is quiet. The wretched occupants of the mud-chinked cabin and of the boxed house know what has happened; their stills are ruined. Each barrel of mash cost at least $5 in money and long hours of hard, careful labor. Again they will have to secure steel oil drums, small kegs, and batteries of discarded liquor barrels and start all over.

The revenue agents recross the hill, dirty and smelling loudly of fermenting mash. As they appear in silhouette on the rim of the woods, a group of mountaineers looks up and sees them and melts away in an instant. In the distance a rickety car starts and labors at full speed. At a country store down the road, a curious woman proprietor makes the ironic observation to the state director of alcoholic taxes, as he munches a cheese and cracker sandwich, "When I seen you fellows go up this morning, I thought you was Sunday-school workers."

22

Politics, Kentucky Style

J
UDGE JAMES H. MULLIGAN published his famous poem, "In Kentucky," [1] in the Lexington *Herald* on February 12, 1902, after he had read it at a banquet in the Phoenix Hotel. It was a fine bit of comic verse which wound up on the sober note: "And politics the damnedest, In Kentucky." In this poem, in which the genial Irish poet sizes up Kentucky in comic verse, the reader is introduced to more of the state than he realizes. It has been repeated thousands of times, and the postcards which bear it have been mailed all over the world. Its final sober line referred partly to recent happenings in Kentucky's political history. No one in Kentucky realized more than did Judge Mulligan that his state had passed through a horrible political ordeal only two years before. His famous concluding line had

[1] After extolling Kentucky's virtues and sins Colonel Mulligan concluded his famous poem:

> The song birds are the sweetest
> In Kentucky;
> The thoroughbreds are fleetest
> In Kentucky;
> Mountains tower proudest,
> Thunder peals the loudest,
> The landscape is the grandest,
> And politics the damnedest,
> In Kentucky.

something of bitter condemnation in it, even though it did come at the end of a jolly poetic satire.

Judge Mulligan was thinking back to that trying day, January 30, 1900, in Frankfort when William Goebel was shot as he and two of his friends approached the legislative office building. There before the famous old classic capitol building with its stately white columns, William Goebel slumped to the ground. An assassin, hidden in the secretary of state's office, had shot him through the chest with a high-powered Marlin rifle.

William Goebel was born of German parents in Pennsylvania. His family moved out to Kentucky in his early youth. Young William became a pupil of the shrewd northern Kentucky politician, John G. Carlisle. It was in Carlisle's office that he learned about both the law and practical politics. Before Goebel had been in Covington long he became an active figure in local politics, and from the local political melee he went to the state senate at Frankfort. When a new constitutional convention was called in 1890, William Goebel was there to represent his county in the framing of a fundamental rule of government for Kentucky. Quickly the young German lawyer became a political leader. He had a burning ambition to become the leader of the Democratic party in Kentucky, and for the next nine years of his life he made careful plans to achieve this end. Goebel, like all other southern demagogues, assumed the role of friend of all downtrodden Kentuckians. He fought the schoolbook companies, the Louisville and Nashville Railroad Company, and anyone else who stood between him and the realization of his personal ambitions.

In 1900 Goebel had fought a vigorous fight in the campaign for the governorship. A few months before his death he had declared to a convention of Democrats: "Mr. Chairman and fellow Democrats; I never got anything in my life that was worth having without a hard fight, and I am always willing to make the best fight I can for anything I believe worth having. I believe the governorship of Kentucky is worth fighting for; and with that purpose in mind I shall now open the campaign and fight for the principles of the Democratic party and the governorship of Kentucky from this day until the November election." His speech rang with militant phrases. The Covington politician had the knife in his teeth. Opening his famous campaign at Bowling Green, Goebel shouted to his opponents, "I ask no quarter, and I fear no foe." Goebel was out to defend his record as a legislator, to protect his political friends, and to guarantee political justice of the "common man" in Kentucky. His opponents were the "solid gold Democrats," the Louisville and Nashville Railroad, and William S. Taylor, the Republican nominee.

Kentuckians were used to hot political campaigns, but that of 1900 was an evil one. Political observers knew there would be serious trouble because there were too many divergent forces set viciously against each other. There was no humor in the campaign. Men's tempers grew short, and ill-tempered partisans went armed, ready for any emergency. Unlike Kentuckians who had campaigned up and down the state from the famous "Big Sandy to Mill's Point" in former years, there were no pleasant high flights of saccharine oratory. Their words were not of the beauties of nature, of the town; likewise, there were no sweet innuendoes about "Kentucky's fairest." Nor was there any clever and witty repartee. The speakers talked in embittered terms of fighting, stealing, robbing, and stuffing ballot boxes. When the campaign was over and the votes had been counted, the shaggy-browed, mustachioed southern Kentucky Republican William S. Taylor was declared elected by the hand-picked Goebel election board.

When it became known that Taylor was to be governor, charges of corruption came thick and fast. Some ingenious Goebel follower made the ludicrous charge that many of the Republican counties in the mountains had used "tissue paper" ballots. It was said that the ballot boxes were stuffed by unscrupulous people who gave the names of trees, names of fictional heroes, or names from the headstones in community graveyards. Up the Kentucky, the voters were in a state of rebellion. Trains came roaring west, down along the river, loaded with mountaineers on their way to Frankfort armed with pistols, rifles, and whisky to seek justice. One of Marse Henry Watterson's *Courier-Journal* reporters said that men were allowed to present pistols in lieu of tickets to the conductors. For several days prior to that cold January 30th that strip of land which nestles in the big bend at Frankfort became a battleground over which irate voters stamped their way. The governor was flanked by troops, and the state buildings were under semimilitary surveillance. Bars and beer parlors were crowded with drinking and armed voters. Republicans and Democrats were literally drawn up in battle array. Then Goebel was shot!

The cry "They have killed Goebel!" spread through Kentucky like wildfire. Up the river at the Pan Bowl the Hargis clan was on a fighting edge. Likewise on the South Fork, Republicans were in a rebellious state of mind. Mountainmen who had gone piling down the river to Frankfort aboard log rafts on the spring freshets were now ready to go downstream to fight in the political war. Charges of the use of tissue-paper ballots were infuriating, and the mountaineers were going to Frankfort to rescue their government from the hands of the highbinders. Democrats in the Bluegrass country along the river said that the sneaking scoundrels from upstream had shot the people's friend. They were for driving the Republican Taylor and his henchmen out of Kentucky and across the Ohio, and then they would search out the murderer who shot Goebel and hang him.

Jim Howard, from the South Fork at Manchester, was one of those accused of killing Goebel. Henry Youtsey, a clerk in the office of Caleb Powers, secretary of state, was another who was suspected of committing the crime. Both these men were tried for the murder and imprisoned, but neither of them has ever divulged the answer to this riddle. It still is an interesting pastime in Kentucky to debate the question of who really shot William Goebel. Several times I have come on an ancient mountain citizen who was quick to say, "I went to Frankfort when the Goebel trouble occurred."

Goebel lived for four days after he was shot. In the excitement which followed the attempted assassination, the Democrats secured control of the state legislature. They were quick to take advantage of the state of confusion, and Goebel was declared to be elected governor. All the electoral controversies then pending before the general assembly were decided in favor of the Democratic party. Governor Taylor and his Republican colleagues left the state. Caleb Powers was arrested and placed in the jail at Georgetown. Back in Frankfort, in the meantime, Goebel fought for his life in a stuffy room at the Capitol Hotel. Crowds of Democrats flocked to his door. His friends stood over him hoping that his powerful physical system would overcome his injury and that he would live to be governor of the state for a full term. His body was badly swollen and in pain. Only once was Goebel able to rally enough strength to perform an official act as governor of Kentucky. His puffed hand managed to withstand the ordeal of scribbling in a ragged zigzag line his signature at the bottom of a proclamation.

When his first and last official act had been performed, William Goebel died. For four days he had fought for the right to live with almost as much vigor as he had fought for election to the governorship. His body was placed in a long black coffin, while outside his room Democrats swore to seek vengeance of the fallen leader's enemies. The coffin was loaded onto a train for one last visit to northern Kentucky before it was laid to rest on top of the great cemetery hill overlooking the long sweep of the Kentucky River. To reach Covington, however, without traveling over some of the Louisville and Nashville Railroad track was difficult, yet Goebel supporters were determined they would not patronize the railroad in any way in this funeral journey. One of the little passenger trains of the ambitious jerkwater line, the Frankfort and Cincinnati Railroad, was hung heavily with crape, and the party of loyal Goebel supporters set out early on the cold wet morning of February 6th to take their chieftain's body home for a brief time where it could lie in state.

Calm and impartial persons in the state appreciated what was happening. Kentucky, they knew, was in a state of unhappy political revolution and at any moment there was liable to be a civil outbreak. Cartoonists throughout the nation depicted the strife of the Bluegrass state in their highly descriptive sketches. This was, perhaps, Kentucky's darkest moment. Not even when Indians invaded the frontier state were the citizens more disturbed and worried.

It was this bitter political fight that caused Judge

Mulligan to add one more philosophical line to his already salty poem. He knew what Kentucky had faced, and perhaps such a bit of humor would relieve the bitter tension of the moment. Perhaps it did; at any rate, Kentuckians laughed heartily at it in a spirit of appreciative good humor.

Turning back the pages of Kentucky's political history, one comes across many strange passages. In the columns of the old *Gazette* in the latter part of the eighteenth century, anonymous writers under the pseudonyms of Cornplanter, Senex, Scaevola, and Vox Populi tugged back and forth over current issues. Several years later Scaevola, or Henry Clay, a raging Jeffersonian Republican, baited the stubborn Federalist, Humphrey Marshall, from the floor of the Kentucky legislature. Marshall was an uncompromising Federalist in a land overwhelmingly Republican. Clay introduced into the House a patriotic resolution to require all legislators to "Clothe themselves in the productions of American manufacturers and abstain from the use of cloth or linens of European fabrics, until the belligerent nations respect the rights of neutrals by repealing their orders and decrees as relates to the United States." This was a reasonable enough resolution or so it seemed to Republican legislators, who had no particular love for the British and who at that very moment were being rapidly convinced that war with England was inevitable. Humphrey Marshall ridiculed Clay, and Clay accused Marshall of being dressed in "belligerent cloth." The two legislators lost their tempers and Marshall called Clay a liar from the floor of the House of Representatives. A challenge followed and was accepted. The two antagonists went across the Ohio River at Louisville to gain honorable satisfaction from each other. It was a somewhat comic-opera affair. Clay wrote James F. Clarke on that cold January 19, 1809:

> I have this moment returned from the field of battle. We had three shots. On the first I grazed him just above the navel—he missed me, on the second my damned pistol snapped and he missed me—on the third I received a flesh wound in the thigh, and owing to my receiving his fire first, etc. I missed him.
>
> My wound is no way serious, as the bone is unhurt, but prudence will require me to remain here some days.

While Clay and Marshall were across the river grazing each other with their poorly aimed pistols, held in chilled hands, William Littell was composing parts of his fine satire on Kentucky politics. In a long-drawn-out account written in Biblical style, Littell laughed at the political scrapping which went on under his nose. He was a keen legal scholar who found much fault in legislation with which to criticize the legislators. They had authorized him to compile the Kentucky laws into convenient volumes. But as he bored his tedious way through the maze of crudely drafted laws of the state, he was quick to see through the sham of most of the legislation. Little men were seeking little special privileges. Men guilty of miscegenation, said he, opposed a divorce law. An act was passed, he said in one of his satires, to keep educated pigs out of Kentucky after one had just embarrassed a member of the legislature. Continuing his jocular criticism, the legal student had two admittedly dishonest legislators present their arguments as to why they were opposed to "an act to promote the impartial administration of justice." The first speaker frankly said, "I shall vote against the passage of this bill, because I apprehend that if it should pass into a law, it may have a tendency to suppress the progress of villainy, vice and barbarism."

In one of his choicest articles, the sly Littell presents a raw bumpkin who has dissipated his life running for office. He was Gregory Woodcock who asked the people of Kentucky to reimburse him to the extent of $1,166.01 due him for services rendered as an able opponent in several elections. Gregory's treacherous descent into a complete state of dissolution is a pitiful one. He informed his constituents "That your petitioner hath grown grey and poor, and become an idler and a drunkard, in attempting to serve his country in the capacity of a legislator. He has been six times a candidate for a seat in the assembly, and twice for one in the senate, but never had the good fortune to be elected. . . ." Among Gregory's expenditures were items such as 100 half-pints of whisky, 41 gallons of whisky, $50 to a doctor for services rendered after he had fought a prospective voter, and finally $25.33 for 200 half-pints of liquor. All these charges were considered by Gregory Woodcock's creator as legitimate expenditures by a man seeking office at the hands of his fellow countrymen.

Of more recent years, Kentuckians recall with a merry twinkle in their eyes the rollicking campaign between the old-fashioned flowery orators, Owsley Stanley and Edwin Morrow. One of the major points at issue between them was that of freeing the mountain-man's "Old Dog Ring." Many times this issue came up in the campaign, and Stanley would howl like a forlorn potlikker hound through his cupped hands at Ed Morrow. Morrow always fought back. They were jovial campaigners, however, and old-timers recall that when the speakings were over they would take a drink together and depart in a jolly mood. Stanley was a ready speaker who had mastered the fine art of ridicule. Once he exclaimed to a doting audience, "Ed Morrow's pronouns wander through a wilderness of words searching vainly for their antecedents."

Kentuckians have always enjoyed their political speakings. Barbecues, burgoos, and speakings have become a sort of institutional combination which has given the state real flavor. During the first quarter of the nineteenth century, Timothy Flint, a closely observant Yankee preacher, wrote in his reminiscent account of his sojourn in the West, "that I have often seen one of these young men [a Kentuckian] in the new states farther west, with no more qualifications than that ease and perfect command of all that they knew, which result from satisfaction, step down into the 'mourning waters' before the tardy, bashful and self-criticising young man from the north had made up his mind, to avail himself of the opportunity." It was this calmness plus an outlandish speaking ability that added color to Kentucky politics. Loud-mouthed sons up and down the river bellowed for attention by yelling "Feller citizens!" from the steps of the courthouses or the stumps throughout the counties.

One honest son of Benson Creek in old Shelby exclaimed to a gaping crowd before him in 1846, "I came to this country about fifteen years ago, not worth a dollar, and by your care, still remain so. And it is well known to this community that my moments of inebriety have been much greater than those of my sobriety. Feller citizens: I am a candidate for the legislature, and by my precept and your example, I have raised up a small and pious family, not numbering more than ten or twelve. It is a fact, gentlemen, I am opposed to all turnpikes, railroads, locks and dams, and they may all be damned together—so I say. Feller citizens: I have three principles on which I intend to run this race. The first is 'Shelby County,' the second is 'Shelby County,' and the third is 'Shelby County,' and mind what I tell you, I'll make Honest Martin and old Judge Tom smoke before the dance is over yet. Feller citizens: there has been but few persons in this state, or Shelby County, who knew that I was going to become a candidate—in fact, there was but two gentlemen who knew anything about it, and one of them was my wife, and the other was Colonel White. Mind what I tell you now, feller citizens, I am a *Dimacrat,* dyed in the wool, and I don't care whether you vote for me or not, and in my last failing moments when the world itself is going into agonies, my last, suspiring convulsive grip shall be a-holt of old Shelby—mind what I tell you."

Kentucky oratory and political maneuvering have always been an interesting aspect of Kentucky culture. But one of the really exciting historical aspects of the state's politics has been the creation of a new county. At one time or another the legislature at Frankfort has been able to take a little time off from its many arduous duties to create one hundred and twenty counties. Always there have been special motives for creating a new county. The name of some prominent Kentuckian or a national statesman or hero deserved to be perpetuated. Then there were the men who wished to escape the jurisdiction of a particularly obnoxious set of officers, so said William Littell. Too, the more counties there were in Kentucky the more opportunities local politicians would have to get into office. If these arguments were not sufficient, then there was the old contention that in a thoroughly democratic state a free honest man should enjoy the privilege of having a courthouse within muleback ride of his front door.

At the forks of the Troublesome, in 1885, there

were three houses built, so a contemporary observer said, by unenterprising men who showed clearly that they had no vision of the future greatness of that spot. Too, the land was the property of the Honorable Robert Bates, member of the Kentucky general assembly from Letcher County. The Honorable Mr. Bates was a shy, shrinking violet of a representative of the people at the head of the rivers. He sat throughout most of his first legislative session staring through his heavy-rimmed spectacles at his amazing fellow legislators. Not once did the retiring, bald-headed representative stir from his seat to indulge himself even in that harmless legislative trick of raising a point of order in order to call attention to himself. This silent representative from the head of Troublesome had only one bill to push. He wanted to create a new county to honor that beloved Kentucky governor, Proctor Knott, who had so distinguished himself as a member of the United States House of Representatives by delivering his famous speech, "Where Is Duluth?" which had tickled a nation. Bates and his prompter and preceptor, Fitzpatrick, were men who believed in paying tribute where such deserving tribute was due. Why should there not be a Knott County? Also, why not call its county seat Hindman in honor of John R. Hindman, lieutenant governor? Since lieutenant governors got so few honors —at least one should enjoy a friendly gesture. The timid Bates was really a man of rare political acumen, and his bill was one to give everybody an honest and deserving break.

Knott County with its new county seat came into actual being on July 7, 1885. The commissioners planned the date of the creation of the new county so as not to compromise presumptuously the famous date on which the American colonies had declared themselves independent of England.

It was a great day at the head of Troublesome on July 7, 1885. A new county was to be formed. People poured into the wide creek bottom from miles around; they came in to be present at the "birthing" of their county. Again the ever-thoughtful Bates and Fitzpatrick had planned carefully for the people's pleasures. They had accumulated an adequate supply of moonshine liquor for the occasion, and this they dispensed at extremely moderate charges. Soon the crowd was jubilant, and there was a great deal of agility on the dancing ground. No one was drunk. A conservative observer said, "They war drinkin' some, but they warn't drunk." Liveliest of all was old man Everidge who came to the meeting without his hat " 'cause it made his head too warm." Likewise he was barefooted because his feet were as sensitive to heat as was his head. To set the old man off in the dance was the belle of the county. She was a natural unspoiled beauty of the hills. Her dress was a plain red calico with a wide yellow ruffle about the bottom and a blue ribbon about the waist. Atop her head was a green sunbonnet. This highland queen became the belle of the ball. Soon the dance was going strong; the guitar and fiddle were ringing out in loud overtones above the merry noise of the crowd. The caller was droning, "All hands up and circle left." The dancers were swinging at a merry pace. They "swung ma, pa and the girl from Arkansas." Old man Everidge's flat bare feet pattered merrily against the ground, and his body galloped up and down the circle as though mounted on a mechanical merry-go-round. The going was fast, and soon the belle in calico with the wide yellow ruffle bolted the set. Like her neighbors, she said she "couldn't dance to do no good with shoes on."

Down the creek a half mile from the dancing ground the earnest commissioners were wrestling with the stubborn problem of creating the new county. Officially the county had been created in the legislature at Frankfort, but the exact boundaries were left to the commissioners. They were to cut off bits of four surrounding counties and to consolidate them into a new county. This was a difficult problem. It was practically impossible to cut off parts of other counties without dislocating public officials of those counties. For instance, they were about to cut off the high sheriff of Letcher, the assessor of Floyd, the coroner of Breathitt, and the surveyor of Perry. At last, however, the ingenious commissioners did some skillful cutting, and they brought into being a geographical unit of government which had a somewhat dissolute amoeboid shape. Once the geographical puzzle was solved, the commissioners were faced with the polite problem of asking the state for funds with which to buy public record books. For years there was a customary charge of $1,200 per county for these records, but the overly conscientious commissioners made a bit of typographical error and asked for $2,100. Rural democracy at the head of Troublesome now was able to hold its own private elections in its own rugged manner.

Years later two forthright Knott County candidates for local office were to make vigorous pleas for votes. Jake Sutton, an ambitious yeoman of honest pretentions and instincts, asked his fellow citizens that he be entrusted with the grave responsibility of caring for them when they got in jail. Jake, like all seriously inclined candidates, had worked out his policies before announcing his candidacy. His simple little handbill was specific in both its promises and its tender pathos. Jake was a practical psychologist, and he made an appeal to those tender emotions of humanity. He said in the beginning that he felt "The good citizens of Knott County should know, who, and what they are voting for." Wrote the forthright candidate:

I know we have been fed up on promises, until we never know whether to believe them or not, but try me ONCE and if I do not try my BEST to do as I say, never risk me again. I was born and raised in this country and am not ashamed of the citizen I have been. I belong to the Baptist [Hard-Shell] Church, and have for the last twenty years and I propose to live up to the standard of religion. If nominated and elected, I shall put a good large table in the jail and let the prisoners set down and eat like men. The best citizens MIGHT happen to be in jail, and they should be treated like real men and citizens. Every man has some of his relatives and friends who get in jail. You want them cared for.

Then with all the humanity of a sensitive, upright man who wished to offer a strong arm to weak and faltering humanity, Jake made one final tender plea: "Mothers, if you want your boy treated right, VOTE FOR ME."

Jake Sutton's plea was a touching one, but it did lack some of the genuine finesse which Lurania Slone made in her mimeographed handbill. She told a kindhearted electorate that she begged its vote:

My husband, Ballard Slone, was elected circuit court clerk of this county and shortly afterwards was stricken with an incurable disease. I followed him to a hospital where he remained until the final summons came and then I followed him to his grave. A short time before he died he motioned me to his bedside and there in the presence of his doctor, his nurse, and his GOD and in the silence of death, he said, "Lurania, I am ready to die and I must go and leave you now. I want you to ask the good people of Knott County to elect you to fill out my unexpired term in order that you may pay my debts, including my hospital bill. They won't fail you, Lurania."

I beg of you to help me fulfill the wishes of my dead husband. . . .

Who could fail to heed such a plea? The good people of Knott stood by this unfortunate candidate, and Ballard's last wish was granted.

When a man in many of the river counties announces his intention to run for office, he generally states who his kinsfolk are. That is, he tells who his kinsfolk are if they are people of some degree of respectability. Oscar Haggin of Breathitt County announced his intention to run for office in the columns of the Jackson paper. He announced that he wished to be county jailer and that "among those to whom I am related by blood or marriage are the following families: Bachs, Lovelys, Allens, McQuinns, Pattons, Landrums, Stampers, Watts, Watkins, Manus, Crafts, Calhouns, and the Nichols. My wife was a Crawford which makes our relation to the Jetts, Johnsons, Combs, Griffiths, Terrys, Amburgys, Bowmans, Heralds, Spences, Lawsons, Capes, Hargises, Days, Haddixes and Evans and many more." In a country where family names are limited in number, Oscar stood a reasonably good chance of getting the votes of everybody in the county, providing he was on good terms with his kinsfolk.

Up the South Fork a rugged native son offered himself as candidate for the office of representative from the Eighty-fifth legislative district. For sheer understanding of local political psychology this handbill has few equals. It gives the following facts: His home was at Mistletoe. He was thirty-one years of age, and he had about two and a half years of college work. For ten years he had taught school, eight of those in Owsley County and two in Clay County. He was a member of the National Guard and stood ready to defend his 85th district in time of both war and peace. In nine years he had become the father of five children. This candidate was clear in his statement of policy. He was in favor of that ancient virtue of "right over wrong." He likewise stood for "freedom and satisfaction, roads and roadwork 100 per cent, education 100 per cent, $30 per month old age and blind pensions, a reasonable teacher retirement act, 100 per cent behind doing away with the dog law and allowing every family one dog free, and the establishment of some industrial schools." This was a clever platform. It promised just exactly the things which the constituency along the South Fork wanted. Ever since Ed Morrow made his "Old Dog Ring" campaign, the tax-free dog has been the most delicate political issue along the river.

In two final sentences in his handbill, the candidate from Clay and Owsley promised to take the advice of any and all his constituents if he was elected. His final appeal was a ringing one: "Vote and talk for me, and I will vote and talk for you at Frankfort." This was reciprocity with a high degree of fairness. This has become a factor in the democratic process along the Kentucky.

Campaigning for local offices in Kentucky, at one time, was a jolly affair. Whichever candidate could think up the most clever schemes was usually elected. Over in "Sweet" Owen the boys lolling around the newspaper office and the courthouse door recall the antics of Bill Swope. Bill was a lively, imaginative candidate who ran for office much of the time just for the sport of the campaign. In 1892 he ran for circuit clerk against Bob Walker. Just before election some slick-talking salesman managed to sell him a wagonload of soap bearing the legend "Vote for Swope" stamped deeply in the sides of the cakes.

This was a fine scheme to get votes. The rural voters over in Owen were glad to get a free cake of soap. Times were hard and they had little money to spend on such luxuries. When news got out, however, that Swope was going to make political headway with his two-horse wagonload of soap, his opponents went into conference to work out the best strategic move possible to offset this ingenious scheme. When at last they had an answer, it all seemed so simple—so simple, in fact, that Swope's opponents began to wonder why he had not foreseen the danger involved. If he had been giving away most anything but soap, his plan would have succeeded, but the soap scheme was a natural to defeat. Workers for Walker started a whispering campaign in which they quietly informed voters on the street of Owenton "that Swope thinks that all the voters of Owen County are so dirty that they need a bath." Too, they asked voters the pointed question, "Is your vote so all-fired cheap that it can be bought with a cake of soap?" The citizens of Owen were unwilling to admit that they were so dirty that they had to get a cake of soap from a candidate with which to take a bath and they were certain they wouldn't sell out for a cake of soap with Bill Swope's name stamped on it.

Bill Swope's imagination had worked overtime. He offered a prize to the man who would come the nearest to guessing the vote he would receive. He hoped, of course, that everybody would guess a majority and that they would all vote for him in order to boost their chances at winning the prize. One bright constituent guessed him to lose; and when his soap scheme went sour, Swope had to give this man a prize for guessing nearest the right number of votes he would receive. P. O. Minor, a genial old-timer, still recalls with a merry twinkle the time he beat Bill Swope for county clerk. P. O. was running a poor second to Bill, and the bad news was coming in from the outlying hustings that Swope was going over big in the country prayer meetings. With a great show of piety Bill was winning votes right and left throughout the county. Minor's chances of winning were fading, and only by some stroke of unusually good luck could he hope to stop the veteran campaigner. By good fortune he was able to get a handful of Swope's posters, which he carried around the circuit in concealment. On one occasion he rode up to a new house which had just been finished but not occupied. It was the property of an influential man in his end of the county, and any injury Minor might do in Swope's name would certainly be a factor in the outcome of the election. Here was a chance to counteract the master prayer-meeting man. P. O. found the biggest rustiest nail on the place and nailed Swope's card to the new front door. The heavy nail went crashing through the paneling and ruined the door. Pretty soon news drifted into Owenton from the northern end of the county "that Swope was trying awful hard to get to be county clerk, but the damn fool didn't have sense enough to be a butcher." There was much whispering about the poster nailed to the new front door, and Swope lost the race.

Kentucky politics have always revolved around the petty personal issues. Perhaps it was from pioneer Kentucky that Abraham Lincoln learned many of his little personal tricks of winning cases in the Illinois courts, and later of staving off assaults by ambitious politicians when he was President of the United States.

This has been true in major as well as in minor elections in Kentucky. Up and down the Kentucky River most of the candidates seeking office have been patronizing and unctuous gentlemen from whose tongues has dripped the sweetest honey of solicitation.

There is another rich Owen County political story. A candidate out on the circuit followed a creek bed road up to a farm, and pretty soon he saw the farmer and his sons setting tobacco up on the side of the steep hill over the creek. They, fortunately for the slick office seeker, had not seen him. When he was even with them, he stepped behind some bushes and yelled up to them that he was his opponent. Any reasonable candidate would have climbed the hill and spent at least an hour passing the time of day. That is the way to get rural votes. But the candidate hidden in the bushes succeeded in convincing the boys at the top of the hill that he was his own opponent. Then he played his trump card by yelling up, "If the hill wasn't so steep and if I wasn't afraid of getting my feet muddy, I would come up and talk with you boys. I want you to vote for me in the election." The answer came quickly. Never before had a candidate been so independent with the free sons of "Sweet" Owen, and their feelings were aroused. They shouted down, "Like hell we will. If you are too good to get a little mud on your feet and too lazy to climb this hill, you ain't fit to be elected to a county office." It was a sharp trick; but when a candidate needs votes, one way of getting them is about as good as another.

The yeomanry of the Kentucky valley is forthright in its politics, and it expects the right sort of treatment from candidates. On the other hand, the humble voter can be tied to a candidate with hoops of steel if given the right sort of treatment. Old Judge Perry, a famous old-time politician, had defeated numerous opponents for the office of county judge, but he had never got the vote of a stubborn old Irishman named Si Cobb. Old Cobb and his crowd voted against the judge in every election just as a matter of principle, and it weighed on the judge's mind. He, however, bided his time when he would win Si's support. One hot summer day the old Irishman drove his ox team up on courthouse square. The oxen were very warm and stood panting as though the next moment would be their last. This was Judge Perry's chance. He rushed out and inspected the team, and then turned to old man Cobb and said, "Si, you have a mighty fine team here, but if you don't get them into a lot where you can unyoke them, they are going to die. Why don't you bring them down to my place and let them cool off?" This was a mighty neighborly thing to do, and Si drove his team down the street to the judge's house. The two men unyoked the steers, and the judge opened the gate to his wife's flower garden and instructed Cobb to drive them in so they could cool off in the shade. Then he turned to the old Irish ox driver and said, "Si, the old lady has dinner on the table. Come on in and eat while your oxen are cooling off." This procedure was tough on the old lady's flowers, but Si Cobb and his crowd voted for the judge as long as he ran for office.

Repartee has always figured as a valuable asset in campaigning for office in Kentucky. A candidate who couldn't be hemmed on the stump was a pretty likely fellow to have in office. Two candidates seeking office down the river raised the issue of where they found their wives. One of them, the man who had married a native daughter and had been in jail for wife beating, damned his opponent for going to West Virginia to find a wife, saying, "The Kentucky girls weren't good enough for a wife." The opponent jumped up and answered, "I'll bet his wife wishes he had gone to some other state to get married." This was the end of that campaign. On another occasion a long-winded candidate went into a tirade about his birthplace. He was born in one county and had lived in all the others where he sought votes. His opponent made the pointed observation "that it takes him a mighty long time to tell about something of so little importance."

William O. Bradley, the first Republican governor of the state and a Kentucky valley boy, was a rollicking campaigner. His ability at yarn spinning on the circuit has never been equaled in Kentucky. He was also a past master at stinging repartee—so much so that only seldom would a Democratic candidate leave an opening for Bradley's biting wit. At Chinquapin Rough in Jackson County in 1887, Bradley was trying to make a speech in behalf of his candidacy for the governorship of the state. Every time he got started, however, the mules hitched about the speaker's stand set up such a commotion with their braying that they drowned him out. A few Democrats sprinkled through the crowd were enjoying this predicament, and every time the mules brayed they roared with laughter. Bradley was equal to the occasion, however. When the braying again started, he shouted, "There it is again. I never can speak without being interrupted by the Democrats."

Politics along the Kentucky River is an amusing pastime. Of course, the candidates take themselves seriously. They become the players in a huge folk drama up and down the valley. Occasionally the constituents also take themselves seriously. When this occurs they lose their tempers, as they did at Frankfort on January 30, 1900, or at Clayhole on the bank of Troublesome Creek in Breathitt County on November 8, 1921.

At the latter place old Aunt Lize Sizemore's right to vote was challenged, and within five minutes nine men were shot to death and six were wounded. Perhaps this, next to the Goebel affair, was the most unfortunate election trouble ever to occur in Kentucky. Usually the local and state campaigns are vigorous exercises in jovial rural democracy, where both campaigns and elections must be an entertainment as well as a political function.

23

Kentuckians Must Eat

NOWHERE else in the United States has food been more a part of human life than up and down the Kentucky River. Eating is a sort of second religion with the folks who live in this valley. It is true that Kentucky foods, like Kentucky whisky, undergo several regional changes before the river runs its full course. One socially minded geologist swore that he could close his eyes, eat dinner, and designate the community in which it had been cooked. Despite these frequent changes, food is the main objective in the country. Long ago the Kentuckian settled the ancient hen and egg argument of whether "man eats to live or lives to eat." Any native along the river can tell you that he lives to eat.

If, beyond the pearly gates, I am permitted to select my place at the table, it will be among Kentuckians, and the food, I hope, will be Kentucky style. Eating dinner in Kentucky is more than a physiological refueling of the human body, it is a joyous social ritual. The table is the great yarning place for the state. Gossip, tall yarns, and laughter punctuate the business at hand of consuming victuals. This, to the Kentuckian, is his great "recalling ground." He drags out his salty little family secrets and laughs about them. A warning to all strangers, however, the family secrets are never quite so secretive or so outrageous as they appear on the surface. There is something about a Kentucky dinner that stretches a yarn or puts spirit into a bit of gossip. A fair example of this is the story of the aged Kentucky judge who claimed himself an excellent shot with a rifle. On a cold shoulder and sober, and before dinner, the judge solemnly repeated his old boast that he could snip a turkey's head off at a hundred yards, but with a round of potent "before dinner" nips of bourbon, in good company, and with a fine meal in prospect, he could raise his ante to three hundred yards. On only one occasion was he ever known to go beyond the three-hundred-yard limit of shooting respectability, and that was when the Japanese ambassador visited Kentucky. The dinner was an extraordinary affair, even among extraordinary dinners, and the judge was in unusually fine fettle. He dragged out his turkey-shooting brag, but it went beyond all previous bounds and he exclaimed to the startled ambassador, "Sir, I shot him at a thousand yards!"

No social historian will ever be able to determine how many Kentucky political battles have been fought and refought at the dinner table. The antics of Ed Morrow and Owsley Stanley have created enough rollicking table conversation to digest the state's entire pork output for the last forty years. Scores of students of folk literature have invaded the Kentucky mountains to search eagerly for snatches of English ballads, but they have overlooked that more important oasis of folk culture known as "Kentucky dinner talk." Even the most stolid banker will sometimes break loose from his sanctimonious shut-mouth financial moorings and be the life of the party. On a few occasions, where it was necessary to curb free and unbridled conversation, one or two of them have done surprisingly good jobs as toast-masters. In fact, some of these bankers have repeated stories which by their very make-up could never have come from a businessman's patent jokebook.

This tradition of good food goes all the way back to the beginning of the state's history. John Ferdinand Dalziel Smythe found game of all kinds plentiful. "A man," said Smythe, "can kill six or eight deer every day, which many do merely for their skins. . . . Wild turkeys, very large and fat are almost beyond number, sometimes five thousand in a flock, of which a man may kill as many as he likes. Elks are also plentiful." He also saw herds of buffalo grazing in the rich savannas, and the Kentucky River was working alive with splendid game fish.

What squirrel stews pioneer Kentuckians could make! Frequently squirrel shoots were held in which wasteful sportsmen fetched home an astounding number of victims of their rifles. The boys at Irvine Lick on the Kentucky counted 7,941 tails and scalps from one day's hunting. They certainly had the makings of an excellent squirrel stew, and it was a very good dish indeed. In fact, it was so good that it won a compliment from the fussy Irish traveler, Thomas Ashe. He ate dinner with a family, the woman of which he pitied because of her hard lot. They had for dinner "a large piece of salt bacon, a dish of homslie [hominy] and a tureen of squirrel broth. I dined entirely on the last dish, which I found incomparably good, and the meat equal to delicate chicken." This dish had to be good to please such a critical visitor.

Other travelers came to visit the western country, and to fuss about what they had to eat. They must have been pleased, however, with Kentucky food because few of them complained about it. Many of them made it their business to investigate the availability of foods in the markets at Lexington and Frankfort. Even yet their lists sound attractive. John Melish found a bounteous supply of venison, fowls, ducks, turkeys, cheese, eggs, butter, potatoes, beans, meal, turnips, and other supplies. William Faux, a little later found the same kind of food for sale in an abundance that would have put a well-stocked cornucopia to shame. No wonder Kentucky cooks learned to fry chickens. They could be had for seventy-five cents a dozen. This bountiful supply of food partly explains how a state gained a national reputation for good eating.

It used to be said that the quickest way to arouse a Kentuckian's anger was to laugh at his horse or to cheat him in a horse trade. This was not altogether true. He could be both angered and persuaded to overlook the shortcomings of a stranger if he either lambasted or bragged on what he had to eat. Alexander Wilson, the American ornithologist, got himself involved in a hot dispute with the Kentuckians. Like all famous visitors to Lexington in the early days, he strolled through the town's market house. In a somewhat humorous vein he wrote of what he saw. There was "black sugar wrapped in gray saddle bags, some cabbage, chewing tobacco, catmint and turnip tops, a few bags of meats, sassafras roots, and skinned squirrels cut in quarters." Local sons forgave Mr. Wilson his light talk about cabbages, chewing tobacco, catmint, and sassafras roots. But not his insult, "skinned squirrels cut in quarters!" Was ever a community so outrageously libeled? What did that Yankee Wilson think? Did he wish to accuse the Kentuckians of being niggardly with their squirrel meat? An angered son wrote in an impassioned heat:

I have too great a respect for Mr. Wilson, as your friend, not to believe he had in mind some other market house than that of Lexington when he speaks of it as "unpaved and unfinished!" But the people of Lexington would be gratified to learn what your ornithologist means by "skinned squirrels cut up into quarters," which curious anatomical preparation he enumerates among the articles he saw in the Lexington market. Does Mr. Wilson mean to joke upon us? If this is wit we must confess that, however abundant our country may be in good substantial matter-of-fact salt, the "attic tart is unknown among us."

Quite in contrast to Alexander Wilson's unfortunate light observations as to the possible food supply of Lexington is the complimentary note of Mortimer Thompson, who, otherwise adopting a cavalier manner toward Kentucky, made himself a welcome visitor by his friendly description of the state's food. Riding aboard the Kentucky River steamer, *Blue Wing,* he found that "they have great fruit in this country: apples as big as pumpkins, just emerged from the blossomhood, and ere they have assumed the golden overcoat which maketh them maturer friends so glorious to view, and pumpkin pies, manufactured by the sable god of the kitchen; pies enormous to behold; where-inafter they are ready to be devoured you might wade up to your knees in that noble compound which filleth the interior thereof, and maketh the pie savory and nectarean; in fact pies celestial, whereof writers in all ages have discoursed eloquently; and sweet potatoes, such s-w-e-e-t p-o-t-a-t-o-e-s! Jiminety! big enough to fill a six foot grave, yellow as rhubarb, and luscious as— 'lasses candy." This was indeed an eloquent tribute to Kentucky's abundant fare, and it is little wonder that the acrid Ohio editor got by with his other observations which were not nearly so complimentary.

There can be little doubt but that Kentuckians know how to dine. Their historical definition of a good dinner is, "a turkey at one end of the table, a ham at the other, six vegetables down one side, and seven down the other with pickles and jelly sprinkled in between, and with a side dish of oysters." This formula must have come over the mountains from Virginia. Colonel William Price, a member of Lewis Craig's traveling congregation, has left an interesting record of banqueting in his letters. Back in Virginia he wrote a friend: "This note is to apprise you that I invite you and all your Baptist friends to my house Christmas day to partake of a big dinner of turkey and oysters, and to conclude with a dance at grandmother's in the evening. No Episcopalian has been invited . . . Tell Robert Craig to bring his fiddle, as we expect a good time generally." A few years later in Kentucky, Colonel Price wrote Governor Isaac Shelby that "I was greatly disappointed by your not coming to my house on yesterday [July 4]. We had a glorious time and a big dinner. Forty men sat down at my tables, who had served in the late struggle for our freedom and independence. It was a glorious sight to behold, and I wish King George III and Lord North could have witnessed the scene in the wilds of America." It is a certainty that if George III and Lord North could have been present at Colonel Price's table they would have been served a royal dinner.

At the head of Dick's River, Colonel William Whitley, famous Indian fighter, pointed the way to high living. He gave a breakfast, in 1813, for his friends who attended the morning races at Sportsman's Hill, which was all that a gourmet's heart could desire. There was chicken soup with rice, baked Ohio River salmon, bacon, cabbage, beans, barbecued lamb, roast duck, applesauce, roast turkey, cranberry sauce, roast beef, broiled squirrel, leg of bear, baked opossum, sweet potatoes, roasting ears, hominy, boiled potatoes, baked sweet potatoes, stewed tomatoes, hot cakes, corn dodgers, buttermilk, plum pudding, rum sauce, pumpkin pie, log cabin pie, sliced apple pie (old style), assorted cakes, fruit, vanilla ice cream, coffee, let-us-smile cider, transy bitters, apple jack, peach and honey, old bourbon, we-smile-again claret, port wine, sherry, and champagne. This was a breakfast for sportsmen indeed, and it is a remarkable fact that they all lived to enjoy future races at this famous track.

In the very beginning of the white man's history in the Kentucky River valley some ingenious soul created a political dish which remains even yet a unique American food. Some dabbler in history has said that this famous stew was first concocted by John Hunt Morgan's men. Long before Morgan was born they were serving burgoo at political gatherings under the shade of huge oaks around Maxwell Springs. An earlier Kentuckian, writing to a friend in the East, invited him to come to Kentucky where he would give him a cup of hot burgoo and a glass of raw whisky. Perhaps the Easterner did not understand what outlandish concoction it was that he was to get in his cup. His dictionary could not tell him what it was. It originated back in the days when hunters counted up their day's kill in the thousands of squirrels, and when pigeons flew through the woods in veritable clouds, and bear, deer, buffalo, and hundreds of turkeys were available. The idea came from Virginia, where Brunswick stew was popular. Vegetables of all kinds were boiled along with the game meats, and the whole mass was highly seasoned with spices. This was a fine temptation with which to attract a crowd. Persons having houses to build, logs to roll, or politicians desiring to get a crowd to their speakings could depend upon the offer of a burgoo dinner to do the trick.

The old recipes have been forgotten because of the disappearance of game. Modern counterparts are still popular at race tracks, political speakings, conventions, and picnics. An all-day political rally without burgoo and barbecue would be about as exciting as a wedding without the bride. Several burgoo kings have placed imaginary crowns upon their brows, and have gone forth with an assortment of battered iron pots, pans, and tattered recipes to make and serve their special concoction. "King Gus" Jaubert became the famous postwar burgoomaster. He had a secret recipe, much of which he never revealed. For more than forty years Gus Jaubert prepared burgoo for the Kentucky meetings. His glorious triumph, however, came in 1895 when he prepared the famous food for 200,000 delegates to the Grand Army of the Republic reunion in Louisville. This Gargantuan meeting required 15,000 gallons of King Gus's delectable brew, along with 45 beeves, 383 sheep, and 544 barbecued pigs.

An earlier burgoomaker along the Kentucky River has left a recipe which has great possibilities of expansion. Based upon the proportions of six persons he used six squirrels, six birds, one and one-half gallons of water, one teacup of pearl barley, one quart of tomatoes, one quart of corn, one quart of oysters, one pint of cream, one-quarter pound of butter, two tablespoonsful of flour, and seasoned to taste with salt.

The modern pretender to the crown, Colonel J. T. Looney, has an elephantine recipe which requires 800 pounds of beef, 200 pounds of fowl, 168 gallons of tomatoes, 36 gallons of corn, 350 pounds of cabbage, 6 bushels of onions, 24 gallons of carrots, 1,800 pounds of potatoes, 2 pounds of red pepper, ½ pound of black pepper, 20 pounds of salt, 8 ounces of angostura, 1 pint of Worcestershire, ½ pound of curry powder, 3 quarts of tomato catsup, and 2 quarts of sherry. All this food is cooked over a slow fire for twenty-two hours. Burgoo cookers guard their secrets with a great deal of care. They tell you with an air of mystery that "this ain't all we use, we put in a few other little things, but that's a secret." They admit, however, that the greatest secret of all "is putting burgoo together." As to how good it is depends purely upon personal taste. Usually it is a tossup as to which has the greater kick in it, the cup of burgoo or the glass of raw whisky. Thus far no student of political affairs in Kentucky has investigated the direct results of burgoo and barbecue upon voting behavior at the polls. If Kentucky politics is "the damnedest," as Judge James H. Mulligan says in his famous poem "In Kentucky," then many of the sins are traceable historically to a languishing electorate gorged on burgoo and raw whisky.

Getting down to the fine points of food, some Kentucky delicacies stand on pedestals of honor. It would be the easiest thing in the world to start an argument among various states on the subject of ham, and of course few of the famous ham states will listen to praise of the product of another. From the day when pioneer drovers herded the first drove of hogs through Cumberland Gap into Kentucky, ham has been a staple commodity in the state's diet. Studious farmer-butchers have given much thought to the art of curing and smoking hams. Recipes for both sugar-curing and dry-salting and smoking have come down from one generation to another, until today it is a matter of genuine pride and distinction that farmers offer fine hams for sale. Virginians have boasted of their hams, but to Kentuckians they are not equal to their choice product. For some strange reason the Kentuckian has never bragged loudly enough outside the state about his famous pork delicacy for it to become a highly commercialized product. When Timothy Flint found the colonels boasting that they had "the best horse, dog, gun, wife, statesmen, and country," they could have honestly added to this list of superlatives their hams. One of the most genuine expressions of gratitude or friendship that a Kentuckian can make is the gift of a ripe old ham. Every Christmas the express offices in the central Kentucky towns are swamped with the familiar little tri-cornered tow-sack packages on their way to the East to be ruined by a greenhorn cook or, perhaps, to be thrown away because the recipient thinks they are spoiled. What sacrilege is committed by many cooks outside of Kentucky in cooking old hams. Many letters of thanks politely hem and haw before they make known the fact that the ham was spoiled. It had, say the naïve authors, "little white spots all through it!" What a blow; a ham that had aged from one to two years was ruined! Those "little white spots" are in reality sterling marks of ham aristocracy.

Perhaps there are dozens of good recipes for cooking an old ham, but no famous Kentucky cook is willing to admit that there is more than one—and that one his own. The author of the *Blue Grass Cook Book* admonishes her readers not to cook a ham under one year of age. Most recipes are somewhat complicated, since they follow the process of cooking the ham from the time it is taken off the hook in the smokehouse until it reaches the table in luscious red slices, bespeckled with tiny white islands of coagulated fat. Few American delicacies can equal a well-baked old Kentucky ham. It is easily in a class by itself.

Kentucky River people have eaten corn bread since the first day a white man kindled his campfire in the valley. Corn bread is as necessary a part of their diet as is salt. Corn bread takes various forms, and all of them, except that with sugar and flour in it, worth eating. There is the "flouncy" kind made with buttermilk and eggs, there is the greasy little corncake, the corn pone, and the rugged pioneer stand-by, corndodger. Kentucky River corndodger, like some of the hardy native sons, is plain unadulterated homemade corn bread without any extraneous ingredients in its make-up. The meal is mixed with scalding-hot water, seasoned with salt, and cooked brown on a greased iron griddle. A simple process, but a glorious asset to a good vegetable dinner. Corn has always been a symbol of food to the Kentucky people. When the first corn crops failed, pioneer communities faced starvation. Fields all the way from the rich rolling Bluegrass to the scrawny little patches clinging to the steep sides of the tall mountain ridges have yielded an abundance of rich flat grains for bread. Earlier it found its way to the little water mills which were turned by the river's strong current, and from these the best-flavored meal in America has come.

A blond sister of the hardy nut-brown corndodger is the beaten biscuit. People have talked about beaten biscuit throughout Kentucky history. This dry-flour bread is a somewhat mysterious and temperamental creation. It is as crusty as the sole maiden survivor of a proud family. There are few combinations in which it can be used with any degree of success. Beaten biscuit and old ham perhaps form the most faithful combination. It takes patience both to make and to eat these cuisine survivals of another age. The recipe calls for hard work; take "a pint of flour, a tablespoonful of lard, a good pinch of salt, mix with cold sweet milk to a stiff dough. Work *one hundred and fifty times through a kneader.* Roll into sheets one-half inch thick. Cut out or make out with the hands, prick with a fork, and bake in a hot oven." This will make a flinty biscuit which people brag on publicly, but which, if the truth be known, they wonder privately whether it is really worth while after all. However, a glass of velvet-smooth eggnog and a generous helping of beaten biscuits and old ham do help to relieve the tedium of life.

There are many other foods in the lower Kentucky valley which have helped out mightily in creating Kentucky's reputation for excellent food. Among these are old ham smothered in sweetbreads, and the fetching combination of golden-brown crisp-fried chicken, chicken gravy and fried mush, likewise, homemade sausage (smoked and unsmoked), lamb fries are not easily forgotten. All these things tend to make an individual bemoan his physiological limitations. Lamb fries are confined almost solely to the Bluegrass. Many a modest hostess has blushed deeply in a public dining room when an uninformed guest has innocently blurted out the question "What are lamb fries?" There is really nothing disgraceful about the dish. In short, lamb fries are lamb testicles cut in thin sections, breaded and fried in deep fat, and served with a thick cream gravy. Many an individual has rebelled at the idea of eating such a thing, only to wind up being fond of this dish.

Moving up the river, the type of food changes as rapidly as does the topography of the country. In adverse ratio, the biscuits, fried pork, and white gravy are dietary stand-bys in the upriver country, and do, perhaps, provoke scientific food specialists to open rebellion. In a land where the tin can was late in making its appearance, thrifty pioneers learned to preserve food by their own homely methods. Apples were cut in pieces, packed in earthen crocks, and saturated with the fumes from sulphur candles. Around the preparation of apples for "sulphuring" there grew up a picturesque folk gathering. Many a mountain cabin on the banks of the Kentucky River has housed riotous merrymakings at apple-cutting time. The young folks came in for the evening to cut apples, and to pack them into earthenware crocks or barrels. They wound up the common working with a square dance. A family had a winter's supply of semifresh apples packed away, and the young folks had a splendid excuse for a frolic.

When mountain sorghum cane reaches maturity just before the first frost appears, it is stripped, cut, topped, and hauled to a clumsy horse-drawn mill to be ground and the juice evaporated into molasses. Kentuckians are fond of sorghum, and hospitable mountaineers give visitors jars of syrup with great flourishes of generosity. To them there is nothing better than large fluffy biscuits, melted yellow butter and golden sorghum molasses. When molasses-making time comes, the people of the community gather for "stir-offs." Courting couples pair off, and dip paddles into the boiling syrup which they lick somewhat after the fashion of lollypop sticks. Stir-offs are the scenes of a great deal of practical joking. Skimmings, or the slimy green impurities of the cane, are dipped off the boiling juice and dumped into "green" holes alongside the pan, and practical jokers spend the evening trying to make an innocent greenhorn step into this filthy mess. Molasses-making season is likewise a dancing season.

Once every mountain kitchen was lined with long brown ropes of shucky beans hanging from the ceiling. In the summer, when cornfield bean vines were loaded with long waxy pods, families picked their beans and invited the neighbors to come in for a bean stringing. Girls came equipped with needles and thread, and they worked away at running the coarse thread through the middle of the beans. When they had strung the last green finger, the fiddlers tuned up, and the gay bean stringers slipped into a whirling square dance. Shucky beans are still found in abundance along the three forks of the Kentucky River. They are very good indeed when cooked with a ham bone. Many a mountain family has weathered a long lean winter because it had an abundant supply of dried string beans hanging along its kitchen walls.

Mountain housewives from the very beginning knew the art of preserving food. Hillside cornfields yielded tons of huge yellow pumpkins, but they would not keep through the winter season. In order to have pumpkin to eat from one harvest season to another, the mountaineer cut them into rings and dried them before his fireplace, or strung them on stout cords overhead on his porch. These rings are stacked on kitchen shelves, and by soaking them in water at the time of cooking they recover their juicy consistency and are suitable for making pies.

Between the mountains and the Bluegrass there is a wide variation in foods. Each in its own way can lay claim to real gastronomic distinction. Underneath Pine Mountain, where Laurel Fork gathers up the first significant floodwaters with which to rush down to a junction with the Greasy Creek to make the Middle Fork, the natives say that "If you ever get your feet wet in the Laurel Fork you will come back to it." I am not so certain that the cold water of the Laurel Fork in one's shoes has such magic power. I am certain, however, that sumptuous breakfasts of glorious home-cured ham, dozens of rich fresh eggs, feathery hot biscuits, mounds of rich country butter, preserves, jellies, and steaming coffee have real drawing power. Apologetic housewives serve meals like this, and offer their regrets that they did not know company was coming or they would "have fixed up a little something extra to eat."

During an earlier day, when Kentucky's public-spirited women wished to raise money for a community cause, they pooled their recipes and published them in books which they sold at a good profit. Many of these books are in existence today, and they constitute a fascinating historical record of Kentucky's famous reputation for sumptuous dining. At any rate, a first-class basis for adjudging the pride of a region in its food is the existence of hundreds of recipes of which the owners are proud enough to have them printed in a community cookbook.

Up and down the Kentucky River, the making and eating of food has been a matter of principal concern. When a Kentuckian goes to live in another part of the country he yearns for the Kentucky dishes. He remembers the water-ground meal which has a flavor all its own, the old hams, or the golden Kentucky sorghum. A homesick native son in Los Angeles decides that he wants richly flavored Kentucky sausage for breakfast, and he has a grocer wire a native sausage maker to send him a three-pound bag by air mail. He could have bought a fat California hog with the money he spent, but California sausage could not have supplied the flavor which he remembered having tasted back in Kentucky. Ever since the day when busybody John Ferdinand Dalziel Smythe came bustling through the Kentucky woods along the river which swarmed with an abundance of game, good food in the region has been a matter of great pride with the settlers.

24

The Onward Flow

THE STEEP PALISADES of the Kentucky stand as ageless monuments to both river and state. Beneath their chalky faces thunderous torrents have swept everything before them. There have followed scorching droughts which have slowed the river to a mere trickle, and have checked its rich loose shoulders with deep dry weather cracks. Even the horse weeds which annually bury the narrow bottoms in jungle growth have at times struggled to find moisture. Nature in the Kenucky Valley has never been a steady and predictable dame though it does have its lucid moments.

At the turn of the century engineers sought to curb the Kentucky in its extreme moments of flood and drought by erecting fourteen locks and dams. Pools created by these man-made barriers helped some, but not enough to check the flood tide or to maintain sufficient channel for commercial boat traffic.

Conservationists of one sort or another have made different approaches to use of the Kentucky. In the early 1920's the newly organized Kentucky Utilities Company dammed the mouth of the Dix with a hydroelectric facility which has generated electrical current for the neighboring bluegrass towns. Down stream at Tyrone this company erected a steam plant where it hauls in coal by river to fire its hungry furnaces, and dips water from the stream to generate steam to turn generators. Near

Boonesboro the Rural Electrification Administration sends electrical current coursing through a wide-spread system of rural lines to bring a revolution in the way of life for hundreds of thousands of isolated country folk.

Where the availability of electrical current has pierced mountain strongholds with radio and television waves, a modern system of highways has ended land barrier isolation. A system of interstate and primary roads slash through the Kentucky Valley with a casualness that makes the task seem as easy as cutting a wedge from a wedding cake. Interstate Highway 75 has ripped deep gashes through the limestone palisades above Frankfort and at Clay's Ferry to permit the construction of matching bridges which create a roadway of easy grade between river bed and bluegrass plateau.

High above the waters of the Kentucky the four matched bridges rest atop slender concrete and steel pylons to hasten Americans in their mad rush around the four points of the compass. Any weekend there passes over these gateway bridges a constant stream of eastern Kentuckians and Tennesseans coming home from Detroit, from Akron, Hamilton, Indianapolis, and Chicago. All of them dashing madly on their way southward as if they begrudged the denial even of a second "back home." To the east a mountain parkway has been dug out of ridges and wild stream valleys toward the northeast corner of Kentucky. This is the direct way into the heartland of Appalachia. Where Daniel Boone, John Finley and their long hunting companions wandered carefree on a summer's hunt, modern automobiles dash across the Red River country in a matter of minutes.

To a large extent these things mark the degree of change which has come to the Kentucky River country. There are others of even greater significance. Atop the picturesque plateau at Lexington, modern industrial plants flanked by acres of parking lots have come to occupy old tobacco and horse farm sites. Sophisticated electric typewriters, paper cups, peanut butter, and electrical supplies are manufactured here to furnish a worldwide market. Nearby the United States Signal Corps Depot at Avon ships an endless stream of materials to armed forces around the globe.

Like giant magnets the plants in Lexington draw in thousands of workers daily. The roads leading into the town from outlying counties become spokes of automobile lights pouring into the giant industrial parking lots. Many a Kentuckian from nearby eastern counties never sees his home in daylight from Sunday evening until Saturday morning.

The Kentucky River flows placidly around the great bend which separates the statehouse from older and more staid Frankfort. High on the west bank occur the political debates, the pulling and hauling, the trading, the pressuring, and the compromising. Governors, legislators, judges, and other state officials struggle mightily with the masses, the past, and the problems of the future.

By no means do all the struggles of Kentucky occur in Frankfort. Higher up the Kentucky and along its three main forks lies the heartland of Appalachia. Here is Kentucky's major problem area. This is indeed complex country populated by a complex people. This region finds itself hounded by so many internal conflicts and contradictions that there can never be a single blueprint for its future, or a single set of solutions for its problems. Clearly it is a region of sharply defined social stratifications. No greater error could be made than to lump all Appalachian highlanders into a common class — one labeled ignorant, shiftless, and dependent upon public relief. There is a disproportionate number of people who fall into the latter categories. It is a paradox indeed that

Appalachian Kentucky has fed a constant stream of migrants who have crowded into the urban slums above the Ohio and around the rim of the eastern Great Lakes. At the same time in this outflow have gone people of genuine talent, business acumen, and rare leadership ability.

No doubt there is justification, whether anthropologically and sociologically sound or not, for believing that large numbers of Kentucky River valley people are just plain hillbillies. They have been caught up in a technological era which is rapidly destroying the last vestiges of their old way of life before they are rooted in the new age. Once the underpinnings of the old era have been destroyed the individual is left amidst the wreckage of social and economic systems which provide little security and limited escape from poverty.

Thus Appalachia has become an exploited land. It is a celebrated cause with national and state politicians, social scientists of many stripes, educational and medical researchers, religious missionaries, economists, authors, and well-meaning college students. An astonishing amount of money has been spent by various private and public agencies in the holding of conferences, making surveys, publishing reports and special studies, in lobbying for special legislation favorable to the region, and in searching out the extent and erosions of poverty.

Stream valleys were cleared by the first settlers, and as population expanded, homesteads were pushed higher and higher up the ridges to the narrow fertile benches, and then onto the flat sterile plateaus themselves. Today the hill country is lined with abandoned house sites, memorialized, as are the graves of former settlers, by heaps of sandstones. A lone decrepit apple tree, an ancient cedar, or a spreading oak shade spots of fond memories, or the scenes of family tragedies. The actors in these homely dramas, most of them, lie in neglected graves, their final resting places marked by uninscribed field stones.

Once the Kentucky hills were covered with magnificent trees — and a wide variety of them. An earlier chapter has described the log run and referred to the exploitation of this virgin forest. Raping of mountain woods has gone on ever since. A log truck hustles down a public road loaded with poles cut before the trees were beyond their maiden growth. Piled up across the landscape are rolling layers of green hills which respond miraculously to care and management. It is doubtful that many other spots in North America respond so rapidly to good forest management as do the hills which drain into the Kentucky River and its branches. An open testimonial to this fact is the miraculous response made by lands in the great Daniel Boone National Forest. In many places Daniel Boone and other long hunters from the Yadkin would feel at home today. There are a few, too few in fact, private holdings which are in the hands of good private management.

By no means is Appalachian Kentucky naturally a poverty-strickened region devoid of rich resources. Perhaps an optimistic Kentuckian had a point when he said the hills "contain minerals that we don't even know about." Only a fractional part of the bituminous coal deposit has been mined. Since the 1880's men have dredged this precious fuel from the bowels of the eastern hills. Opening of the commercial mines reshaped the lives of a large number of highlanders. They moved in from their lonely hillside cabins to huddle in coal camps. Here they became dependent, not upon corn patches and tiny gardens, but upon cash wages, credit at the company store, and close neighbors for company. If they left problems behind at the head of the hollows, they developed new ones in the company villages. During World War I coal mining boomed, and there was a short post-war period in which wages remained high, and production boomed. Once demand for coal dropped off and wages sagged there was trouble. Blood flowed in the Battle of Evarts. Benham, Lynch, Harlan, Whitesburg, Hazard, and dozens of smaller places were torn by labor strife. John L. Lewis and his United Mine Workers organized the miners, defied the operators, built five workers' hospitals from a royalty levy on coal tonnage, they upped wages, and otherwise brought improvement in the lives of miners. They, however, could not withstay the use of automatic coal mining machines in the mines.

The ever-increasing use of mining machinery up the Kentucky River replaced men in such numbers that from year to year the drop in the ranks of coal miners became a social and economic phenomenon. Machines sent men and their families in flight to the "outside" in search of new means of gaining a livelihood, and to find new homes. The machines did more than this. Giant shovels laid the stony ribs of the mountains bare while gargantuan augurs bored holes through mountain crests and spilled hundreds of thousands of tons of fine grained coal onto conveyer belts to be loaded into endless coal trains.

Kentucky coal was dumped by the thousands of tons into the maws of furnaces about the Great Lakes, to smelt steel, to generate electricity and steam, and to enrich huge industries.

The augurs created enough havoc in the mountain slopes, but the vast crawling behemoths which tore the earth apart in millions of tons from atop thin seams of coal have done irreparable damage to the countryside. For miles on end they dump their staggering burdens of spoil down the slopes to block stream beds, to overburden timber, and even to tumble down upon highland homes. Whatever the arguments in favor of this type of mining, the depressing fact remains that the earth has been disturbed and misshapen for all time to come. Bit by bit legislators on the bank of the Kentucky at Frankfort have dealt with the strip mining issue. The mining lobby has been powerful and noisy, while the protests against the practice have been angry. Both governor and legislator have been caught up in the fight to stop the practice altogether or to adopt laws which would insure minimal restoration of the contour of the land.

Strip mining is not the only fundamental issue threatening water and land use in the Kentucky Valley. Rising urban and industrial communities in central Kentucky present an altogether new perspective of the surrounding hills. Water and recreational facilities have grown enormously in importance in the past decade. There has been some discussion of turning the Kentucky Valley into a recreational facility in which water can be conserved as a natural joint enterprise. Already a major impoundment has been constructed at Buckhorn. Elsewhere along the Kentucky, United States Army Engineers have explored sites for future impoundments to supply the rising industrial needs for water and flood control.

There will always be some sort of conflict going on in the Kentucky River country over land use. There is such a scarcity of flat lands adaptable to satisfactory industrial plant location that burying any of it under water would limit future possibilities of new economic developments. Paradoxically an uncontrolled river offers such serious threats of floods that industrial development is severely limited. Beyond this large impoundments threaten with extinction the remaining agricultural activities in much of the valley.

The dispute over the location and construction of dams only reflects the pressures of change which have occurred in all of Kentucky. In fields other than industrial expansion Kentuckians have sought new sources of economic income which would not exhaust the state's resources. No part of the state offers more opportunities than does the land along the Kentucky and its lateral streams. Two major state parks have been created along the Red and Kentucky rivers. At Boonesboro the State Park Commission established a park on the site of Boonesboro. No one will ever know the amount of energy and anxiety expended on the part of dedicated people who in the past sought to have this historic spot commemorated in some dignified way.

In a land where a farmer once could plant as much burley tobacco as he chose, he is now either limited in the amount of ground he can plant or by a lack of labor to grow and harvest it. All through the valley farmers have bought out little landholders and consolidated their fractional acre tobacco bases into bigger plantings. Each time this has happened a rural farm family has been dispossessed, and the fabric of the old pattern further rent. Land holdings have grown larger, and the number of farmers on the land smaller.

Reduction of tobacco acreage obviously is not the only reason for the great transformation of life along the Kentucky. Once the county seat towns were the scenes of noisy and feverish activity on county court days in the spring. Farmers brought in their young mules to be sold to drovers on their way South to the cotton belt. Mule and horse trading was one of the most exciting pastimes many a Kentuckian enjoyed. Old timers still reminisce about the shrewd horse and mule trades they made in their younger days. This is a thing of the dim past. Farms have become mechanized. One man can now tend as much land as a half dozen used to work. A modern tractor with the necessary implements can do more work than ten mules did in the old days, and they do not have to be fed every day of the year.

An equally important revolution has occurred in the type of crops which are now being produced. Burley tobacco which now arrives on auction floors in December bears little kinship to that sold from the same floors in 1940. Scientists have produced new strains of plants which resist disease, and which possess certain quality characteristics demanded by modern cigarette smokers. Constantly the process of plant breeding goes on to keep tobacco-growing a modern enterprise. Before the first quarter of the nineteenth century had ended Kentucky cattle, sheep, and horses had established fine reputations. By 1880 Kentucky was the principle livestock producing region of the South, and many a bluegrass farmer was as proud of the ancestry of his animals as of that of his own family. Meadows which once grew large crops of hemp and tobacco are now in grass which graze purebred cattle and sheep.

Though there are larger bluegrass areas in the United States, it is the Bluegrass region of Kentucky which is best known. This has been partly true because of the grass, but largely because of the way of life developed in the region. Today grasses in Kentucky are more important than ever before. Not only is there bluegrass, but throughout the Valley of the Kentucky the recently discovered Kentucky fescue grows lusciously in pastures and on roadside shoulders. This tenacious plant is not at all discriminating as to the type of soil in which it will grow. Whether or not grazing animals prefer other grass over it is largely an academic issue. The introduction of fescue has resulted in the checking of erosion on lands which were being too heavily cultivated and grazed.

For a century and a half Kentuckians have boasted of the fertility of their soils without knowing the facts of their depletion. A pioneer in soils management preached the heretical doctrine of depletion, but his preachments fell largely on deaf ears. The lands were being eroded, and they lacked nutriments which would make them productive. It was not until the introduction of superior phosphatic and nitrogenous fertilizers by the Tennessee Valley Authority that farmers saw the validity of the old soil specialist's arguments.

In a more fundamental manner the Kentucky Valley is already deeply involved in the future of the state, and it cannot hope to escape further and drastic changes. Older inhabitants along the river's course may cherish their rich memories of a less complex past, and bemoan the conditions of the moment. The old survivors love the folksiness of earlier days, and too often they veil the realities of a former time with the gentle fog of romantic myth. A derelict apple or cherry tree hovering as the last survivor over an old home place sets them to recalling the days when the trees produced some of the sweetest apples or cherries in all Kentucky. The old folks ate all they could in season and dried or preserved the rest from which the old master cook made fried pies as light as the down from an angel's wing, and as sweet as the notes of the harp of heaven.

A stroll through the woods with a veteran brings out stories of the days when towering giants of trees were brought crashing down to feed an insatiable outside lumber market, or they bull-whacked ponderous loads of oil machinery up impossible slopes to search for oil and gas. Old coal miners have largely forgotten the dirt and drudgery of the pits and recall their coal shoveling days as the good old times.

One can stand on the bridge in the heart of old

Frankfort and contemplate not only the scenes from whence the Kentucky flows, but likewise the shifts which have been made in those scenes. Upstream lies a green land enshrouded in great rolls of undergrowth forests which outwardly conceal the wounds which woods and land have suffered. The water of the Kentucky itself gives a placid appearance, but actually it carries the poisonous chemicals of the mines, the pollutions of the towns, and the silt of uncontrolled currents. Paradoxically there is interlaced in the current the flow of some of the finest springs and fresh water streams this side of the Appalachian watershed.

Like the myths and reality of Kentucky history itself the Kentucky River flows on incessantly, unable to separate the pure from the polluted, thus making an uneasy promise to people of its valley. Today the stream is almost free and unfettered, but tomorrow it may be curbed behind high rise dams and converted into sluggish pools which, like the carp which now scour the river's bed, will give little notion of its force. Certainly the two extreme conditions of Kentucky's population will be called upon to make enormous compromises in order to enjoy the full benefits of the future even if it does displace the present balances of nature and society.